LOW-INTENSITY CONFLICT IN THE THIRD WORLD

by

STEPHEN BLANK
LAWRENCE E. GRINTER
JEROME W. KLINGAMAN
THOMAS P. OFCANSKY
LEWIS B. WARE
BYNUM E. WEATHERS

Air University Press
Maxwell Air Force Base, Alabama 36112-5532

August 1988

Library of Congress Cataloging-in-Publication Data

Low-Intensity Conflict in the Third World by Lewis B. Ware, et al.

  "August 1988"
  Includes bibliographies
    1. Low-Intensity conflicts (Military science)—Developing countries. 2. United States—Military relations—Developing countries. 3. Developing countries—Military relations—United States. 4. World politics, 1945-. I. Blank, Stephen. II. Air University (US). Center for Aerospace Doctrine, Research , and Education.
    U240.L69 1988
    355'.0215—dc19   88-19395
                                                                                                        CIP

DISCLAIMER

For Sale by the Superintendent of Documents
US Government Printing Office
Washington DC 20402

Contents

FOREWORD

The United States must improve its ability to cope with low-intensity conflict. We must become a great deal better at fighting this kind of war. We may learn quickly, in which case we will be able to cope with low-intensity conflict in the near-term; or we may learn slowly, in which case we will suffer years of frustration.

Low-intensity warfare represents an arena of conflict for today and for tomorrow. There can be little doubt that it poses important problems for American interests and policy. And yet, because of the confusion that surrounds the understanding of low-intensity conflict, the United States has been ill-prepared to face its consequences. This book is a serious effort to make thinking about low-intensity conflict more understandable and, thus, more accessible to those who would form our national response to this pressing issue. It counsels the reader that low-intensity conflict appears in the guise of proxy warfare, religious extremism, ethnic and racial rivalries, and on the heels of failed developmental projects. All these events threaten our friends, our allies, and ourselves.

The Soviet Union and its proxies have come to the conclusion that the global system is vulnerable to low-intensity conflict. We can therefore expect more of it. Only when the United States has developed a flexible capacity to deal with its root causes around the world can we better secure our own interests and suppress Soviet efforts in this domain.

The present volume takes a significant step toward framing the context in which a creative set of policies for low-intensity conflict can evolve. We all have a need to better understand this new, disturbing, and growing phenomenon. With that need in mind, we highly recommend it.

SIDNEY J. WISE
Colonel, USAF
Commander
Center for Aerospace Doctrine,
    Research, and Education

ABOUT THE AUTHORS

Dr Stephen Blank is a research associate in the Political-Military Affairs Division at the Air University Center for Aerospace Doctrine, Research, and Education (AUCADRE), Maxwell AFB, Alabama. He has been an assistant professor of Russian and Soviet history at the University of Texas, San Antonio, and a visiting assistant professor of Russian history at the University of California, Riverside. He serves as a consultant on Soviet affairs to GE TEMPO (a General Electric think tank) and the Center for Strategic Technology at Texas A&M University. He has published many articles on Soviet nationality policy, foreign policies, and, more recent, military policy. Doctor Blank is presently completing a manuscript on the first years of Soviet nationality policy and the Commissariat of Nationalities under Joseph Stalin.

Dr Lawrence E. Grinter is professor of Asian studies in the Political-Military Affairs Division at AUCADRE. A former faculty member of the National War College and the Air War College, Doctor Grinter has published widely in his field, including *Asian-Pacific Security* (1986, coeditor), and *East Asian Conflict Zones* (1987, coeditor); and he has undertaken numerous studies for the National Security Council and the Office of the Secretary of Defense.

Jerome W. Klingaman is a retired Air Force pilot with nine years experience in special operations and low-intensity conflict activities. He is presently a senior research fellow at AUCADRE, where he serves as chairman of the Low-Intensity Conflict Research Support Group and conducts studies on the problems of low-intensity warfare. Klingaman teaches a seminar on strategy and air power doctrine for low-intensity conflict at the Air War College, and he lectures regularly on these subjects at other military and civilian institutions. He is active in doctrine development with the joint services and has assisted the Office of the Secretary of Defense and the National Security Council in formulating national defense strategy for low-intensity conflict.

Dr Thomas P. Ofcansky is currently serving as assistant professor of African studies in the Political-Military Affairs Division at AUCADRE. He has been an Air Force historian with the Air Force Communications Command, Scott AFB, Illinois; the Tactical Air Command, Langley AFB, Virginia; and the Military Airlift Command, Dover AFB, Delaware. Prior to joining government service, Doctor Ofcansky held teaching positions at

West Virginia University and Harcum Junior College. Doctor Ofcansky's publications have appeared in a number of journals and magazines, including *Africana Journal, Journal of African Studies, African Defence Journal, Journal of Third World Studies*, and the *Christian Science Monitor*. He has authored two books about Africa.

Dr Lewis B. Ware is professor of Middle East studies and chief of the Political-Military Affairs Division at AUCADRE. Before entering service with the Air Force, he taught at New York University, Boston State College, and Northeastern University. He has published numerous articles on a wide range of subjects in such journals as the *Middle East Journal, Military Review*, and the *Journal of South Asian and Middle Eastern Studies*. Doctor Ware has also produced a series of monographs on the Middle East for the Air University Press.

Dr Bynum E. Weathers, a member of Phi Beta Kappa, is associate professor of Latin American studies in the Political-Military Affairs Divsion of AUCADRE. He has taught at the University of Puerto Rico; the Air Force Academy; Northeast Louisiana University; St. Mary's University, San Antonio; University of Alabama, Montgomery; and Huntingdon College, Montgomery. Doctor Weathers's research has taken him to Argentina, Uruguay, Mexico, and Central America. He has published several studies on low-intensity conflict, including *Guerrilla Warfare in Nicaragua, 1975–1979.*

PREFACE

In the summer of 1986, the Airpower Research Institute—a directorate of the Air University Center for Aerospace Doctrine, Research, and Education (AUCADRE)—decided to devote a substantial part of its energies to the question of low-intensity conflict (LIC). This decision came about in recognition of the changing nature of modern warfare and the need to transform attitudes toward its theory and practice.

From the very beginning, the study and understanding of low-intensity conflict has been beset by problems of definition. Is LIC merely an operational construct that deals with measurable levels of escalating violence, or is it a concept that depends for its validity on an examination of the cultures in which it evolves? The task of grappling with the problem fell to the Political-Military Affairs Division. Without denying the importance of the former, the division concentrated its efforts on an investigation of the latter in the belief that an understanding of the LIC environment provides the key to correct policy assessments. The result is the present volume, in which each member of the division explores the LIC environment in his particular area of regional specialization.

A common thread ties together the five studies of this collection. Each study views the persistence with which the bilateral relationship between the United States and the Soviet Union continues to dominate American foreign and regional policies. Indeed, the LIC environment has often been obscured behind a heavy curtain of myth that depicts all low-intensity conflicts as manifestations of superpower global rivalry. And it is certainly true that Soviet activities must not be discounted in any discussion of the LIC potential for instability. But it is also true that such discussions must recognize the paramount importance of a global diffusion of military force and the evolution of a political polycentrism; LIC policies based on superpower rivalry may be unresponsive to regional issues. The risk is great that LIC studies will become overly discrete and subject to an unacceptable reductionism.

These studies analyze the LIC environments in Central Asia, the Middle East, Southeast Asia, Latin America, and sub-Saharan Africa. For each region, history, politics, economics, and ideological currents are emphasized so as to illustrate best the wide variety of LIC phenomena that affect the societies under scrutiny. A final study puts into the perspective of a long-term LIC strategy the implications each contribution draws for US policies.

Dr Stephen Blank's study examines low-intensity conflict in Central Asia from the perspective of three case histories: the Basmachi insurgency of the 1920s, the Soviet invasions of Iran in 1920–21 and 1941–46, and the post–1979 struggle between the Red Army and the Afghan resistance. Using comparative historical data, Doctor Blank establishes a consistent pattern of Soviet political, military, and ideological responses to regional insurrectional movements. The thrust of his contribution is not on the sources as much as on the dynamics of conflict. This emphasis enables him to draw certain conclusions about the ultimate outcome of the Afghan situation and to take the full measure of future LIC regional environments.

In his study on the Middle East, Dr Lewis Ware argues that Islamism is the most important factor shaping the present-day LIC environment. Yet, apart from a common characteristic of protest against the failure of the Middle Eastern secular state system to provide prosperity and security for Muslims, Islamism is not ideologically monolithic. Rather, it demonstrates a wide range of flexible responses on both the strategic and tactical levels to local conditions. This underscores Islamism's protean nature and the fact that Khomeinism relates to it *in grosso modo* more as an inspiration than as a guiding force. Operating generally as an urban phenomenon with insurrectionary potential, Islamism poses grave problems for a coordinated US regional LIC policy.

Dr Lawrence Grinter, taking up the theme of the state's relationship to the LIC environment in Southeast Asia, develops an extensive typology of national reactions to internal and external challenges. Here, LIC manifests itself across a broad spectrum of interregional and international rivalries against the background of attempts by individual regimes to contain domestic dissension. What we find in Southeast Asia is perhaps the widest possible variety of conditions that produce LIC: insurgency of conflicting political factions in the Philippines; application of state counterterrorism against enemies in Indonesia; and imperial expansion into Cambodia by the Vietnamese in the aftermath of the Second Indochina War and the anarchic civil war between Cambodians of differing political persuasions. Complicated by the interplay of Soviet, American, and Chinese interests in a region of growing global importance, the need for priority of objectives, and clarity about them, is imperative.

Dr Bynum Weathers looks at Latin America and analyzes the history of its low-intensity conflicts in Nicaragua, Chile, and Peru. He provides a comprehensive survey of Cuban involvement in these struggles. While careful not to overplay the direct influence of Guevarism on the LIC environment, Doctor Weathers counsels that the Cuban interest in ideological hegemony in Latin America must always be taken into consideration when assessing the indigenous factors for upheaval. In his study, the reader will detect a strong tendency of the regional regimes to filter their experiences through the prism of Cuban-American-Soviet relations, thus reducing their ability to deal with the causes of LIC in an autonomous manner. By the same token, this tendency also accounts for a significant myopia in the evolution of US policy.

Dr Thomas Ofcansky advances the provocative thesis that, in sub-Saharan Africa, the LIC environment displays the strong and continual influence exerted by ethnic rivalries. He argues that colonialism has done little to mitigate this constant of the African experience other than to mask its fundamental nature and its threat to regional stability. It flows from this that LIC does not express itself solely in ideological or racial terms, but rather, as Doctor Ofcansky attempts to demonstrate for South Africa, in terms of a violent intertribal feuding that erupts whenever central governmental controls are relaxed. This is a corrective, Doctor Ofcansky contends, that might well balance the US political-military position in favor of a less globalist orientation.

In the final section, Jerome Klingaman assesses the regional analyses for their implications at the level of strategic planning. His assessment focuses on specific implications for our understanding of low-intensity conflict, and he draws from these implications a critical perspective on the broad policy guidelines contained in present and future low-intensity conflict strategies. Klingaman demonstrates that thinking about low-intensity conflict has only recently entered the strategy development process on the national level but is likely to remain in the forefront of official concern for the remainder of this century.

Many people at AUCADRE made this book happen, but special recognition must go to Preston Bryant, the Air University Press editor who worked hard to bring it to its present form. And special thanks go to AUCADRE's production division: Marcia Williams, John Westcott, Carolyn Ward, Charlie Wallace, Hattie Minter, Dot McCluskie, Anna Leavell, Tom Howell, Joann Guastella, Steve Garst, Marshall Fulmer, Joan Dawson, Susan Carr, Patricia Boyle, Debra Beal, and Lula Barnes. Their work in producing this book exemplifies their dedication to AUCADRE.

L. B. Ware
Chief, Political-Military
Affairs Division
Airpower Research Institute

Low-Intensity Conflict in the Middle East

Dr Lewis B. Ware

All things merge in one another—Good into evil, generosity into justice, religion into politics.

—Thomas Hardy

In the past few years, the academic and military communities have been paying increased attention to the phenomenon of low-intensity conflict (LIC). There is general agreement that, for the foreseeable future, LIC will remain the dominant form of violent confrontation in most parts of the world.[1] Yet, despite this apparent consensus, there exists no universally accepted definition of LIC on which to construct a strategy of containment.[2] Rather, LIC studies have invariably concentrated on tactics and operational responses to isolated hostilities with little effort to extrapolate from them the principal characteristics of the low-intensity environment.

The present study will suggest, on the contrary, that in the Middle East the causes and general characteristics of the low-intensity conflict environment are readily discernible and that, by analyzing five case histories of low-intensity conflict, an argument can be made for the unique way LIC has evolved in the region. This, in turn, may aid in both clarifying the definitional issue and facilitating the writing of a coherent national LIC policy.

Apart from the perennial Arab-Israeli crisis and the Iran-Iraq war, violent confrontation in the Middle East is historically of short duration, involves relatively low material expenditure, and reflects ad hoc alliance-building as well as extreme political fragmentation. Until modern times, the interpenetration of Middle Eastern society by the European colonial powers, which linked the region to the European power balance, severely constrained the outbreak of conventional warfare between rivals. The devolution of power during the period of decolonization into nationalist, independent, and secular regimes resulted in a weak state system that had no central political pivot. Moreover, the substitution of superpower for colonial interests acted to suppress further, though not eliminate, interstate violence in the contemporary period. Consequently, during the past half

1

century, low-intensity conflict has increased proportionately to the weakness of the state system, bringing the Middle Eastern secular state under direct attack.

There are a number of reasons for this situation. First, the modern, secular state is seen to represent the prolongation of Western colonialism and therefore suggests the possibility that neocolonialism will be imposed on the region; second, the imposition of a secular Western political system is considered alien to the historical political culture of the region; third, and most important, the secular state has not succeeded in bringing prosperity to the regional peoples. This absence of prosperity is everywhere manifested in a rising tide of unemployment, severe balance of payment deficits, unequal distribution of national wealth, uncontrolled urbanization, and economic stagnation. Such conditions, with their important ramification in the uneven distribution of political influence between the secular elites and those they have mobilized to elitist values, are felt by the dispossessed as a sociopolitical malaise, and they provide an index of the volatility of low-intensity warfare against the state.

What makes the present Middle Eastern LIC environment unique is that politicized and highly ideologized religion in its Islamist form shapes the common reaction to this malaise and that urban-based Islamist protest movements best articulate these contemporary social and political realities.[3] Thus, this study will confine itself to a discussion of the relationship between varieties of Islamism and the LIC regional environment in the context of incipient conflict that challenges the stability of the Muslim secular state. In order to grasp the essence of these relationships, one must understand the fundamental principles of Islamist ideology and how that ideology is expressed as an alternative political culture.

Islamism imbues its adherents with an exalted sense of personal worth and translates this sense of worth into political action. Historically speaking, Islam established an imperium that gave form and substance to God's program for the salvation of believers. Even the modern Middle Eastern state has not been able to divorce fully the spiritual from the temporal realm and render religion a matter of personal conscience. Inasmuch as all Middle Eastern governments (apart from Turkey, where Islam is disestablished, and Lebanon, where Islam is the majority sect) are constitutionally Muslim governments, they are enjoined to underwrite Islam and at the same time to promote often contradictory nationalist values. Some states have "desacralized" Islam to a large extent and transformed it into a "national" religion; but the historical religiopolitical culture has suffered only a temporary eclipse. When the postindependence state was strong, all tendencies to reassert older Islamic political traditions could be suppressed as reactionary. Once the state entered its nation-building stage, however, these values resurged, gaining new prominence; and their propagandists became adept in employing all the means of mass communication to re-

2

create a community of the faithful (just as the state itself had done in forming a national secular society): hence the claim of Islamists that religion should once again direct the activities of the state.

Within this general Islamist framework, variations exist that depend on ethnolinguistic circumstances, the sociohistorical differences between the Sunni and Shii Islamic worldviews, and the national policies of the states in which LIC poses a significant threat. Five insurgencies illustrate today the major variations of Islamist political activism. Some aim at overturning the established and legitimate order, whereas others aim at making the legitimate order conform more explicitly to Islamic values. Yet all operate within prescribed limits while responding to a wide variety of regional conditions of conflict.

Most prominent is the Khomeinist revolution. Only in Iran has an Islamic activist insurgency attempted to grapple with the dilemma of modern life by gaining control of a state apparatus in the name of Allah. Not unlike the theocracy of right belief that John Calvin founded in Geneva, the Khomeinist state refers to the myth of a fixed point in time when Islamic political traditions were uncontaminated by outside influences. And Khomeinism has provided inspiration for insurgencies elsewhere in the Middle East. In 1981, Khomeini sponsored a Shiite uprising in Bahrain. His objectives were to alter the Gulf power balance and promote Iranian imperial goals in its war with Iraq. In Lebanon, Iranian-supported Islamist factions fight with each other for the right to redesign the Lebanese confessional system in favor of Lebanon's dispossessed Shia majority. In Egypt, where an indigenous Islamism predates the Iranian experiment by 30 years, Islamists compete with the state to define the Muslim content of pan-Arab political action. In Tunisia, Islamism concentrates on reforming society without challenging the legitimacy of the modern secular state.

Analysis of these five case histories reveals an emerging pattern of low-intensity conflict in which the common environment of violence derives from the instability of present Middle Eastern secular political culture. Islamism proposes to substitute order for chaos, and that order is predicated on a thoroughgoing moral renovation of Islamic society. This being said, it should be noted that the unity of Islamism with respect to a political program is more hypothetical than real; and so the notion that an interregional Islamist subversion of secular regimes, directed and funded by Tehran, is hereby challenged. In point of fact, beneath the apparent Islamist monolith, a diversity of local and regional conditions determine the character of the actual LICs to which Islamism has skillfully and flexibly adapted its tactical goals.

If, despite the rhetoric of Islamism as to its anticolonial, anti-imperialist, and internationalist mission, the object of Islamist protest focuses primarily on the Middle Eastern state system, then the implications for a LIC strategy are clear. Such a strategy must take into consideration the internal threats to particular regimes and the role Islamism plays in their political evolution. Furthermore, such strategy must avoid an interpretation of the LIC environment as an extension of either the US-Iran or the US-Soviet bilateral relationship. Scrupulous attention to the local context in which political forces struggle to refashion Muslim society will produce a well-formulated strategy that recognizes the inapplicability of conventional military means to the resolution of regional problems. By the same token, a Middle Eastern LIC strategy acknowledges that diplomatic and political support of the regional elites remains the condition sine qua non of a successful US policy.

The Khomeinist Revolution

To grasp the significance of Islamism for the evolution of Middle Eastern LIC environments, we must first understand the basic assumptions that Islam makes about the political order and how these assumptions transform faith in a comprehensible universe of eternal spiritual values into a course of temporal political action.

Khomeinism is an excellent point of departure for this discussion because the Khomeinist revolution has, for the first time in Muslim history, given these assumptions an operative form as a political theory of the state. It must be cautioned, however, that when we speak of Khomeinism we are not speaking of Islamic fundamentalism. All religion is basically fundamental in that all religions rely for the exposition of their truth on the literalism of revealed scripture. What we are talking about here is religion as ideology. Ideology comprises an identification of and a justification for a preferred political order; it demonstrates the "rightness" of that order by opposing it to other orders; it proposes a plan for the realization of the "right" order and thus gives a sense of purpose to its political activities in terms of policies; and last, ideology furnishes a coherent picture of future historical outcomes.[4] As an ideology, Khomeinism satisfies these criteria; but Khomeinism does not exist in a vacuum. Rather, the manner by which Khomeini has ideologized and politicized Islam illuminates the Shiite roots of the Iranian religious ethos under the impact of Persian political culture.

In Islam, the moral universe, ordered by the creative act of God, is immanent in all the affairs of His creatures. This implies that political and moral prescriptions are inseparable because they derive from the same source and underpin a just society.[5] As the immutable revelation of God, the Quran lays out clearly God's prescriptions for His community and so represents a perfected social and political constitution not dependent on the vagaries of time or circumstance. All other political orders are false because they are the constructions of the fallible human intellect without reference to God's revelation of a "straight path." But Muslims can be "negligent" in acknowledging and applying God's commandments, and

4

thus may fall under the corrupting influence of non-Muslims.

This preoccupation with corruption is central to Khomeinist ideology. For Khomeini, it is axiomatic that Western imperialism has brought about the moral decadence of the Muslim world through economic, political, and geostrategic exploitation. Europe, and by extension America, has conspired against the Islamic moral order in the continuing historical confrontation of evil and good. Islam must answer the challenge of exploitation in two ways. First, Muslims are responsible for purifying their own society according to the principle of internal jihad (jihad al-dakhali). In this sense, jihad means a "striving" to reconcile the present corrupted social reality with the just and perfect society. Such reconciliation requires that Westernism in all forms be purged from Iran. Second, this concept of the just society must be imposed on the Muslim world at large, especially in those countries whose governments either exhibit a secular Western orientation or have military and technological relations with the West. Here, Khomeini conceives of jihad as an external modality of reconciliation (jihad al-khariji)—a principle most closely, if somewhat erroneously, associated with the notion of "holy war." For Khomeini, the triumph of Islamist ideology is inevitable; Islam will regain its rightful place in the forefront of world civilization.

All ideologies possess political theories that suggest the means by which assumptions about the universe can be effectively translated into practical reality. An extreme and irreducible utilitarianism makes Khomeini's political theory accessible to the individual believer. His ideology posits a Manichean universe of irreconcilable forces in which good and evil can easily be transposed into exploiters and exploited. Moreover, these forces inhere in the global political system. Whether one sees this conflict as one between communism and capitalism, liberal democracy and fascism, the rich "North" and the deprived "South," or the superpowers and the third world, the effect is to impose duties on the believer to rectify injustices. In Khomeinist theory, every good Muslim is enjoined by the Quran to "command good and forbid evil" by establishing Islamist governments everywhere tyranny reigns.[6] To the Iranian Shiite Muslim, Khomeini appears as a "guide" whose task is to restore the status quo ante through the mobilization of the nation; to those who are the objects of the Khomeinist attacks, jihad is an offensive principle that portends a continuing cycle of low-intensity conflicts. Directed against "tyrannical" regimes that paradoxically approve the use of force to bring about an end to the use of force, Khomeinist political solutions become moral imperatives.

In general, the characteristics of Khomeinism can be found in most varieties of Islamism. What sets Khomeinism apart is the role the charismatic leader assumes in the exercise of internal and external jihad. While considerable debate rages within the Iranian Islamic Republic as to the relationship between jihad and Khomeinist goals, there is little doubt that

Khomeini himself perceives both aspects of jihad as emanations of his divinely inspired mission. Khomeini's role gives his ideology its highly aggressive content and presupposes that his authority rests on a doctrine which both transcends and enhances his personal charisma; but this doctrine of authority is intelligible only in the context of the interaction between Shiite religious precepts and Iranian political culture.

Shiism was born out of the competition for leadership in the early Islamic community. The traditional Bedouin Arab model of authority was one that vested power in an elected member of the Prophet's tribe. Accepted by the majority of Muslims, this model reflected the normative practice or "sunna" of the Prophet. At the same time, a theory of governance based on designated succession and representing the imperial Perso-Byzantine environment openly strove to supplant the Sunni perspective. Upon embracing Islam, the Persians eagerly championed the imperial theory as consonant with both their anti-Arab bias and their imperial traditions. Within the space of several centuries, this minority perspective acquired a distinctly messianic character. The authority of the designated successor passed theoretically in the family of the Prophet from father to eldest son for 12 generations before the mysterious disappearance of the last in the prophetic line. The Persian partisans of this theory of governance, the Shia, believe that the universe is ruled by an absent leader (the "imam") who will return under conditions of oppression to recreate a world in which spiritual and temporal values are reconciled in an age of justice. Such a theory was well suited to the psychological needs of the oppressed Persian minority to refuse allegiance to the non-Shiite regimes under which they were obliged to live.

In the absence of the Hidden Imam, the Shia clergy arrogated to itself the prerogative to act as the Imam's general agents and to interpret imamic law for the multitudes. All those clerics (mujtahid, plural mujtahidun) capable of rendering such interpretations were ranked according to their abilities; and the higher echelon, the ayatollahs, chose from among themselves a spokesman for their consensus. But this Grand Ayatollah neither spoke for the incommunicado Imam nor ruled the community. Rather, he was the mujtahid to whom believers deferred in matters of law and social ethics. That the function of social guide (wilayat al-faqih) was gradually transformed into a political office is due to internal decadence and external imperialism.

When the Persian imperium was resurrected in the early sixteenth century, Shiism gained for the first time official patronage. This immediately posed a dilemma for the clergy, who had for centuries adjudicated the legal affairs of the community. The state now openly demanded a monopoly of control over society. The clergy was obliged to decide whether or to what extent it was willing to compromise its sociopolitical predominance in exchange for state sanction and protection.

During the next three centuries, this tension greatly affected the direction

6

of state-clergy relationships. Impacted by internal modernization and external pressures from the British and the Russians, the state attempted to centralize its authority and reduce the clergy's autonomy; but the state became weaker and more despotic. Already disposed theoretically to deny legitimacy to any state, Sunni or Shii, the clergy slowly abandoned its attitude of practical accommodation and transformed its quietist, pietistic religiosity into a conservative but highly activist instrument of political protest; this, however, without impugning the legitimacy of secular power per se.

The process of deterioration accelerated in the last decades of the nineteenth century; and Iran has been living through an extended period of low-intensity conflict. Further, periodic European interventions have complicated Iran's adjustment to social transformation. Nevertheless, when the Pahlavi regime came to power in the 1920s, the clergy had already progressed far in reestablishing itself as a class independent of, and opposed to, the concept of secular monarchy. Thus the clergy has been as much an influence on, as an object of, these momentous changes; and the doctrine of wilayat al-faqih permitted the clergy to extend its complete control over the state when the Pahlavi regime crumbled.[7]

The political culture, then, in which Ayatollah Khomeini operates is one where the ground has already been prepared for radical theocracy and clerical authoritarianism. Khomeini played a personal role in focusing the demands of a clergy and a people for fundamental change, but he did not make the revolution. It was the late shah, Muhammad Reza, who determined the course, tempo, and scope of the revolution. He sought to translate his belief in a revitalized imperial Iran into an expression of his own personal power at a time when the country could not support the grandiosity of such pretensions. Under Muhammad Reza, the country suffered from profound social dislocation, economic hardship, corruption in the ruling elites, a political and ideological vacuum, uncontrolled urbanization, a deteriorating public sector, and the disruptive influence of American culture. The political upheaval of 1978–79 coincided with the decline of Iranian hegemony in the Gulf under American auspices.

This was the situation Khomeini manipulated from exile. The crowds that heeded his words, through a network of clerics and rapidly reproduced cassette recordings of his sermons, were semi-industrialized and possessed great potential for political mobilization. To this seething but as yet politically unformed mass, Khomeini introduced the concept of right belief. Right belief included appeals to scripturalism, divinely inspired clerical leadership, the historical Shiite martyrdom of the Imams, and that particular kind of sober and orderly unitarianism which chimed in nicely with the requirements of industrial society for progress and prosperity.[8] Thus, in the absence of a determined effort by the shah's disaffected military to defend the state after his departure, Khomeini used religion to channel the impulse of a popular, conservative, and activist sentiment toward the destruction of the last vestiges of secularism in Iran; and within a short time, Khomeini's Islamism had swept away the remains of the weakly rooted Pahlavi imperium.

The consolidation of post-1979 Khomeinism is the history of how the brutal moralism of a popular insurgency destroyed all traces of the ancien régime at the cost of thousands of lives. But it was an insurgency whose ideology lacked a program. Now that power had been seized, the question of the nature of an Islamic government had to be answered. Although the new Islamic Republic of Iran had an "Islamic" constitution, the right of the clergy and of their "guide" Khomeini to govern still rested on theoretical premises over which the religious establishment itself did not altogether agree. This disagreement extended to the imposition of Islamic norms on national economic structures and to the relative importance of Islamism for export as opposed to Islamism as an instrument of internal social reconstruction.

Within several years of Khomeini's accession to supreme authority in Iran, three events had established priority for the immediate expansion abroad of the Islamic order: first was the American hostage crisis of November 1979; second, the war with Iraq that began on 22 September 1980; and third, the Israeli invasion of Lebanon in June of 1982. Discreet as these events were, they revealed the extent to which external "satanic" powers threatened the Shiite communities of Iran and the Middle East. Thus, these events directly contributed to the final triumph of clerical rule.

By 1983, an apparatus, however unsophisticated, was in place for expanding Khomeinist Islamism. The natural locus for the first experiment was the Gulf, for it was in the Gulf that the new Islamic Republic of Iran felt itself most vulnerable. The attempt to subvert the Gulf failed. Nevertheless, it bears scrutiny if only as an indication of Khomeini's early ineptitude in exporting his Islamist revolution and of the kind of pressure his regime could apply to the Gulf states.

The Attempted Coup in Bahrain

On 16 December 1981, Bahraini authorities arrested 52 Gulf Arab nationals on charges of plotting to overthrow the Bahrain government. Within a day, another 13 were arrested on the same charge in Saudi Arabia.[9] It was no coincidence that all the plotters were Shiite Muslims who belonged to the Islamic Front for the Liberation of Bahrain, a shadowy organization housed in Tehran and associated with the Hojjat al-Islam Muhammad Mudarrisi, Khomeini's chief operative for exporting the Iranian revolution abroad. Since the mid-seventies, Mudarrisi, an Iranian cleric and founder of the Islamic Action Organization in Iraq, had been preparing the terrain for Khomeinist revolution in the Gulf region.[10] When Khomeini took control in Iran, Bahraini authorities asked Mudarrisi to leave Bahrain, an overwhelmingly Shiite island-state; but Mudarrisi had already gained the support of many prominent Bahraini Shiites for an eventual coup. That coup was to be carried out by trained insurgents against civil and military targets using weapons that had been prepositioned throughout the island in carefully concealed caches. Fortunately, the coup, programmed to occur simultaneously with the celebration of the tenth anniversary of Bahrain independence, was foiled by the watchfulness of the Bahraini police. Five days later, a group of five armed Iranians appeared at the Bahrain embassy in Tehran, identified themselves as members of the group that had staged the abortive overthrow of the Manama government, and demanded the release of the captured prisoners.[11]

The Bahrain incident may be explained in two ways. Some see it as the first attempt to wage a holy jihad outside Iran to unite all the Muslim nations of the Middle East under the aegis of Persian Shiism. Bahrain certainly had the potential for low-intensity conflict and Islamic revolution. It had experienced all the sociopolitical dislocations of a burgeoning oil economy. Moreover, it is an island where up to 70 percent of the population professes Shiism and where many are Arabs of Persian extraction, yet where Sunni authority nevertheless prevailed. A coup in Bahrain would have established Khomeinism on the other side of the Gulf and would have had paramount importance in securing the sympathy of several hundred thousand native Saudi Shia living in the oases on the peninsula's eastern shore. Khomeini had been sending his propagandists on pilgrimage to Mecca since 1979 to challenge the legitimacy of Saudi control over the Holy Places; and when the Grand Mosque was attacked by Saudi dissidents in November 1979, Khomeini did not hesitate to accuse the Saudi authorities of acting against Islam by suppressing the riots within the sacred precincts. This blatant appeal to the pan-Islamic sensitivities of the Muslim community against the Saudi regime may have been the preliminary step in a grandiose scheme to subvert the peninsula.

A more persuasive view of the Bahrain incident is the argument that the military conditions on the Iran-Iraq war front dictated a flanking movement that would isolate Iraq from its Arab support and secure for Iran a commanding position on the maritime oil route out of the Gulf. During the 14 months between the beginning of the war and the Bahrain coup, military activities had settled into stalemate along a thousand-kilometer front. The Iraqis had occupied the portion of Iranian Khuzistan that was ethnically Arab and were at the gates of Ahwāz and Dezfūl, the two principal oil-producing towns of the province. But they were unable to exploit their advantage. The war had also degenerated into a contest of personalities between Khomeini and Saddam Hussein, each of whom demanded the dismantlement of the other's government as a precondition of peace; and

9

the Arabs were beginning to choose up sides. Jordan joined Iraq and forced the radical Arabs to espouse the Iranian cause. Only Saudi Arabia and the Gulf states remained technically neutral.

By unleashing the forces of Islamic revolutionism in Bahrain, Khomeini was betting that he could physically outflank Iraq and capitalize politically on the Gulf Arabs' failure to support Iraq. Bahrain was the logical object for a demonstration of *force majeure*; the late shah had once hinted at action against the island in a bid to make the Gulf a *mare Iranicum*. Only reluctantly did he relinquish the imperial claim to Bahrain in 1971 when Bahrain gained independence—and then not without first extracting Arab acquiescence to the Iranian occupation of the Gulf islands of Tunb and Abū Mūsá. If the Ayatollah's mission was to reassert Iranian imperial policy in an Islamist guise and thus to project Iranian power once again in the Gulf, he failed miserably. Neither Bahrain fell nor did Iraq waver in its determination to prosecute the war on Iranian territory. On the contrary, the Bahrain situation served to increase Arab vigilance; and measures were taken to lay the groundwork for the transformation of the infant Gulf Cooperation Council into a mutual security organization.[12]

It is possible that this failure dictated a fundamental shift in the direction of the Islamic revolution. By June 1982, the principle of wilayat al-faqih had finally triumphed. The coordination of the revolution abroad fell under the Ministry of Islamic Guidance and became the exclusive province of the clergy. For the remainder of 1982 and throughout 1983, the Ministry of Islamic Guidance (under the leadership of Hojjat al-Islam Mudarrisi) organized seminars in Islamic government and liberation for participants from the third world and the Arab Middle East. The emphasis was pan-Islamic; and the new president of the Iranian Republic, Hojjat al-Islam Khamene'i, declared in June 1983 that no expense would be spared in spreading the word of Islam.[13]

The evolution of this new direction coincided with the March 1982 offensive that drove the Iraqis from two thousand square kilometers of Iranian land, with the dispatch of one thousand Pasdaran (Revolutionary Guards) to Lebanon following the Israeli invasion in June, and with the subsequent appointment of Hojjat al-Islam Ali Mohtashemi as ambassador in Damascus to coordinate their activities. By the autumn of 1983, the Iranians were already implicated in the bombing of the US embassy and the Marine headquarters in Beirut.[14] Thus a new phase of jihad al-khariji opened. It was to involve Khomeinism in the tortuous labyrinth of pan-Arab affairs.

The Lebanese Imbroglio

Since 1975, the battle for Lebanon has been a battle to redefine the

Lebanese system of government. The battle has been as much a political as a physical contest, but force has been applied for relative advantage whenever negotiations break down between the contestants. The conflict centers in Beirut; but in a small country whose countryside remains in close proximity to its major city, fighting between rival political factions spills over into the surrounding villages and towns. Anarchy characterizes this low-intensity environment. As new armed factions appear, whether based in the urban areas or in their satellite villages, political demands are re-negotiated in attempts to find a center of gravity amidst a continual competition for ascendancy in a state void of central control.

The introduction of Iranian Islamism into Lebanon added a new factor to the anarchic environment, which has in turn shaped it to its own political contours. That Iranian Islamism already had resonances in the precivil war Lebanese Shiite community and that the Lebanese and the Iranian movements share common ideological concerns suggest that the conditions which made for the success of Khomeinism in Iran—a charismatic leader, a clerical institution historically opposed to secular central authority, a homogenous majority Shiite population undergoing socioeconomic dislocation and political repression, solid connections to a Shiite urban middle class, and the open rivalry of the superpowers for influence in a country of great geostrategic importance—were to a certain degree absent from the Lebanese equation. Evolving under local conditions of competition, Lebanese Islamism is attempting to reestablish the status quo in favor of the growing demographic shift toward the Shiite community; it is just one alternative, albeit an important one, available to mobilize Lebanese political sentiment.

The indigenous Shiite community makes up approximately 40 percent of the total Lebanese population and is today the predominant Muslim sect. This remarkable demographic shift is of fairly recent origin; it can be traced to the 1920 French policy of enlarging the Lebanese state at Syrian expense when the Shia of the Biqa valley were added to the already existing Shiite community in the Jabal Amil on the southern border next to British Palestine. The modernization of Lebanon's infrastructure provided access for the Shia to the capital city. As the demographic and commercial weight of the community increased in Beirut, Shia sought actively to transform that reality into new means of presenting their political aspirations. A number of factors influenced that transformation: the shift away from representation by the traditional Shiite landed aristocracy (zuama) to a dependence on clerical leadership; the growth of a Shiite urban bourgeoisie; and the events of the post-1970 PLO exodus from Jordan to Lebanon.

Until the arrival in 1958 of the Iranian cleric Musa al-Sadr as religious head of the Lebanese Shiite community, Shia dissatisfied with the rule of their zuama tended to associate themselves with the parties of the Lebanese left. Musa al-Sadr succeeded in reversing this trend by laying the groundwork for community self-help institutions. Al-Sadr first chose to invest his

11

political capital in the Supreme Shiite Council, which spoke officially through the Shiite religious hierarchy to the Lebanese government. But soon after the Palestinian retreat from Jordan, he shifted his activity to Shiite South Lebanon where, in founding the Majlis al-Janub (Council of the South), he began to fight the attempt of the PLO to draw off community energies for the pan-Arab, anti-Israeli struggle.

Because the Majlis al-Janub failed to answer the problems posed by the increasing politicization of the Lebanese Shia, al-Sadr replaced it, on the eve of the Lebanese civil war, with the Harakat al-Mahrumin (Movement of the Deprived). In 1975, the Harakat al-Mahrumin spawned a paramilitary wing, the Afwaj al-Muqawama al-Lubnaniya (Battalions of the Lebanese Resistance), for which the acronym is Amal or "hope."[15] In the opening days of the civil war, Amal's initial impulse was to bide its time by spreading its resources among the warring militias. But with the introduction in 1976 of Syrian forces, which entered Lebanon to ensure that the Palestinians did not consolidate their hold on Beirut, Amal shifted its allegiance to Damascus. As the PLO became progressively weaker in southern Lebanon, the Amal grew in strength. That strength increased with the 1978 Israeli incursion, the disappearance of the Imam al-Sadr,[16] and the Iranian Islamist revolution of 1979.

These events were crucial for the survival of the Shia community and for the stability of Amal. Once the leader was lost, his personality began to accrue the myths and aura of martyrdom—confirmed in no small way by the example of Khomeini himself. This occurred at an important juncture in time; that is, when the international, regional, and national direction of Iranian Shia politics was a matter for hot debate.

In 1982, two factions—the Islamic Amal under Hussein Mussawi and the Hizbollah (Party of God) associated with the clerical successors to al-Sadr on the Supreme Shiite Council—rose as Islamist alternatives to the Amal. This split not only reflected the growing influence of the Iranian experience on Lebanese Shiites but served as yet another example of the fragmented character of the Lebanese political culture.

The Islamic Amal gave militant expression to a number of concerns that Musa al-Sadr had voiced before his disappearance. It aimed at reversing the underpriviledged class status of the Shia by associating their struggle for dignity with the universal struggle of the downtrodden against Western imperialism. This internationalist point of view received tactical support from other radicals such as Muammar al-Qadhafi and Hafiz al-Asad, and it chimed in very well with Khomeini's political goals for the Iranian revolution. From its safe haven in the Syrian-controlled Biqa valley, the Islamic Amal unleashed a jihad against both the US presence in Lebanon and American ties to Israeli and Christian Lebanese forces. The October 1983 bombing of the Marine headquarters in Beirut and the kidnappings and airline hijackings that followed were the direct consequences of this jihad.

Although it has some shady links to the Islamic Amal, Hizbollah defined its role in the more limited context of successorship to Musa al-Sadr. The Hizbollah party, under the direction of Shaykh Muhammad Fadlallah, created a forum for the mobilization of the large Shiite community in West Beirut; thus, it found itself in direct competition with both the parent Amal and the considerably weakened Shiite zuama. Recognizing that the Lebanese government preferred to deal with institutions rather than personalities, Fadlallah used the council to pressure the Lebanese president, Amin Jumayyil, for communal concessions. He failed—largely because the Beirut government believed that a larger American role might reverse the popularity of the Christian-dominated state apparatus; but this event accentuated the latent radical tendencies of Hizbollah. By 1983, a new political direction was evident.

A cursory examination of the Hizbollah pronouncements shows that the clergy dominates the organization and that Fadlallah is attempting to adapt the Khomeinist interpretation of wilayat al-faqih to the Lebanese environment. An important point to keep in mind here is that the Lebanese clergy differs from its Iranian counterpart in that it does not control Shiite religious endowments;[17] hence, the Lebanese clergy could not expect to have the necessary independent source of income that guaranteed the Iranian clergy freedom to remain outside state patronage and oppose state power. But this did not prevent the Hizbollah from adopting the Khomeinist position on an Islamic republic in Lebanon. Its efforts have centered on transforming the Jabal Amil into a "homeland" endowed with Islamist state structures and on regrouping the Shiite population in the south.[18] In advocating the partition of Lebanon, Hizbollah was obliged to confront the dual problems of a physically separated Shiite constituency and the concentration of the Israelis and their South Lebanon Army proxy on the southern border.

The split of both the Islamic Amal and the Hizbollah from their parent body caused a divergence between the two strands that make up Khomeini's political theory in the Lebanese context. The first strand clearly reserves the primary institutional role in Islamist resurgence to the clergy; but this Hizbollah position is challenged by the Islamic Amal and militated against by the Lebanese political system. The second strand commits all believers to work with zeal for the elimination of all governments that exercise tyranny over Muslims—and to replace them with Islamist governments. The Islamic Amal has interpreted the latter to mean a regional confrontation with Israel and an international showdown with its imperial proxies. Hizbollah, on the other hand, works within the narrower confines of actual Lebanese realities as it attempts to build a Lebanese Shiite republic in the south.

The parent Amal organization had regained its secular leadership at the time of the disappearance of Musa al-Sadr. When Israel invaded Lebanon

13

in 1982, power was passing rapidly to Nabih Barri, a relative newcomer in the Shiite community. Barri represented the introduction of the overseas Shiite merchant community into Lebanese Shiite politics. Relative to the Christian Lebanese, whose overseas role has traditionally been a source of economic strength at home, the Shiite entrepreneurial class has only recently developed importance commensurate with its demographic preponderance in Beirut. Barri has tried to mobilize the Shiite bourgeoisie to challenge the stranglehold the Christian oligarchs have had on the Lebanese economy and political system. This makes Barri and the class he represents qualitatively different from his Iranian counterparts: whereas the Iranian merchant class maintained close economic, political, and family relationships with the religious establishment, the Lebanese Shiite merchant class wants power over the religious authorities so as to compete unhindered with the Christian elements that dominate the government.[19] Thus, Barri's Amal has attracted the opposition of the Hizbollah. Moreover, because it has committed itself to compete with the Christians for greater representation in the Lebanese parliament and for a redistribution of political, social, and economic resources, Barri's Amal has earned the opprobrium of the Islamic Amal, which works to replace the status quo nature of Lebanese democracy with a radical vision of Lebanon's political role in the region.

When the Jumayyil government signed a truce agreement with the Israelis in May 1983, Barri and the Amal did not join the National Salvation Front that opposed the truce; they tacitly supported the government side. Under attack by this new coalition of Druze, Sunni Muslim, and elements of the Lebanese left, the Jumayyil government called in US support. The subsequent bombardment by US naval forces of the mountains overlooking Beirut caused a rise in extremism among the Front militias that were competing with the Amal.

In the struggle for West Beirut, the Amal was militarily victorious but remained politically isolated from the rest of the Shiite community. The key player in the isolation of the Amal was Syria; and for opportunistic reasons, Syria supported the Amal. But Syria had also to consider the wishes of her Iranian ally; and as long as Syria permits a large number of Iranian Pasdaran to operate from the sanctuary of the Biqa valley, the power of Barri's Amal to unite the community will be severely undercut.

In the intense struggle for power that has marked low-intensity conflict in Lebanon since 1975, it would appear that the focal point of competition will once again be the south. The PLO is for the moment gone, and elements of a disunited Shiite community have filled the vacuum. The Islamic Amal and the Hizbollah are already well entrenched in the south; it will not be long before Barri's Amal is obliged to compete in force. Facing these Shiite factions is the South Lebanon Army, a surrogate of the departed Israeli occupation force. And the Syrians are certain to ensure that their own interests are protected.

In Bahrain, the aborted coup of 1981 temporarily halted the expansion of Khomeinism on the Arab side of the Gulf, demonstrated the weakness of Iranian revolutionary Islamism as a strategic substitute for the late shah's imperialism, and denied Iran the possibility of isolating Arab support for Iraq. Lebanon, however, was a different matter. The presence of Pasdaran in the Biqa valley signaled the first venture of the revolution of right belief into the uncertain world of Arab tactical alliances. Here, Khomeinism occupied unfamiliar ground. While the Ayatollah could depend on Syria for aid against Iraq, Syria could not be sure that Khomeini's zealots would not disturb the delicate political balance that served Damascus's hegemonical interests in Lebanon. Thus, tension arose from an asymmetry of goals between the two partners. Whereas the Khomeinists wished to sweep into Lebanon to organize the fragmented Shiite community and impose an Islamic republic as the antidote to Lebanese anarchy, Syria occasionally cultivated that anarchy as a hedge against a strong Lebanese government acting to promote Israeli aims in the south. Moreover, the Syrian regime was having its own variety of Islamist troubles at home; it feared domestic interference from the uncontrollable Persians. Such an asymmetry rendered the low-intensity conflict environment all the more lethal.

The Iranians entered the arena of competition for Lebanese spoils intending to organize the country politically and ideologically but ended up playing the role of just another outside factor in a smoldering civil war. Hence, a number of competing Shiite groups, enmeshed in the contradictions of the Lebanese system, continue to struggle for the right to define the role of Islamist precepts in a meaningful political community.

Egypt and the Muslim Brotherhood

Egypt, too, has been bedeviled by the Islamist phenomenon. In Egypt, however, Islamism operates in a society whose social institutions developed from a common pre-Islamic historical matrix and whose territorial boundaries and religious communities are coterminous. Under these circumstances, religion plays an integrative role in the creation of the modern nation-state.[20] Such a role for religion is possible because Islam is uniquely suited, by virtue of its doctrinal comprehensiveness, its ideological congruence, its historical link with polity, and the all-encompassing scope of its teaching, its symbols, and its rituals, to give institutional support to the nation-building enterprise.[21] As such, Islam—and most appropriately in its Sunni form—has always provided the polity with legitimacy. In Egypt, this has been historically true; Sunnism, in contradistinction to the Shiite oppositional tradition, has acted to stabilize society.

The rise of Gamal Abd al-Nasir and his revolutionary pan-Arab ideology

15

challenged the role Islam had played in Egyptian Sunni Arab society. Nasir's pan-Arabism was preoccupied with the question of Western imperialism. Based on the idea that the political unity of Arab states remained the best defense against Western intervention, and predicated on the cultural, linguistic, ethnic, and historical affinities of the Arab peoples, pan-Arabism demanded loyalty to the transcendental ideal of an Arab "nation." Such an ideal stressed the secular nature of pan-Arab political unity, the potential of pan-Arabism for social integration through rapid modernization, pan-Arabism's historical inevitability, and the pan-Arab commitment to social justice and redistribution of economic resources. Elitist, pragmatic, and supranational in that it called into question the rationale of individual state sovereignty and territorial integrity, pan-Arabism legitimized the struggle of the Arab peoples for a middle-road socialist solution that was neither capitalist nor Communist. In Nasir's view, Arab socialism was the only acceptable means by which the Arab nation could be rejuvenated, take its rightful place in world history, and secure prosperity for the Arab peoples. But this new set of sociopolitical and economic norms stood in opposition to Islamic values.

The triumph of the 1952 revolution in Egypt and the elaboration of Nasir's pan-Arab aspirations responded not only to a relative imbalance of power in Egypt's favor vis-à-vis other Arab states but to the real grievances that underpinned a palpable social crisis.[22] In exploiting that crisis, Nasir raised to the pantheon of pan-Arab virtues the destruction of Israel. For him, Israel represented the last vestige of transitional Western imperialism in the Middle East. Without its elimination, the Arabs could never be free to realize their drive toward unity. In committing Egypt militarily to this task, he assured her a paramount role in the pan-Arab alliance. Thereafter, pan-Arab unity would be inextricably linked to Nasir's assumption that Egypt had the right and the duty to marshal Arab regional forces under the banner of Egyptian one-state nationalism. And so while riding the crest of the wave of supranational ideology, Nasir was also subjecting the patterns of political interaction between Egypt and other Arab countries to considerable strain.

The strain was also evident within Egypt, where Nasir worked to socialize the Egyptian people to the goals of his pan-Arab revolution. He created a new class of military and civilian technocrats to carry out its programs, reorganized Egyptian state structures, and manipulated the internal sociopolitical relationships between traditional classes of people. And by subordinating religion and the religious establishment to the state, Nasir undercut the ability of Islam to play an integrative part in the maintaining of Egyptian social coherence.

Religion, however, had staked out its claim to guide Egypt's destiny long before the coming of Nasir. By the last decades of the nineteenth century, a new generation of Islamic thinkers had appeared in Egypt. They were

16

obliged to grapple with the question of the relationship of traditional religion to the requirements of the modern world. The Ottoman Turkish Empire, which had been the historical focus of Muslim political loyalty, was collapsing under the pressure of Western imperialism. The Arabo-Muslim world was looking for a new political identity.

The Islamic reformers proposed a revision of Islamic law so as to make it consonant with the idea of Western technology, social progressivism, and constitutional law. These modernists—for the most part, clerics who had had experience in the West—were essentially synthesizers and reconcilers of Western and Islamic opinions. They espoused a pan-Islamic union of all Muslim peoples against the domination of the West. Freedom of the Muslim peoples from colonialism and the assimilation to Islam of selectively borrowed Western ideas and practices seemed to these reformers sufficient for the rehabilitation of the Muslim world. As a great center of Islamic learning, Egypt occupied pride of place in the dissemination of this message; but the reformers lacked a program and were unable to gain political authority for their ideas. Nevertheless, this failed pan-Islamism did succeed in providing an ideological context for the rise of the Muslim Brotherhood (Jamiyyat al-Ikhwan al-Muslimin), the first native Islamist movement to propose itself as an organized alternative to the colonial Egyptian state and, later, to Nasir's pan-Arabism.

The Muslim Brotherhood was founded in 1928 by the reformer Hassan al-Banna. In elaborating the Brotherhood's political concerns, al-Banna parted company with the modernists over whether Western political concepts were of value for recreating a Muslim identity. The rejection of Western concepts was to al-Banna a logical reaction to Britain's failure to grant Egypt the political freedom necessary to implement Islamic sociopolitical ideals. Through the Brotherhood, al-Banna argued that Islam would foster a new identity by furnishing all Muslims with a comprehensive set of scientific, economic, pragmatic, philanthropic, humanitarian, and nationalistic principles; scientific in the sense that the Quran can be explained "scientifically" (i.e., literally); economic inasmuch as the mission of Islam is to encourage the growth of national wealth and to promote social justice, equality, and opportunity; pragmatic because Quranic belief requires the unity of Egyptians and all Islamic peoples; philanthropic since Islam demands a struggle against ignorance, poverty, and disease; humanitarian through the universal precepts of Islam; and nationalistic in its quest to liberate Egypt and all the Arab countries from foreign rule. To al-Banna, jihad alone (the fusion of community improvement and political struggle) could achieve the final goal of freedom.[23]

To this end, al-Banna fashioned his movement into a community of belief; and he had a clear strategy for propagating his comprehensive Islamic worldview. He first emphasized social cohesion and self-sufficiency by encouraging his followers to construct private (ahli) neighborhood mosques, endow religious educational centers for their children, fund small hospitals and dispensaries, capitalize small commercial and industrial enterprises, and form social clubs for the discussion of issues vital to the Brotherhood.[24] The actual political deliberations of the Brotherhood took place in "cells" under the leadership of an "amir" (commander, both secular and religious) and were linked in an organizational hierarchy to al-Banna, the "Amir al-Mu'minin" (Commander of the Faithful).

Early in the life of the Brotherhood, al-Banna set down its strategy for political ascendancy. He counseled the Brothers to avoid theological disputes with nonbelievers, domination by the British-controlled Egyptian elites, and political divisiveness. He sanctioned the occasional use of violence for political ends but preferred a gradual accession to power. He exhorted the Brothers to keep before them the ultimate aims of Islamic unity and the restoration of the caliphate. Most important, al-Banna demanded that any country which denied the primacy of Islam as the sole source of political loyalty be considered a tyrannical state.[25]

In al-Banna's movement, then, there existed the embryo of a new Islamic social order that faithfully replicated an older Islamic experience solidly anchored in the Quran and the early prophetic community. In projecting Muslim experience back into time, indexed against specific verses of the Quran, the Brotherhood aimed at recreating a utopian society unencumbered by traditional, linguistic, historical, and philological interpretations of the past.[26] This allowed the Brotherhood to address its message to Muslims with all the power of the psychological moment, to require all prevailing sociopolitical systems to accommodate to Holy Writ, and to provide a revolutionary ideological perspective that liberated believers from the oppression of alien sociopolitical systems.[27] Al-Banna and the leading ideologues of the movement, such as Sayyid Qutb, had recast Islam in positive social and political terms. They reconfirmed the metahistorical aspects of Islam and resacralized the faith. Once again, Islam emerged triumphantly to lead good against evil and belief against unbelief; and the Brotherhood reestablished the authenticity of Islam as a sociopolitical system guaranteed by God who, by extending social justice to all believers, affirmed the absolute equality of all believers in the struggle for a better future.[28] Because of its all-encompassing ideology, the Brotherhood was able to adapt to the vagaries of Egyptian political change and thus to absorb failures and disappointments during the troubled times between its founding and Nasir's ascendancy to power. But like all movements of its kind, it was not able to provide a programmatic answer to the problems it had posed.[29] This was one of its weaknesses when confronted with Nasir's new pan-Arab order.

The Nasirist state relied for its legitimacy on the power of its leader, charted its political and economic course by shifting its personnel to suit the needs of the state, practiced a form of limited political association, attempted to create a new political and administrative elite from the urban middle classes, and extended its control down to the lowest levels of the population by means of a mass-based single-party system.[30] Initially, the state was conciliatory to the Brotherhood because it wished to use both Islamic institutions and other representations of Islamic political interests as a basis for Egypt's regional dominance; but that was to change once the Nasirist revolution was consolidated.

By 1954, Nasir had subordinated the Muslim clergy and the large institutions of Islamic learning (such as the Azhar Mosque-University) under the Ministry of Religious Endowments (Awqaf), which served to enunciate state religious policy and pay the salaries of the clergy in government mosques. In 1958, Nasir announced the formation of the United Arab Republic with Syria, which resulted in closer coordination between the socioeconomic program of his revolution and the socialist objectives of the Syrian Baath party. The Brotherhood eventually ran afoul of Nasir's formula of Arabism, Islamism, Egyptian nationalism, and socialism because it was unable to tolerate Nasir's secular pro-Baathist philosophy as an alternative to Islamic government. After the Brothers made an attempt on his life, Nasir subjected them to periods of suppression until his death in 1970. In the meantime, and especially during the early 1960s, Nasir pressed forward his campaign to have the "socialist" basis of Islam recognized and to "nationalize" religion by bringing the private mosques, which were the strongholds of the Brotherhood, under the supervision of the government. These actions precipitated the final break of the Brotherhood with the Nasirist state.

In 1970, Anwar Sadat began his struggle for Nasir's mantle, having inherited the political problems that the June War of 1967 and the unresolved contest in the Yemen had generated. A series of economic crises also faced Sadat—crises that Saudi Arabian financial assistance could only partially alleviate. The deteriorating economy favored the solutions of the Egyptian Left, which also benefited greatly from Egypt's military connection with the Soviet Union.

Anwar Sadat's answer to these multiple pressures was to engage in a war with Israel that led to the 1979 peace treaty. It also led to Egypt's turning away from pan-Arabism and the Palestinian issue and toward a more self-contained perception of national priorities. Simultaneously, Sadat purged the Left and paved the way for a state retreat from intervention in the economic sphere—the latter designed to attract the kind of capital for reconstruction now unavailable from Arab sources. Sadat opened the country to American and Western investment. He called his new economic liberalization "infitah" or the "great opening," but its benefits did not extend to the poorer strata of the society; the very people whom Nasir made socially mobile, Sadat's policies deprived of opportunities for advancement.

Sadat failed because he was unable to address in a meaningful way the structural problems that had given rise to crisis under Nasir. This invited a revenge. The social classes that Nasir had made available for the appeal of pan-Arabism were now available in Sadat's time—especially after the Iranian revolution, the peace treaty, and the new friendship with America—for mobilization in the name of Islamist revolutionism.[31] These classes were formed from the rural immigrants who were flocking daily into the cities in search of work and from the recently educated urban dwellers who had received state jobs with no real possibility of professional mobility. Such people furnished the Brotherhood and other Islamist groups with fresh cadres. In retrospect, then, because the processes disruptive to Egypt's socioeconomic structures did not abate under Sadat, a crisis of political legitimacy occurred that simply exacerbated earlier anomalies; and sociopolitical circumstances provided propitiously for the repoliticization of Islam.[32]

If Nasir believed that Islam possessed "socialist" roots and should be subordinated to the state, Sadat claimed that the state and religion were compatible because both reflected "science and faith." Sadat's more accommodating position represented his attempt to build a tactical alliance with the Brotherhood in order to vitiate the appeal of the Egyptian Left. This meant that Islamism too would be permitted to benefit from the political liberalization of the 1970s implied by infitah. When Sadat began cautiously to extend certain political rights to the opposition parties and to associate them, through open parliamentary competition, in the decisionmaking process, the Brotherhood entered a new phase of political activism that centered around the media and the national assembly.

In 1976, the Brotherhood resurrected al-Banna's newspaper, *al-Dawa* (*The Call*), to capitalize on Sadat's relaxation of censorship. They propagandized for a new constitution which would elevate the sharia (the corpus of Islamic law) to the primary source of national legislation. The Brothers' goal was clearly to reestablish the official status of Islam in Egypt and to apply sharia to all aspects of personal statute. For the Brotherhood, changes needed in personal statute included promulgation of the Islamic criminal code, a woman's dress code, mandatory memorization of the Quran in the state bureaucracy, prohibition of alcohol, and a prohibition against men working in women's hairdressing salons.[33] Faced with the fear of alienating a large and important Coptic Christian community, Sadat argued that sharia should constitute the principal but not sole source of legislation; hence, all of the Brotherhood's proposals, with the exception of the ban on alcohol, were effectively tabled.

Sadat's accommodationist policies also affected the Brotherhood's ideological stance on a number of other issues. The Brothers had always held tenaciously to the ideal of the recovery of Palestine; but in accepting Sadat's prejudice against the Nasirist form of pan-Arab liberation, they began to insist that the question was a Muslim-Jewish affair that had to be solved in the context of pan-Islamic unity.[34] No doubt encouraged by the Iranian revolution, the Brotherhood nevertheless chose to pursue this objective as a "party of Islamic democracy." Had they been successful in gaining a deciding voice in parliament, they might have forced the Egyptian government to espouse their cause. Sadat may have been interested in accommodation, but he was not prepared for competition. Even when the Brotherhood adjusted its economic view of the world to suit the modified capitalism implied in the politics of infitah, Sadat believed their motives were purely tactical. He resisted all efforts to construct a modus vivendi on Brotherhood terms. What the gradual shift in Brotherhood views did illustrate was that the petite bourgeoisie made mobile by Nasir's reforms of the previous decade were coming back to haunt Sadat, since it was these people together with a growing class of professionals who, though they were the net beneficiaries of infitah, were now joining the ranks of the Islamists.[35]

Sadat's response was to crack down in 1979 on the increasing power of the Brothers. The Brothers' politics of jihad against Israel had made their political participation irreconcilable with Sadat's policy of rapprochement with the West, détente with Israel, and hostility toward the Iranian revolution. It was not surprising that Sadat felt an ambiguity toward the reforms demanded by the Brotherhood; these reforms might frighten away Western business and upset the Coptic population.[36]

Sadat used the pretext of the January 1977 riots, which radical elements of the Brotherhood had unleashed against Cairo pleasure spots, to suppress the organization. But it was too late. By the end of 1979, the Brotherhood had penetrated the universities and created a front, the al-Jami'ah al-Islamiyyah, which took over most of the student councils. Islamism was now already well established within the ranks of the army, setting the stage for the eventual assassination of Sadat in 1981 and the enduring problem that his successor, Hosni Mubarak, would have to face.[37]

The Muslim Brotherhood had arisen in Egypt as a reaction to Nasirist internal and external policics. Thc Islamist groups spawncd in the universities and in the army during the late 1970s, such as the Jihad, represented the accumulated frustration of those for whom Nasirism was a failure and Sadat the unregenerated revisionist. The Jihad in particular, from which the army assassins of Sadat derived their inspiration, gave a new twist to Islamic militancy. Egyptian Marxists contended that the rise of the Jihad was related directly to Sadat's encouragement of religion to check political leftism; the sociologists tended to think that the Jihad came about in response to the breakdown of traditional Egyptian communal values under the impact of rapid urbanization, rural migrations to the cities, and the ensuing poverty of the citizenry. The secularists saw in the Jihad the decline of the Nasirist secular state. The psychologists and economists believed that adherence to the Jihad demonstrated an effort of youth to flee sexual repression and economic deprivation by taking to the sanctuary of private mosques as a cover for petty crime. The traditional ruling establishment viewed the Jihad as the work of "outside agitators" such as Khomeini.[38] All these explanations contain a germ of truth; and collectively they were potent factors for the Jihad's overall success.

The Jihad emerged in 1974, engineering a failed coup in the Cairo Military Technical Academy. Reorganized, it reappeared to challenge security forces in Alexandria in 1978. Sadat included the Jihad in his 1979 suppression of all Islamist groups. By 1980, Jihad was reconstituting itself all over the country in cells that resembled the organizational structure of the Brotherhood. Each cell had its amir (commander) who reported to the Amir al-Mu'minin (Commander of the Faithful), president of the Jihad's Majlis al-Shura (consultative council), which set policy for the entire organization. The Amir al-Mu'minin was usually a man of some religious competency, since he was required to issue a "fatwa" (juridical decision) on whether policy was at variance with Holy Writ. The first amir al-Mu'minin, a former professor of Quranic studies at Asyut University, provided the connection of the Jihad with the university Islamists.[39] That the Jihad colluded with like-minded extremists in places like Asyut, and that it found provincial universities there a good source of recruits, illustrates how heavily the traditional regions of the countries were coming under the assault of urbanization and how rapidly the discontinuities between rural and urban societies were accelerating.[40]

The growth of Jihad cells depended primarily on remittances from Egyptian workers abroad. The extremists purchased weapons and propagandized their cause on cassette tapes.[41] Because of Sadat's liberal policy concerning private mosques, the Jihad was free to enlarge its structure through personal contacts among believers and to establish centers for more intensive study of its doctrine.[42] Thus, Sadat provided the Jihad with the means for his own downfall. On the eighth anniversary of the 1973 October War, while reviewing a military parade, Sadat was assassinated by a group of Jihadists (the Takfir wa Hijra faction: "Repentance and Holy Flight") that had formed within the army.

In the subsequent trial of the assassins, much valuable information about the new Egyptian Islamism came to light. The leadership came from the middle professional classes and from the army, often reflecting the small town and rural background of the national leadership itself; but the vast bulk of the militants were young students and people from lower and middle income jobs—the very classes created by the Egyptian revolution.[43] This was in sharp contradistinction to the Iranian model where the Khomeinist revolution was carried on the backs of the traditional religious elites and the urban merchant class who had always been the traditional historical ally of the clergy.[44] Furthermore, the purpose of Takfir wa Hijra in killing Sadat was not to foment a revolt or a revolution. No evidence was produced during the trial that suggested a master plan to overthrow the Egyptian government; but the assassination did conform to the idea that revolt against a sitting government, in accordance with the Quranic injunction to "command the good and forbid the evil," was legitimate. This established at least an ideological link between Takfir and the Muslim Brotherhood. Both believed that their creed gave them the right to exercise authority in and over society and to interpret those rules by which society was to live. Insofar as society was ordained by God, any contravention of God's rules by a secular government immediately put that government outside the purview of God's society; consequently, Sadat and his government were guilty of kufr (apostasy). In the eyes of Takfir, Sadat had committed kufr by not applying sharia law as an antidote for the ills of the nation. He was not a true believer, required no allegiance, and could become the legitimate object of a Jihad for his removal. Moreover, Sadat had conspired with the Americans and the Israelis, sworn enemies of Islam, which further enraged the assassins and led them to proclaim that Muslims should no longer consider the Jews and the Christians a "tolerated people" (Ahl al-Kitab).

The difference between the old and the new Egyptian Islamism can be found in the Jihadist charge that the Muslim Brotherhood and some of the more moderate Islamists showed no activism in the promotion of jihad. The Brothers had insisted that a broad base of support was necessary if jihad was to be successful; thus the Brotherhood justified its entry into post-Nasirist politics. The Jihad, on the other hand, believed strongly that only through the direct and immediate imposition of its will on the state could the majority of Egyptians be brought to an understanding of what God demanded of them.[45] On the general level of political strategy, therefore, the Jihad showed an affinity for the romantic nihilism of the Brotherhood's ideologue, Sayyid Qutb, from whom many of the ideas mentioned above are derived. On the tactical level, the Jihad practiced a complementary "Islamic Guevarism."

Islamism presents one of the most dangerous problems faced today by Hosni Mubarak. As long as the Jihad's adherents believe that their vision of the just society is correct and that contemporary Egyptian society is doomed to degenerate, the organization may be capable of producing charismatic leaders in the style of Khomeini. No argument from the traditional religious elites of the Egyptian community can undercut the Jihadist appeal. The Jihadists are no longer available to these arguments, since they contend that the old traditional elites—as well as the hard-line Nasirists and Communists—have forfeited the right to speak for Islamic authenticity. It is a matter of time before the Jihad uses the same reasoning to justify a final break with the more moderate Brotherhood.

It is extremely difficult to gauge the probability of success of an Islamist insurgency in Egypt. If such an insurgency should occur outside Iran, Egypt may well be the LIC environment in which it will succeed. Were Islamist forces to come to power in Egypt, they would benefit from more than fifty years of organizational experience and from their relatively knowledgeable understanding of Western categories of thought and political process. In the momentary absence of a charismatic leader, due to the Sunni tradition of consensual leadership, such forces would be obliged to rely more heavily on those organizational talents and on the control of the media. Thus, there might exist the possibility of the institutionalization of an Islamist power that reflects the socialization of the middle and petit bourgeois classes from which Egyptian Islamism derives is strength. And these classes have learned to survive their leaders.[46]

Egyptian Islamism has indigenous roots in modern Egyptian history, reflects the LIC environment in which it operates, and takes its unique character from the social crisis that history has produced. But the relationship of Egyptian Islamism to other Islamist ideologies such as Khomeinism is circumstantial. Iran has always lacked the liberal tradition of Egypt, the background of nationalism shared by elites and middle classes, and the long period of acculturation to poverty that the Egyptian poor have endured.[47] At best, Khomeini has given Egypt inspiration for change along Islamist lines; he has had no direct hand in shaping the confrontation that is to come.

Islamism in Tunisia

Although it is of more recent vintage, Islamism is no less a potent force for insurgency in Tunisia than it is in Egypt. Like the Egyptian Brothers, Tunisian Islamists have attempted to point out the deficiencies of the state in securing prosperity for its citizens. The fact that the state has so deeply permeated the sociocultural life of the average Tunisian with the message of modernity and development makes these deficiencies all the more glaring. Islamism speaks to Tunisians as an alternative political language.[48] Islamists find themselves in opposition to the Tunisian single-party system and the values of Habib Bourguiba's Destourian Socialist party (PSD), whose monopolization of the political process has been theoretically limited by Bourguiba's acquiescence to the concept of multipartyism. Up to the present, however, the state has not permitted the Islamists to enter the political arena legally; and so the Tunisian Movement of Islamic Tendency (MTI) remains a protest movement on the fringe of organized political life but one which endeavors, like the state, to co-opt religious symbols in a fierce competition for the allegiance of the populace. On the level of humanistic values, no differences exist between the state and the MTI with respect to the application of religion to the improvement of the Tunisian moral milieu. The principal point of contention between them is not with moral theology but with the place Islam will occupy as a practical institution of national reconstruction.

The MTI professes the need for a religious state anchored in Sunni consensus whereas the PSD insists on the subordination of Islam to the secular state and its French rationalist tradition. And the situation is complicated by another important issue—succession to the leadership of a country where no real rule of law with respect to the institutionalization of power has been established.

This makes the Tunisian Islamist dilemma distinct from that of Egypt and Lebanon. In Lebanon, Islamist groups do not struggle against a central authority, an army, a bureaucracy, or any oppressive state force because none of these exist. In Egypt, Islamist forces were repressed by a strong state married to a pan-Arab philosophy that fuels Egypt's regional political aspirations. In Tunisia, the MTI and PSD do not disagree over the historical right of the state to exist and to define its relationship with other states. Rather, it is that the MTI contests the probity of the present Tunisian regime. And the ways both party and Islamists go about translating their demands into reality are marked by a remarkable similarity in sociopolitical assumptions.

This has occurred because Islam and nationalist politics have been linked in the struggle for independence. The great genius of Habib Bourguiba, the architect of the Tunisian state, was to make Islam a crucial element in the struggle for decolonization by portraying it as a repository of purely Tunisian values. But after 1956 and the shift from independence politics to the politics of nation-building, Bourguiba opened a campaign against organized Islam because the Islamic reformist views of the Tunisian religious establishment were too closely associated with his political rivals, the Old Destour (Constitutionalist) party.

Bourguiba's determination to secularize religion has never wavered significantly. Official Islam was to be reconstructed along the lines of a "political" religion with the state serving in place of the "imamate" and Bourguiba as its "imam." To accomplish this task, Bourguiba brought the religious authorities under the control of the state by placing the major mosques, their religious endowments, and the curricula of their schools in the hands of a minister for religious affairs. At the same time, he promulgated a new Code of Personal Statute which effectively made matters of marriage, divorce, inheritance, and civil rights for women the prerogative of the civil courts. Thus Bourguiba, like Nasir, left organized Islam with a carefully delineated sphere of influence shorn of any real power.

This state of affairs held sway in Tunisia during the 1960s while the PSD concentrated on the fight against underdevelopment. However, when the Tunisian socialist economy began to break down in the 1970s, Islam reappeared to protest the moral excesses of secular PSD economics and the party's political oppression. Interestingly, this protest erupted, as in Egypt, both in the countryside and in the cities, among the lower middle classes that had not shared in the economic and political gains of modernization during the first decade of independence. This happened for two basic reasons: first, the government was interested in industrialization rather than agriculture and therefore favored the development of urban areas and the coastal regions where the infrastructure for rapid industrialization was already in place; and second, the party, which was already synonymous with the state and the accepted political instrument of development, reflected in its distribution of resources the native regions of its elites. Thus the economically and politically dispossessed, not having access to the fruits of the society—especially in terms of the educational opportunities on which the creation of the human resources necessary to fuel development was founded—turned increasingly to the Islamist alternative.

A number of important events determined the fortunes of the new Islamism.[49] In the autumn of 1969, the experiment in agricultural collectivization failed because the PSD was unable to provide the necessary leadership and expertise for the success of a guided economy. The end of collectivization coincided with the fall from grace of Minister of Economy and Plan Ahmad Ben Salah, who had used his position as a stepping-stone to presidential succession.[50] Thus the economic crisis, with its barely concealed overtones of political competition, highlighted the potentially dangerous consequences of a country without an institutional procedure for the transfer of power. Played out against this background of economic instability, a succession crisis and the disintegration of national unity, which resulted from the inability of the PSD to carry out its role as the motor of development, Muslim sentiment resurged to demand the return to an authentic Islamic culture (asala) void of reference to the West.

At the beginning of the 1970s, the new Islamism wanted nothing more than cultural autonomy from the Bourguibist state. The Islamists resented Bourguiba's usurpation of "imamic" charisma and his imposition, through the policies of state and party, of Western positivism in the sphere of personal law. The students of the Zitouna Mosque in Tunis, now the theological faculty of the University of Tunis, gave form to this resentment when, in early 1970, they asked the government to permit the organization of a Society for the Preservation of the Quran. Fearing a shift of student sympathy toward more radical pan-Arab causes, such as Baathism and Colonel Qadhafi's variety of Nasirism, the government acquiesced. Furthermore, the government relaxed its surveillance of the private mosques as an extension of the spirit of economic liberalization that was intended to redirect the public sector toward a more aggressive capitalistic orientation. The mosques rapidly became the locus for the coalescing of Islamist sentiment, which led to formation of a loosely knit Movement of Islamic Tendency; hence, the government played a role in undercutting the social basis for single-party supremacy.

In January 1978, the General Union of Tunisian Workers declared a nationwide strike in response to the government policy of holding down

26

the minimum wage for industrial and agricultural laborers in the face of mounting inflation. As the strike quickly spread throughout the country, it was savagely put down, thus ending the historic cooperation between the syndicalist movement and the single party. Many other issues surfaced in the wake of this event. It was now obvious that the previous decade of laissez-faire capitalism had not succeeded in attracting needed capital into the country, that the population was growing younger and less responsive to Bourguibist values, and that the state could no longer provide employment for the graduates of its universities and technical schools.

More than any other event, the 1978 disturbances acted to politicize the Islamist movement; and in 1981, the MTI petitioned the government to recognize it as a legal political party. The government was preparing for elections to municipal and national office and had promised to enfranchise opposing political opinion. But the rigged elections were engineered in such a way as to deny all but the Communists legal status and so belied the government's pledge to encourage multipartyism. Deceived by the government, the MTI joined the active opposition. This prompted the government to begin a campaign to control the private mosques, forcing the MTI into acts of defiance for which its leaders were incarcerated.

In the winter of 1984, rioters took to the streets to protest the suspension of subsidies for staples such as bread, sugar, and tea. The subsidies had long served to drain Tunisia's hard currency reserves and this austerity was considered a necessary measure if the government was to continue to qualify for assistance from the International Monetary Fund. Troubles erupted immediately in the countryside, where the effects of the price rises were most keenly felt among the poorest classes; but they quickly spread north to the large cities. It was rumored that the MTI was involved in the instigation of these riots. But there is no proof of the government's contention that the MTI willfully concocted the violence to challenge government control, even though it is true that Islamist elements stood in the forefront of the disturbances.

In fact, nothing leads us to believe that the MTI was as tightly organized as the Egyptian Brotherhood or their Jihadist competitors. Certainly the MTI was technically capable of sparking an urban insurrection, but it possessed no cell structure to speak of, did not resort to clandestine activity with the aim of overthrowing the republic, and was not blessed with a central leadership capable of enunciating the interests of all Tunisian Islamists. Like the Brotherhood's relationship with the Jihad, the MTI had also undergone its internal schisms over the issue of Islamist representation in political life.[51] To a certain degree, internal dissension within the MTI replicated the tensions between the Brotherhood and the Jihad over the proper attitude that Islamists ought to adopt toward the state within an elected parliamentary structure.

Like the Jihad in Egypt, the MTI appeals to university students; and,

27

indeed, the University of Tunis has been a hotbed of Islamist agitation since the appearance of the Society for the Preservation of the Quran. The few sociological studies that have been done on its membership concur that, within the core of its activists, the student from rural, petit bourgeois origins—the class most highly mobilized by the Bourguibist philosophy— is overrepresented.[52] The sympathizers with the movement, however, come from the urban lower middle classes and the unemployed. The leaders of the MTI, on the other hand, are those who possess a background in the liberal professions such as law, medicine, and the exact sciences—precisely those on whom the state and the party have drawn for their postindependence elites.[53]

This phenomenon deserves some explanation because therein may lie the key to an understanding of the conditions under which Islamism could mount a successful challenge to the established order. Economic and political arguments are usually the first to be proposed as reasons for the appeal of Islamism to this particular class of protestors. Both arguments, however, are flawed. Although it is true that Islamism often makes a greater impression on the lower socioeconomic ranks, the argument from economic deprivation does not provide an adequate explanation for the popularity of Islamism among the professionals, technocrats, and women whom the Tunisian educational system has assiduously cultivated by giving them accelerated access to training. And, whereas there is no doubt that the Tunisian political system has failed to furnish a multiparty context for the expression of diverse political views, the system continues to generate a forum for the ideas of the very same class from which the MTI draws its leadership. The presence of women in the Islamist movement is likewise anomalous; but among all the women of the Middle East, Tunisian women possess the most civil rights.[54]

In the Tunisian context, the argument from a psychosocial deprivation perspective appears to be more cogent and plausible. This argument stresses the lack of continuity between the independence and postindependence generations in terms of ideological identity and social orientation. Inasmuch as the state has not fulfilled its mandate to promote social justice but has instead perpetuated inequalities, Islam becomes the language of secular rejection.

The Western model of social organization is founded on the rationalism of the Western technological and scientific order. Just as that order, with its material raison d'être, has undermined Western social morality and accelerated its decay, so has technology exercised a similar effect on Muslim societies, such as Tunisia, which have chosen to modernize on Western lines. The rationalism of Western technology makes no inherent normative assumptions; therefore, when in times of extreme socioeconomic dislocation Tunisian technocrats turn to technology for moral guidance, they find no readily available answers. Often, they will submerge their ambiguities about technology and modernization by returning to the explicit social and moral teaching of the Quran, which represents the sum total of societal aspirations for such individuals in terms of a recreation of the historical community of believers under the Prophet. In the Tunisian context, this variety of Islamism presents itself as superior to, and a substitute for, the secular, modernizing, and Westernizing Tunisian political outlook. In espousing such Islamism through association with the MTI, the technocrat avoids the pain of having to deal morally with the rapid transformation of his social circumstances. This has led to an Islamist revolt against the consumerist orientation of the Tunisian state implied in its acceptance of the material basis of Western technology, and it has ensured that the MTI would advocate a social and material puritanism, a striving for individual self-reliance, and a recovery of Islamic authenticity.[55]

In 1956, when Tunisia gained its autonomy from France, Bourguiba set about to circumscribe Islam and to cast religion in the role of enemy to secularization. Unfortunately, his campaign has not worked. Bourguiba's failed vision of a Tunisia modernized along purely Western lines is juxtaposed today to the resurgent Islamist vision of restored national unity organized according to Muslim precepts. That juxtaposition expresses itself in the vocabulary of social anxiety.[56] The principal actors in the Islamist drama are those who have most to gain and most to lose by the present tension.

Despite these circumstances, the Islamists have not necessarily opted for an Islamist state. Rather, they insist that the moral leadership of the national community should be theirs because only they are capable of understanding how to obtain the benefits of modern civilization without losing a traditional religious ethos.[57] Inasmuch as the MTI is willing to pursue its goal peacefully, the burden will fall on the state to make good on its promise of democratic pluralism. Notwithstanding the conflicting interpretation of what pluralism means, the MTI is more marked by Bourguibist political culture than is Bourguibism by Islam.[58]

The chances, then, of the MTI leading an insurrection against the state are slim. The political values shared by both Islamists and the PSD, and the weakness of the MTI as regards a theory of state, mitigate against this possibility. Moreover, the influence of the Khomeinist phenomenon on the MTI is for the moment indirect—offering an example to be emulated rather than a strategy and tactic to be followed.

In Tunisia and elsewhere, the real threat may come from the armed forces, were the military, as a legitimate instrument of state coercion, to become infected with the virus of radical Islamism. Islamism has, in fact, made some progress in that domain. In the autumn of 1983, a number of officers were arrested for participating in the formation of a cell of the Islamic Liberation Party within the air force.[59] But the Islamic Liberation Party has been associated with a Jordanian branch of the Egyptian Brotherhood;

hence, no evidence exists at present that points to the involvement of the indigenous Islamist movement in the suborning of the Tunisian military.

In the past few years, other non-MTI Islamist cells have been uncovered. As late as July 1986, four Islamist radicals were sentenced to death for carrying out military attacks against a variety of targets. These radicals claimed allegiance to the "Islamic Jihad." Their aim was the creation of an atmosphere of anarchy, the encouragement of a suitable climate for revolution, and the procurement of arms to fight against the Tunisian regime which in their eyes had sold out to French and American imperialism. Among those condemned to death was a lieutenant in the Tunisian army.[60]

As long as political and socioeconomic immobilism persists in Tunisia, the ground for the growth of a native Islamism will remain fertile. By the same token, the deeper Tunisia is dragged into the conflicts of her neighbors to the east, the greater the chance for a radical non-Tunisian variety of Islamism to take root. The combination of these forces can be disastrous under conditions of instability.

For the present, the Tunisian situation more closely mirrors the Egyptian situation than the predicaments faced by Arab nations elsewhere. In Egypt, Jihadists in the army very nearly brought down the government with the assassination of Sadat. Though an Islamist-inspired Tunisian army coup against an aged president is hardly likely, Islamist elements within the army may make common cause with the MTI at the time of his death if Bourguiba's successors do not face squarely the problem brought about by the national socioeconomic and political crisis. Such a common cause would be a terrible irony since the Tunisian armed forces have always been considered the least praetorian, most apolitical and most pro-Western military establishment in the Arab world.[61]

Conclusion

The true school of command lies in the general culture. Behind the victories of Alexander one always finds Aristotle.

—Charles de Gaulle

Conventional military confrontations in the Middle East tend to catch our attention because of their violence. But, historically speaking, such confrontations are becoming less frequent and may indeed be passing phenomena. The struggles with the greatest potential for redistributing political power are occurring within the Arab state system as a protest against the legitimacy of the secular state itself. These unconventional conflicts are fought on battlefields whose contours are indeterminate and shifting and where the actual battle has nothing to do with questions of state sovereignty, territoriality, or the maintenance of alliances. The battlefield exists everywhere; in cities, in towns, in villages, in the bush, in parliament, in trade union halls, in the corridors of government buildings, in the streets even, because the battle is for access to the minds and hearts of people.

The environment in which these battles take place fits the broad range of assumptions we make about the nature of low-intensity conflict. Low-intensity conflict is not programmatic, not prioritized as to objective, not materially intensive, not amenable to superpower intervention and arbitration, and not subject to the rules of conventional engagement. Low-intensity conflict is fluid in the scope of its operations; flexible in adjusting to conditions; geopolitically transregional; temporary and ad hoc in alliance-building; and, as regards its most salient feature in the Middle East, highly ideological.

This study has argued that Islamism is the most aggressive form of political ideology in the region today, and that the circumstances of its appeal will guarantee its prominence in the low-intensity environment. This being said, it must be recognized that despite some superficial affinities to Western categories of thought, Islamism is not derivative of Western political culture. The Western observer has too often tended to equate Islamism with a Leninist model of organization and a Marxist worldview. Whereas the Islamist worldview certainly demonstrates a striking similarity to the Marxist concept of historical determinism, nothing supports the thesis that Islamism acts as a single unified expression of inevitable historical forces. For example, Khomeinism, the only variation of Islamism to gain control of a state apparatus, may provide revolutionary incentive for Islamist movements everywhere; yet we have no reason to believe that Khomeinism furnishes a central political direction for like-minded Islamists outside of the Iranian sociopolitical milieu in which the development of Khomeini's movement took place. In contradistinction to Marxism-Leninism, Islamism espouses puritanism rather than social radicalism, relies on mass consciousness-raising rather than on the vanguardism of an elite party structure, tends to operate openly rather than subversively in society, denies the material—and therefore secular—concept of the historical process, and depends for its success on scriptural literalism. This not only implies that Islamism is directly opposed to the Marxist-Leninist formula; it underscores the Islamist belief that all forms of Western sociopolitical and economic ideology are alien to Middle Eastern society. In point of fact, Islamism has worked to expose the claim that Western modernization theory provides a guide for the physical security and economic prosperity of the Muslim world. But to the Islamist, modernization itself is not the problem. It is moral corruption, brought about by modernization and Western imperialism, for which Islam offers itself as the necessary corrective.

The means by which Islamism seeks to purify society differ vastly. These means exist within, and respond to, distinct sets of social and political conditions. In Bahrain, Khomeini sponsored an internal insurgency to establish Iranian power in a region Iran considers its ethnic, religious, and historical irredenta. Hence, the Bahrain incident may be understood in the light of historical Iranian state imperialism. In Lebanon, on the other hand, Islamism rallies the sentiment of a previously fragmented Shiite community for recognition of its rights to political authority based on the demographic formula of Lebanese confessionalism.

Egypt presents a somewhat different picture. Islamist roots reach deep into Egyptian society, reflecting the historic Sunni tendencies toward a consensual reformism of moral and intellectual life. Under the Muslim Brotherhood, a new Islamic humanism arose. Under conditions of a deteriorating economic situation, it competed with the West to define Islam's relation to modernism, Egypt's Arab destiny, and the right to determine the course of the pan-Arab polity. The competition was prolonged well into the Nasirist period; and by the time Anwar Sadat acceded to power, the social concepts of the Brotherhood had hardened into a turgid antistate orthodoxy that led, in the wake of the Israeli-Egyptian peace treaty, to the radical revisionism of the Jihad.

Tunisian Islamism also confronted the question of modernism, but the confrontation took place within a context circumscribed by the theory of the secular state. The Movement of Islamic Tendency attacked the Tunisian state not so much because the state resembled a structure alien to Islam but because the state acted to colonize the country internally. In a state without provisions for the institutionalization of power, it is not surprising that the Movement of Islamic Tendency accept Bourguibist political assumptions while it rejects Bourguibist political remedies. The danger for Tunisia lies in the growing influence within the armed forces of nonindigenous Islamism that threatens to involve Tunisia in extraregional and international issues.

On first view, then, the similarity of the four case studies of Islamism presented in this paper is more apparent than real. While it is true that on the plane of social ethics, Islamism from Iran to Tunisia stresses the importance of a puritanical morality, the weight of precedent in history, and the truth of dogma, it is likewise true that on the level of the political relationship of state to religion, Islamism reveals a surprising ambiguity. This ambiguity accounts for the protean character of Islamism and the wide range of variation in its sociopolitical characteristics. The farther afield one moves from the charismatic model of Iranian Shiite religious organization and into the Sunni Arab world, the more pronounced this ambiguity becomes with respect to the issues of secularism, anti-Westernism, the colonial struggle, and one-state nationalism. Faced with the task of formulating a political-military policy to contain the potential of Islamism for low-intensity conflict, the policymaker must ground his decision firmly on a tolerance for such ambiguity.

The solution to the Islamist problem rests in the final analysis with the regional elites in power.[62] No solution may be affected that eschews careful long-term study of regional geopolitical realities in favor of immediate military interventionism; the problem does not and will not respond to the managerial logic of conventional military thinking. For US political-military strategists, nothing less than a change in their understanding of Middle Eastern culture is required. To take a liberty with de Gaulle's epigram, the strategist must realize that behind the victories of Saladin the presence of the Prophet Muhammad looms large. Failure to understand this is to confirm the dictum of the historian Thomas Carlyle that collective wisdom often reflects individual ignorance.

If low-intensity warfare in the Middle East is to be contained, the US military will be obliged to adjust to thinking in terms of these regional realities and to cease filtering its attitudes through its relationship with the Soviet Union. Once freed from the poverty of globalist thinking, policymakers may devise policies that aim at strengthening Middle Eastern allies through aid and training programs of visible worth. Such programs should include instruction in counterinsurgency techniques, the encouragement of regional security by means of judicious military transfers and defense arrangements, and the necessary provisions for the creation of a regional rapid deployment force.[63] In this way, the United States will be able to avoid the political liability of a counterproductive presence in the region while, at the same time, ensuring for itself the diplomatic flexibility that future conflict resolution in the Middle East will surely demand.

NOTES

1. For an overview of low-intensity conflict and its global implications, see Yehezkel Dror, "High Intensity Aggressive Ideologies as an International Threat," *Jerusalem Journal of International Relations* 9, no. 1 (March 1987): 153–69.

2. *Low Intensity Conflict and the Principles and Strategies of War* (Carlisle Barracks, Pa.: Strategic Studies Institute, US Army War College, 20 May 1986), 15.

3. Ibid., 16.

4. Alexander George presents a theoretical consideration of the characteristics of ideology in his article "Ideology and International Relations: A Conceptual Analysis," *Jerusalem Journal of International Relations* 9, no. 1 (March 1987): 2.

5. Two particularly good introductory essays on the nature of the Islamic worldview as it touches on political society are W. M. Watt, *Islamic Political Thought* (Edinburgh: Edinburgh University Press, 1968); and Hamid Enayat, *Modern Islamic Political Thought* (Austin: University of Texas Press, 1982).

6. For an elaboration of Khomeini's political theory, see Elie Kedourie, *Islam in the Modern World* (New York: Holt and Rhinehart, 1980), 43–66.

7. An excellent summation of the development of contemporary Iranian politics as it applies to the Shiite clergy can be found in the introduction to Shahrough Ahkavi's *Religion and*

Politics in Contemporary Iran (Albany: State University Press of New York, 1980).

8. For an extended discussion of these points in the context of a typology of Khomeini's revolution see Ernest Gellner, "Inside Khomeini's Mind," *New Republic*, 18 June 1984, 29–30.

9. "65 Arabs Arrested in Sabotage Plot," *New York Times*, 16 December 1981; "Arrests Continue in Bahrain," *New York Times*, 17 December 1981; "Also of Note in the Middle East," *Christian Science Monitor*, 18 December 1981.

10. Sa'id Arjomand, "The Shi'a in the Middle East: Communal and Transnational Goals" iddle and Transnational Goals" (Washington, D.C.: Middle East Consultants, Inc., 10 February 1986), 7.

11. For details of the coup, see Robin Wright, *Sacred Rage* (New York: Simon and Schuster, 1985), 114–19. Wright differs with the *New York Times* account as to the political affiliation of the five armed Iranians. The *Times* claims that they belonged to al-Dawa, a Shiite revolutionary group operating in Iraq. *New York Times*, 16 December 1981.

12. *Middle East International*, 9 April 1982, 4–5.

13. Arjomand, 7–8.

14. Ibid., 8–10.

15. For an in-depth look at the creation of Amal, see Augustus Richard Norton, "Harakat Amal" (Paper delivered at the American Political Science Association annual meeting, Denver, 2–5 September 1982.

16. The disappearance of Musa al-Sadr in Libya remains today cloaked in mystery. It has been hinted that Colonel Qadhafi was somehow involved in his presumed assassination and that his death was linked to the Imam's violent anti-PLO stance. Fouad Ajami puts Musa al-Sadr into the context of these events; see his article, "Lebanon and Its Inheritors," *Foreign Affairs*, Spring 1985, 778–99.

17. Arjomand, 49.

18. At least this seems to be the present direction of the Hizbollah. See "The Iranian hand that stirs the Lebanese pot," *The Economist*, 27 September 1986, 37–38.

19. Arjomand, 49.

20. Terrance Carroll, "Islam and Political Community," *International Journal of Middle East Studies* 18, no. 2 (May 1986): 200.

21. Ibid.

22. Maridi Nahas, "State Systems and Revolutionary Change," *International Journal of Middle East Studies* 17, no. 4 (November 1985): 523.

23. Abd al-Moneim Sa'id Aly and Manfred W. Wenner, "Modern Islamic Reform Movements: The Muslim Brotherhood in Contemporary Egypt," *Middle East Journal* 36, no. 3 (Summer 1982): 340.

24. Ibid., 338.

25. Ibid., 341.

26. Yvonne Haddad, "The Quranic Justification for an Islamic Revolution: The View of Sayyid Qutb," *Middle East Journal* 37, no. 1 (1983): 17.

27. Ibid.

28. Ibid., 28.

29. Bassam Tibi, "The Renewed Role of Islam in the Political and Social Development of the Middle East," *Middle East Journal* 37, no. 1 (1983): 13; Tibi, "Islam and Modern Ideologies," *International Journal of Middle East Studies* 18, no. 1 (February 1986): 24.

30. I. William Zartman, "Beyond Coercion: The Stability of the Arab State" (Paper presented at the 1986 Middle East Studies Association annual meeting, Boston), 14–17.

31. Nahas, 508.

32. Tibi, "Islam and Modern Ideologies," 24.

33. Aly and Wenner, 349.

34. Ibid., 351–52.

35. Ibid., 352.

36. Ibid., 355.

37. Ibid. On the general question of the relationship of modern Middle Eastern militaries to the political process, see Nazih N. M. Ayubi, "The Military Elite in the Contemporary Middle East" (Unpublished paper presented at the Middle East Institute, Washington, D.C. 8–9 June 1983).

38. Hamied N. Ansari, "The Islamic Militants in Egyptian Politics," *International Journal of Middle East Studies* 16, no. 1 (March 1984): 123–24.

39. Ibid., 126.

40. Ibid., 130–33. Jihad seemed to develop most rapidly in Upper Egypt because, as Ansari points out, this was the region of traditionally slower development, scarce resources, limited land for farming, and benign neglect of the government. Asyut and Minya were the cities of Upper Egypt where such glaring disparities were most visible. The population of Asyut province doubled in the last two decades and 45 percent of its inhabitants were crowded into the provincial capital. This was reflected in an increased enrollment in the university from 15,000 in 1971 to 28,000 in 1976. Islamic extremism of the Jihad variety was first felt as a distinct urban phenomenon in Asyut in 1975 and it was not surprising that the bloodiest confrontations between state and Islamists occurred there two days after Sadat's death. Similarly, Cairo's migrant belts experienced the same kind of disruption especially where housing was bad and where scarce agricultural lands were being developed on the outskirts of the city for urban and recreational properties as in the Giza area.

41. Ibid., 127.

42. Ibid., 129. Again Ansari indicates that the increase in "ahli" mosques seems to be the key to the successful organization of Jihad in the 1970s and into the 1980s. In a single decade, their number doubled to 40,000; and in 1986, Egypt had 436,000 mosques of which only 6,000 were under the control of the government.

43. Ibid., 133.

44. This point is put into the context of modern Iranian political culture by Hamid Algar. See his article "The Oppositional Role of the Ulama in Twentieth-Century Iran," in *Scholars, Saints and Sufis*, ed. Nikkie Keddie (Los Angeles: University of California Press, 1972), 231–56.

45. Ansari, 137.

46. The concluding argument is drawn from Aly and Wenner, 359–60.

47. Ibid.

48. The following points of comparison and explanation draw heavily on the arguments of Jean-Claude Vatin in his article "Revival in the Maghreb: Islam as an Alternative Political Language," in *Islamic Resurgence in the Arab World*, ed. Ali E. Hilal Dessouki (New York: Praeger, 1982), 221–48.

49. For a full discussion of these events in the context of contemporary Tunisian political history see Lewis Ware, *Tunisia in the Post-Bourguiba Era: The Role of the Military in a Civil Arab Rebublic* (Maxwell AFB, Ala.: Air University Press, February 1985); and Susan Waltz, "Islamist Appeal in Tunisia," *Middle East Journal* 40, no. 4 (Autumn 1986): 651–70.

50. The importance of the Ben Salah affair for the contemporary Tunisian predicament is summed up in Douglas Ashford's seminal article "Succession and Social Change in Tunisia," *International Journal of Middle East Studies* 4, no. 1 (January 1973): 23–39.

51. Within the MTI there exists a number of factions which separate the hard-liners and antidemocratic elements from the centrists who are willing to work within the system according to the Bourguibist rules of political engagement. This underscores the fact that the MTI is not a cohesive group on the strategic, tactical, or even ideological level. For implications of splits in the MTI, see Waltz, 659.

52. Ibid., 654–56.

53. Ware, 31–33.

54. Waltz, 662–65.

55. Ibid., 665–69.

56. Vatin, 243.

57. Ibid., 244.

58. Ibid., 247.

59. Ware, 34.

60. *Middle East*, October 1986, 60.

61. For a comparison of the structure, organization, and Bourguibist philosophy of the Tunisian military with other Arab militaries, see Ware, 47–48.

62. In this I am in complete agreement with the analysis of Professor Jerrold Green. See his contribution, "Ideological Challenges to American Involvements in the Persian Gulf," in *US Strategic Interests in the Gulf Region*, ed. William J. Olson (Carlisle Barracks, Pa.: Strategic Studies Institute, US Army War College, 10 October 1986), 107–21.

63. Of all the recommendations made by the above study, Professor Olson's suggestion of an Arab Rapid Deployment Force deserves the most careful consideration. See his concluding chapter, "An Alternative Strategy for Southwest Asia," in Olson, 203–25.

Soviet Russia and Low-Intensity Conflict in Central Asia: Three Case Studies

Dr Stephen Blank

The Soviet experience with low-intensity conflict is extensive and varied. Whether as participant or supplier to an external proxy, Moscow has bequeathed a significant legacy to students of this phenomenon. For example, the civil war and the widespread ethnic and peasant uprisings of 1918–24 were low-intensity conflicts. These conflicts left a profound mark on Bolshevik outlook and military history that conforms to the obsession with historical study for lessons applicable today. Thus, both Western and Soviet commentators point to the parallels between the Basmachi revolt and the present war in Afghanistan.

A study of selected Soviet experiences in such conflicts yields important clues as to what works and what fails in such conflicts, thus materially aiding the formation of US policy to deal with Communist insurgency tactics. For reasons of economy and of comparison within one region, we have deliberately restricted our study to action against Central Asian Muslims. This entails three low-intensity conflicts: the Basmachi uprising in 1918–31, the Soviet interventions in Iran, 1920–21 and 1941–46, and in Afghanistan since 1978. In ascertaining what has succeeded and what has failed, we inquire into the possibility of cataloging a possible inventory of tactics that would bring about desirable outcomes in Afghanistan and in future conflicts.

In studying these regions, one quickly finds that they all occurred in backward areas of intense religious loyalty that were increasingly under pressure from modernizing forces, pronounced ethnic fragmentation, and intense sociopolitical polarization. Common religious identity, intensely felt, animated the anti-Soviet movement. And, in all three arenas, the "Great Game" between Russia and its Anglo-American rival was always present.

Not surprisingly, therefore, Soviet practice has explicitly built on and refined the military-political tactics first developed in reintegrating and Sovietizing multinational Soviet Russia during the civil war and its aftermath. This Soviet "solution" of the national question and the related one of internal Sovietization was a constant source of inspiration in devising the means of extending the revolution abroad. Since much of the activity and rationale of Soviet foreign policy is the unending search for the most expeditious way of generating or Sovietizing such revolutions, this initial experience and subsequent refinements are of great importance for those who wish to compile the inventory previously mentioned.

Early on, Soviet leaders grasped that they could not prevail without their joint military-political leadership enjoying some basis of public support; that is, a cadre, even if small and controlled and propped up from Moscow. And on the morrow of the initial revolution, Moscow instantly began forming Communist parties among minorities within Russia. These groups consistently failed to seize power; therefore, by late 1918, the Red Army first started to conduct its own "liberation mission" under Lenin's guidance.

> With the advance of our troops to the west and into the Ukraine, regional provisional Soviet governments are being created to strengthen local Soviets. This situation has a positive side to it, in that it deprives the chauvinists of the Ukraine, Lithuania, Latvia, Estonia, of the credibility of the possibility of seeing in the movement of our troops an occupation and creates favorable conditions for the further movement of our troops. Without this situation, our troops in the occupied areas would be placed in an impossible situation and the population would not greet them as liberators.[1]

Such a military combination became indispensable to the Soviet leaders; and it has to include at least the potential for, if not the reality of, native mass support. By 1920, the same mold was cast for Bukhara and Khiva in Central Asia. They served as models, as Mongolia did later, for Sovietization of foreign countries. In May 1920, Deputy Foreign Commissar Karakhan recommended to Lenin that the Emirate of Bukhara be replaced with a pro-Soviet regime headed by the Young Bukharans. By August, they had been organized, along with Bukhara's first Communist, into a new Bukharan Communist party. Karakhan continued, stating that once this group was consolidated, an internal uprising, supported from Soviet territory by Bukharan troops—mainly deserters—should occur, after which Soviet troops would intervene, ostensibly to restore order, protect railroads, borders, and so forth.[2] Frunze, the Soviet commander, duly carried out these military-political tasks and added the fabrication of a foreign conspiracy (just as in Afghanistan) to justify the invasion.[3] In September 1920, the invasion took place according to script. So useful was the model that Joseph Stalin applied it six months later in Georgia. Soviet leaders have refined and updated it ever since.

However, as today in Afghanistan, the initial Sovietization attempts in Russia and the borderlands of the Soviet Union ran into violent opposition. From 1920–24, all the nationalities of Russia rose against Soviet rule. The tactics used by the Soviets in these counterinsurgency operations prefigured those used in Afghanistan today. Recent citations indicate the relevance of these insurgencies in the Ukraine and in Russia to operations in Central Asia from 1918–31 and in Afghanistan.

Tactics varied among these peasant uprisings. There were groups that fought pitched battles in Siberia and along the Volga, but the most well-known uprisings in Tambov and the Ukraine were guerrilla-type insurgencies. Soviet authorities reacted by lavishly (for those days) equipping the military with artillery, machine guns, cannons, armored cars, airplanes, thousands of bayonets, and even 10,000 swords. Mikhail Tukhachevsky likened the Soviet operation to a campaign, a war of serious urgency. These rebellions against Soviet rule then experienced systematic terror and war. It must be stressed that the tactics summarized here are taken from Soviet sources and are used in Afghanistan today. Not only were regular military units used, but Antonov's Tambov command staff was penetrated by Chekists and hostages were taken (they would be shot if rebel units appeared in the region). Those harboring "bandits" or their families would be shot. Starting in March 1921, the families of rebels were deported and, in June, despite admission of Soviet preeminence, all involved in any way with the uprising were deported, including entire villages. Tukhachevsky, the commander in Tambov, summed up pacification in the following terms.

> The Sovietization of the centers of rebellion in Tambov province followed a definite progression, district by district. After troops were brought into a given district, we would concentrate maximum force there—the army, the Cheka (secret police), and the party and Soviet apparatuses. While the military units were busy wiping out the bands based in the district and establishing revolutionary committees, the Cheka was catching any surviving bandits. After Soviet power was consolidated in one district all our forces were transferred to the next.[4]

The Central Committee, in April 1921, ordered provincial party and Cheka committees to join forces in suppressing outbreaks throughout the region.[5] It should be noted that the elevation of Najibullah in Afghanistan represents an analogous process.

Combating the Nestor Makhno-led insurgency in the Ukraine, Michael Frunze utilized tactics he had developed in Central Asia against the Basmachi insurgency. Politically, he mobilized all political organizations—party, Soviet, and Cheka—to split the basic mass from their leaders. Militarily, he used operations derived from his Turkestan experience against the rebels. Since Col Gen M. A. Gareev's book is intended to be an authoritative exposition of Soviet strategic doctrine, it is worth noting that these tactics were used in Afghanistan about the time Gareev sent the book to press. Operating against guerrillas, Frunze

> decided to operate against the bands in small, highly mobile detachments, using predominantly cavalry units and machine gun carts. A special "flying corps" was organized which was to constantly pursue, surround, and destroy the bandit detachments. All the garrisons, troop units, and facilities were given specific missions to combat the bandits. The establishing of the Communist special purpose units (ChON) (ancestors of Spetsnaz troops—SJB) was a new form of military training and involvement of the workers in the active struggle against the bands.[6]

If one substitutes armored helicopters for cavalry and mobile land forces, one immediately grasps the contemporary message in this historical discussion.

Frunze's further observations on local wars, summed up in his writing on the French in Morocco, are also relevant in this connection. He criticized them for mechanically transplanting the lessons of World War I and the European theater to Morocco. (Gareev's real targets were Soviet officers who did the same thing in Afghanistan.) Gareev, through Frunze, reprimands those who fought a positional war using heavy artillery and bombing to occupy land. Soviet, and supposedly French, commanders did not switch over to fluid practicality as to local conditions of war, to the need for fighting both offensively and defensively, or to the political goals of the campaign.[7] But it is in Central Asia, against the Basmachi insurgency, that the experience of counterinsurgency is most profound.

The Basmachi Insurgency

The Basmachi insurgency was largely staffed by peasants; but some elements of the commercial classes of Central Asia, motivated by the Soviets' attacks on religious institutions as much as by economic devastation and terror, were also involved. Pro-Russian land and water policy, cavalry raids against religious organizations, and policies that facilitated the death by famine of 1,000,000 Muslims, facilitated the revolt. It began in 1918, lasted until 1931, and hit its high-water marks in 1920–22 and again in 1929. The revolutionary goal was reactionary and theocratic, though not untouched by pan-Turkic or pan-Islamic agitation. The revolution's greak weakness, like that of the Afghan rebels, was its inability to settle on an agreed leadership and to advance a coherent program for governing the region. Militarily, the Basmachi earned the respect of their enemies as fearsome warriors.

The revival of Soviet and Western interest in them can be attributed to the clear parallel, noted by both, with events in Afghanistan.[8] The Basmachi insurgency typified low-intensity conflict or insurgency warfare. Their tactics took the form of ambushes, hit-and-run attacks, raids, and small unit combat against Soviet formations of superior size and equipment. They received little help from abroad—far less than Soviet fantasies allege; and they were frequently underarmed as well as isolated. Their motivations were largely religious, clannic, tribal, and fiercely held. But their strength was in rural areas. They could not seriously imperil Soviet power in the main cities and arteries. Their military shortcomings were certainly contributing factors in their ultimate defeat; but their political failures were the decisive ones. The Basmachi never devised a political program that commanded mass support other than the negative demand for expulsion of the infidel. Thus, they had no positive political message—and you cannot beat something with nothing! Certainly, they could not appeal to the rising younger generation of Central Asia, which was considerably more exposed to and receptive of Soviet-style modernization. Much of their failure is also attributable to their own lack of cohesion and leadership. They never accepted any one program or any one man as their leader; instead, they fought under tribal and clannic flags. And this disunity promoted skillful exploitation by the Bolsheviks.

The Bolsheviks, after 1922, blended terror with inducements to exploit these differences among the Basmachi and to intimidate Basmachi supporters at home and abroad. They played off urban versus rural, Uzbek versus Turkmen, young versus old, and so forth. Every opportunity to fractionate the Muslim community was eagerly seized. Yet they sought persistently to construct networks of mass native support, bringing Muslim modernizing leaders like Faizulla Khodzhaev and Akmal Ikramov to the fore. These mass bases were incorporated quickly and were steadily purged of harmful elements. They also generated tremendous mass propaganda about the glorious future the regime was building. By these two devices, the state opened a channel to potential leaders of upward social mobility and linked it to a positive, constructive sociopolitical vision—something the Basmachi did not even conceive of. Moscow also secured the allegiance of a minority of Muslim clerics after 1922, thereby splintering the religious opposition. It did this by temporarily legalizing Muslim courts and schools, allowing religious instruction, and permitting Mosques to operate without persecution. They also accepted the Shariat law in Soviet codes. Further, land and water reforms reduced much of the socioeconomic motives that had fueled the Basmachi's recruitment. Finally, in 1924, the regime divided Central Asia into five separate republics (four then, five after the 1929 creation of the Tadzhik republic), each of which was internally divided to abort sustained, organized resistance.

These moves, coupled with the death in battle of the charismatic Basmachi leader, Enver Pasha, eliminated much of the support for the Basmachi by 1925. Until then, Soviet troops had generally fought in large-scale formations. Now, they adopted new battlefield tactics. Defeat forced the Basmachi leader, Ibrahim Bek, chief of the Lokai tribe, to levy harsh taxes on his followers, prompting some to move back to the Soviet side and form volunteer units. Indeed, units of Lokai tribesmen formed a posse to hunt Bek down.

From 1925 to 1930, the Basmachi continued raids on Soviet Central Asia from Afghanistan where they enjoyed a carte blanche to move around and organize. But from 1925, the Soviets offered neutrality in return for cessation of Afghan support to the Basmachi and simultaneously conducted raids into Afghan territories. In 1929, a coup toppled Amanullah in Afghanistan and gave rise to a common peasant, Bacha i Saqao, who was

41

staunchly anti-Soviet. This led to a Basmachi renaissance.

Moscow now sent large troop contingents to Central Asia. They fought a brutal counterinsurgency war; and they deported 270,000 Central Asians. Dushanbe, Namangan, Andizhan, and Margelan were burned to the ground, another 1,200 villages were destroyed, and other cities were severely damaged. Nevertheless, the fighting raged on. Moscow then decided to invade Afghanistan to establish a local Communist party which could proclaim a Soviet regime and then invite Soviet assistance. Air power was beefed up, as was general preparedness in Tadzhikistan. Soviet troops invaded, but the flight of Amanullah apparently pulled the political rug out from under Moscow, prompting the Soviets to retreat. But again in 1930, Moscow adopted a policy of hot pursuit, thus abrogating the 1926 neutrality treaty. Now, the Afghan army acted; it chased the Basmachi into the Soviet Union where, after several months of bitter fighting in 1931, Ibrahim Bek was captured, tried, and executed. A new treaty with Kabul sealed the border and led to the speedy termination of the revolt.[9]

First among the lessons of the insurrection is the need to engage successfully in an adroit policy of divide and rule among rival ethnic and other factions, offering inducements to one against the other. Moscow successfully executed this among different ethnic groups and within the clergy. It also fashioned a basis for mass support among pro-Moscow natives who joined the Soviets because of divisions with their elders and with the more traditionalist clergy. At the same time it was offering masses of new political forces a "career open to talent" and a matching vision, Moscow was terrorizing potential resistants.

Divide and conquer tactics worked equally well with the tribes. But the other side of divide and rule was the co-optation of elites, which was crucial in facilitating penetration of the Basmachi by pro-Soviet elements. Indeed, this point is too little stressed; whether one studies Vietnam or Central Asia, it is clear that intelligence as to the indigenous military-political situation is vital to combatants. It enabled Moscow to neutralize both military and political objectives even in the planning and preinvasion stages. Such intelligence networks deny the anti-Soviet forces strategic or tactical surprise and the solid bases of political support that are critical to insurgency operations. Construction of a native cadre and the attendant co-optation of elites are absolutely essential—a truism still lost on those who believe a revolution can be stage-managed from the outside by external means.

Moscow's verifiable ability to construct ramified native intelligence networks is of vital significance. Intelligence was almost certainly influential in leading Moscow to combine appropriate military tactics with unremitting terror (which, under the right circumstances, is highly effective). And Moscow's repeated military failures did not ever seriously jeopardize its control of the urban centers. Political skill and terror can, it seems, go a long way, even in the absence of military victory.

Finally, Moscow also succeeded in diplomatically isolating the rebels and in insulating its borders. Afghan support for the Basmachi terminated when Soviet invasion materialized as a real option, thus eliminating the "privileged sanctuary." Combined with internal lack of cohesion, the lack of foreign support doomed the Basmachi. And the limits on aid to the mujahidin, just as were imposed on the Basmachi, have effectively limited the military scope of the Afghan insurrection, ultimately conferring the strategic political advantage on Moscow until 1986. Thus, one can observe the fundamental importance of intimidating insurgency's suppliers and of insulating the rebels. The force that can achieve these political goals, and maintain them, has gone a long way toward ensuring ultimate victory. This chronicle is there for Moscow to read; and if it carefully applies these lessons, it can achieve at least its minimum goals in Afghanistan. From 1978 to 1984 (at least), it disregarded these lessons at its peril. But the Soviets have begun to apply the lessons of the Basmachi insurgency and of its two forays into Iran, which are of equal validity for the present experience in Afghanistan.[10]

The Iran Invasions

In the Soviet invasions of Iran in 1920–21 and 1941–46, we find the further evolution of Soviet outlooks and practice concerning low-intensity conflicts abroad. Soviet power was associated with insurgency operations in Iran, a rather different perspective from that of their counterinsurgency in Central Asia. The invasions into Iran were linked to the collapse of the Iranian government and to what the Soviets perceived as major threats to their security. Both interventions also came to be major turning points in Soviet relations with Great Britain and the United States.

In 1941, the original invasion was a conventional one—conducted along classical military lines for definable military objectives and in tandem with the British occupation. Their objectives were to cleanse Iran of Axis agents and influence and to forge a secure channel of supplies and communications. The subsequent insurgency developed from the postinvasion conditions. The Red Army intimidated the regular Iranian army and prevented it from countering the Soviets' military-political movement. When a second invasion occurred in 1945–46, the Red Army acted as a screen, running interference for the Tudeh and those under its patronage.

The 1920 military operation seems to have been less clearly defined. It appears to have been a probe aimed first at dislodging the British from the Caspian and second at frightening the weak Iranian regime into breaking with London and negotiating with Moscow. The third aim was to enable the Iranian Communists (IKP) to link up with the Jangali revolutionary movement led by Kuchuk Khan, a religiously motivated anti-English and

43

anti-Qajar (the ruling dynasty in Tehran) leader. To the best of our knowledge, the Red Army received no operational instructions after it occupied Resht and Enzeli and facilitated the work of the Iranian Communists; therefore, one cannot be certain as to the mission's ultimate objectives.

Whether Moscow sought to trigger a Communist takeover, a nationalist one antecedent to a revolution, or a neutralization of Iran and the British presence there, its actions constituted a threat to Iran and British interests.[11] Soviet interest in Iran had mounted during 1918–19 even while Moscow was preoccupied with its own survival.[12] By 1920, the Soviets had captured Azerbaidzhan and saw it as a starting point for Eastern operations against the main enemy, the British Empire. Stalin, in particular, directed the military operation with this aim in mind. In 1919–20, a substantial domestic debate over tactics and objectives in Iran occurred in Moscow.[13] The Red Army landed both Iranians and Russians at Enzeli in May 1920 and sealed off Iran's Caspian provinces. Thus, both English and Iranian influences were ousted from the region. Working with Iranian Marxists and workers, Moscow's agents there formed the IKP and effected an alliance with Kuchuk Khan's clerical-nationalist movement. His motives were essentially clerical and anti-imperialist; but the IKP's program was a radical one that encompassed socialist as well as nationalist goals. Meanwhile, the Soviet troops in Resht forced Tehran to negotiate a neutrality treaty with Soviet Russia and threatened the vital but vulnerable British position.[14] These threats were conducted simultaneously with negotiations for mutual recognition between Iran and Great Britain. This method of negotiating has not lost its appeal to Communist regimes.

Moscow ultimately achieved its coveted recognition, but did so at the expense of the revolution in Iran. The reasons can be traced to the multitude of options Moscow faced without sufficient prior consideration. At the time of the invasion, belief in the liberation mission of the Red Army was at its height; nobody seems to have given any serious thought to the consequences of revolutionary warfare on the borders of the British Empire. Soviet leaders were divided as to tactics and goals. Soviet Muslims apparently pressed for creation of a Muslim Red Army to invade Iran in depth and trigger a vast anti-imperialist pan-Islamic conflagration. These Muslim elites called for arming the East to the teeth. Essentially, they sought to hijack Soviet Eastern policy for their own pan-Islamic goals. Undoubtedly, this would have triggered a major conflict with Great Britain. But the country's exhaustion after seven years of war, revolution, civil war, and another round of foreign intervention and wars, as well as Moscow's determination to control its foreign policy for Soviet goals, ruled this out as a viable policy.[15]

Though all were adamantly against pan-Islamism, Soviet leaders were themselves divided. Leon Trotsky and Commissar of Foreign Affairs Georgii Chicherin viewed Iran's Sovietization as an arduous process. They sought to use the Red Army to frighten both states into negotiations and diplomatic relations. By midsummer of 1920, however, Trotsky had evidently come to believe that a direct invasion backed by the resources of the Communist International was desirable. Gregorii Zinoviev, head of the Comintern, favored a propaganda campaign led by the Comintern. By September, he had organized a congress of the peoples of the East in Baku. Himself a Russian Jew, Zinoviev summoned the Muslim masses to a Jihad against British imperialism. Stalin, the operational director of both Soviet national policy and Eastern policy, scored the plan for its grandiloquent but empty phrase-mongering; and he evidently persuaded Lenin. However, Stalin, too advocated an ultimately unrealistic policy, hoping to launch a purely Russian invasion of Iran with troops loyal to himself and directed by his local Transcaucasian clients. As for the Iranian Communists, they wished to impose a direct socialist revolution and to launch a class war based on Kuchuk Khan's movement.

Aggravating these difficulties was the fact that Soviet Russia was emerging as an Eastern power, forcing Lenin to announce to the Comintern and his coadjutors a doctrine for Eastern revolution. He imposed on the Comintern the doctrine that Soviet interests took precedence over indigenous revolutionary strivings. This position took the form of a reasoned proclamation of supporting, through organizationally separate parties, so-called progressive bourgeois nationalist reformers of anti-imperialist outlook (e.g., Atatürk). Thus, Lenin rebuffed the extravagant revolutionary aspirations of the IKP; but for some time, Moscow lacked the power to discipline them.

Essentially what ensued was a policy that moved along parallel tracks. Improved diplomatic relations were pursued by Chicherin and his diplomats at the level of state-to-state relations. In Iran, the goal was neutrality and recognition. Recognition was also Lenin's goal in London in order to end war and isolation. The second policy track was that of fostering subversion within Iran (and Great Britain) through all means of revolutionary insurgency, including invasion. These tracks were mutually reinforcing; that is, one could bring pressure to bear along one track in order to attain the objectives of the other. What doomed this to fail was the ineptness and impatience of the IKP, the fact that the policy's multiple threads were not held in one leader's hand, and the military weakness of the Soviet state.

Because the IKP's rash policy of immediate Sovietization included not just the formation of peasant Soviets, but also the fomenting of peasant uprisings against landlords,[16] Kuchuk Khan ruptured the alliance in late 1920; so when the treaty with Iran was signed, the Soviets found themselves deprived of a card to play and not fully in control of the IKP. And though the IKP and Kuchuk Khan soon mended fences, this entente also proved to be a short-lived and ill-fated marriage of convenience. Within a few months, Kuchuk Khan killed the leader of the IKP and was, in turn, killed by Reza Khan's troops. Because the treaty with Iran stipulated Soviet troop departure once England withdrew its troops, Stalin's recalcitrance in keeping troops there threatened to induce Tehran and London to renounce their treaties with Moscow.[17] Lenin therefore forced Stalin to withdraw his "private" army.

Despite the failure to induce an Iranian revolution, Moscow achieved a considerable victory over Britain and the desired neutrality of Iran. Iran now recognized Moscow, which provided a cover for a network of Soviet agents and Communists abetted by the embassy. And the Soviets learned some instructive and important lessons. Since then, notwithstanding differences among Soviet institutions and individuals over elements of policy, no faction (e.g., Muslim) or subordinate individual (e.g., Stalin) has been allowed to conduct foreign policy or revolutionary operations abroad. Moscow has preferred to direct such operations and to shield itself by minimizing combat roles for its military personnel.

Soviet policy has sought to fashion a reliable political-military instrument that can induce or catalyze foreign revolutions without committing the Soviet regime to dangerous risks. The Soviets have also sought to develop a policy of pursuing minimum and maximum goals at the same time, using the parallel tracks of diplomacy and subversion. The use of these two tracks allows the Soviets or their surrogates to get off the crisis escalator or to ride it further as the situation warrants. One track can substitute for the other and shield it at any time. Coupled with the overextension of the British Empire, this allowed the Soviets to secure their minimum aims of recognition and neutralization of Iran; but Iranian national resurgence under Reza Khan and British determination to hold onto the oil fields precluded the conversion of northern Iran into a Soviet sphere of influence and the subsequent Sovietization of Iran.[18]

Such a policy can only succeed where the indigenous party is fully receptive to Moscow's control and does not precipitate too quickly a revolutionary crisis. One of the lessons of Iran is that the impatience of the IKP threatened vital Soviet security and state interests. Controlled parties, working in tandem with certifiable "nationalists," progressives, and so forth, through covert fronts, provide a much more reliable basis for Sovietization.[19] This enables Moscow to harvest the benefits of Sovietization while denying responsibility for the foreign state's internal processes. In the initial stages of their rise to power, Communist parties must, with Moscow's or Havana's urging, pursue policies of seeming moderation on the way to consolidating authority. This lesson was lost on the Afghan leaders discussed below. Such a policy shields the Soviet Union, paralyzes native support for opponents, confuses Western reactions, and gains time for consolidating an unassailable position. Iran provides one of the first examples of this process; and it was reinforced by later events in Iran, Chile, and Afghanistan.

Other lessons of the Iranian gambit in 1920–21 refer not just to political organization of the native Communist party. It is not enough that insurgents follow an agreed-upon and tightly imposed political strategy; Soviet military power must be sufficiently strong to deny or minimize unfavorable external or third-party reaction. It is not surprising, therefore, that Soviet commentators have attributed recent successes in third world "wars of national liberation" to their attainment of parity with the United States. Absent this military "deterrence" capability with regard to foreign intervention, the Soviet-sponsored forces will find little success in their search for consolidation. Isolation of Western forces is a major condition of success in such contests.

Thus, in 1921, Soviet forces in Iran could not promote the domestic insurgency because of overriding international security concerns and because of the IKP's unreliability. Military and political success in such contests must be mutually reinforcing; otherwise, they will be mutually endangering. In 1921 and 1946, the risks attached to the insurgency outweighed the likely benefits; so the Soviets harvested their gains and decamped. Since 1955, the Soviets have applied the lesson learned here: they have built a military capacity capable of supporting friends and deterring enemies in such contests.

In this military-political relationship, the local Communist party must organize the masses through political fronts likened by Comintern leader Otto Kuusinen to a solar system revolving around the party core in Moscow. This solar system can and must be duplicated at the native level. Only the presence of a viable political organization can provide the basis for successful military action. Military force cannot substitute for political support, even if committed en masse. The political immaturity of the IKP in 1920–21 made it impossible for the USSR to reap maximum benefit from its invasion of Iran. No amount of force can compensate for the absence of a viable mass political organization.

In the intervening period of 1921–41, Soviet relations with Iran developed from the baseline of their 1921 treaty. Article VI of that treaty permitted the Soviet Union to intervene if an anti-Soviet threat developed in Iran. Soviet espionage and subversion flourished there, with the Soviet embassy often being used as cover for these activities.[20] Moreover, Soviet policy enforced its own brand of colonialist exploitation on Iran's foreign trade and economic development.[21] One of the most visible implications of the economic imperialism was the clear Soviet intent to create a potentially detachable "sphere of influence" in northern Iran.[22]

These phenomena point not only to imperialist Soviet designs on Iran but also to an enhanced capacity to use economics to manipulate its economy in service of insurgency. After 1941, Soviet economic policies constituted a clear and present danger to Iranian sovereignty and integrity. And the Soviets' intelligence, espionage, and subversion work of 1921–41 made possible the development of substantial clandestine assets that could emerge quickly.

The lessons learned by the Soviets from 1921 to 1941, and the diffusion of this learning among the requisite military and political elites, can be found in the translated Soviet command study of 1941 for Iran.[23] This manual reveals how the Soviet military planned to invade and occupy Iran if so commanded. A profound study of every possible military and political target and every logistical asset, it reflects hours of painstaking work by a superbly functioning intelligence network. The authors of this study commanded an extensive knowledge of all key Iranian geographical features and their military significance. The manual also displays a total familiarity with ongoing domestic legislation, class structures, class stratification patterns, and the history, evolution, and composition of *every single ethnic group in Iran.* It also includes a detailed description of landholding practices, a branch-by-branch detailed enumeration of Iranian industries and factories, and the locations of minerals, fuels, roads, highways, railroad lines, and crossings. It gives a thorough description of all frontier fortifications, defenses, and the Iranian army order of battle. As a testament to Soviet thoroughness, one finds on page 100 a province-by-province listing of all horses, donkeys, mules, and camels to be found in Iran. The report also includes a detailed picture of Iranian communication networks, health care facilities, airfields, weather conditions, and defense installations. Finally, the report also considers the possibility of war spilling over to Iraq, India, or Afghanistan.

> It is self-evident that the territory of Iraq which is allied to Iran must be regarded as the hinterland of the theater of war as well as the northwestern part of India (i.e., Pakistan). Nor can it be ruled out that the territory of Afghanistan might be used as a starting point for hostile action against the Soviet Union.[24]

The entire purpose of the report is to determine the most effective theater of operations for the Red Army. The bottom line for each operational axis is the size of Soviet troop concentrations that could be effectively deployed there. It is hard-nosed military and political analysis of a high order; it aims to discover and exploit the economic-political weaknesses of Iran for Soviet purposes. It notes that the peasants were thoroughly suppressed by the shah. Due to insufficient political maturity and the absence of a political organization, they could not be counted on to seize power. On the other hand, a crisis, such as World War II, could trigger a sudden fall in foreign trade and exchange and a steep decline in industrial construction, thus generating a general worsening of economic conditions. And under such conditions, prior economic encroachments and the Soviet trade treaty of 1940 with Iran could be of great importance.[25] However, the greatest attention of the Soviets was focused on ethnic and tribal disaffection. They saw this as the Achilles' heel of a regime stuck in a difficult transition to modernity. Class analysis took a decided backseat to national questions as focused on by Soviet authors.

The dissatisfaction of different nationalities and ethnic groups, as the Azerbaidzhani Turks, Kurds, Turkomen, Armenians, and Jews, is heightened by the fact that despite a thousand barriers, the truth of the conditions of the minorities in the Soviet Union— in the Soviet Azerbaidzhan, Soviet Turkmen Republic and Tadzhik SSR—does trickle through. Reports which we have received suggest that in the territories occupied by the national minorities and tribes, the Iranian leadership cannot count on the political reliability or loyalty of the hinterland.[26]

This analysis went on to note that while centralization and suppression of the tribes had temporarily ended, the minority problem remained unsolved. Accordingly, the smallest foreign conflict would immeasurably escalate the national problem; and the Soviet solution (annexation under the guise of self-determination, Balkanization, or merger with Soviet Azerbaidzhan, Turkmenistan, and Tadzhikistan) could extraordinarily influence hostilities in Iran.[27] In considering possible axes of attack, the Soviets downgraded Khorassan because of the citizens' loyalty to Tehran. They played up the provinces of Gilan, Azerbaidzhan, and Masandaran because they would have a chance to win over the Kurds and other minorities suffering social and ethnic discrimination.[28]

While there is no talk of movement south or of the south being the final objective of any campaign, it is unlikely that nothing more than a northern campaign was contemplated. The contemplated military operations afforded the regime a menu of choices that ranged from occupation and assimilation to outright annexation or to war and revolution. The pronounced and characteristic Soviet emphasis on speed betrays a desire for a quick end to the war and may signal the willingness to settle for strictly limited political gains if need be. Once again, there are minimum and maximum goals in Soviet policy; and once again, military operations are merely handmaidens to larger political goals.

The joint Anglo-Soviet occupation of Iran in 1941 was designed to remove the Nazi threat. The Soviets followed the routes that offered the most promising political advantages—Azerbaidzhan, Gilan, and Masandaran. And they did the same for the second invasion in 1945–46. The results of the first invasion were predictable. Reza Khan fell to be replaced by his weaker son; and Iranian society began to disintegrate. Strong anti-Tehran trends, repressed before 1941, now complicated Iranian politics—which was already compromised greatly by the interallied competition for influence there.[29]

At first, the Soviets were cautious about altering the local socioeconomic structure in their zone; but they inserted experts into their consular service and began to seal off the region both economically and administratively.[30] Early on, the Soviets displayed a disdain for the sovereignty of Iran while treating the locals better than Tehran did. And they maintained a strict military discipline and bearing, which attracted favorable notice.[31] By 1942–43, they had begun to negotiate new exploitative accords with a Teh-

49

ran that was too frightened to resist. Soviet food and grain policies demonstrated a capacity—and probably the intention—to seal off the north and starve out the Tehran region.[32] By 1943, terror and censorship were commonplace and the Soviets had established a substantial nationwide propaganda apparatus.[33]

Also in 1943, the Tudeh party appeared. Composed of both homegrown and veteran Comintern figures, it soon constituted a political monopoly in the Soviet zone. The Tudeh party used its local monopoly to extort money from those serving and living there, making them contribute if they hoped to hold their positions. The Tudeh rapidly expanded to include a broad network of front organizations, a massive propaganda network, and the only national party organization operating across Iran. Typical of Tudeh at this time, and later of their many imitators (e.g., the PDPA in Afghanistan), was its systematic obfuscation of its links with the Soviets and its reiteration of the fact that it was not a Communist party.[34] It had learned from its unfortunate predecessor the virtues of camouflage.

The Iranian crisis of 1944–46, brought on by Great Power rivalry and Soviet imperialism, need not be repeated in detail here. Some points need, however, to be stressed. The Soviet personnel in Iran manifested a lordly and chauvinistic attitude toward Iranians.[35] On the other hand, they shrewdly exploited real grievances brought on by the harshness and economic ineptitude of Tehran. They recruited shrewdly, and they maintained a seemingly egalitarian policy to cement a genuine political mass movement which they reinforced and protected with Soviet troops. Thus, the importance of the political aspect of low-intensity conflict was highlighted, as was the importance of exploiting ethno-national grievances. Tudeh and Soviet army troops successfully posed as nationalists in both Tehran and Azerbaidzhan.[36]

The technique of indirect aggression pioneered here by the Soviets proved to be very difficult to counter. Only through firm and rising US military-diplomatic pressure, extremely supple and wily Iranian diplomacy, and the building of a countercadre in the guise of a police force, were the Soviets blocked. Iran proved to be a test case for the United States in learning how to contain Soviet imperial ambitions. The experience testified to the need for developing a viable reply to Soviet-sponsored insurgency. Host access to significant international support and viable domestic countercadres were the main replies. Of equal if not greater importance of such a cadre is for the United States or other outside power to learn the country. Intelligence and efficient deployment of those who understand its significance are crucial to blunting the threat of a locally based mass Communist insurgency. Because this method counters mass with mass and knowledge with knowledge, it enables the government or its patron to devise viable military, political, and economic policies in response to the insurgency.

The Iranian USSR's expedition of 1941–46 demonstrated the ongoing refinement of Soviet thinking and practice in low-intensity conflict situations. A much more effective military and political synergy emerged only to run up against American superior force combined with Iranian cunning. Nationalist grievances were expertly ventilated and exploited, and economic and propaganda warfare were skillfully used to both intimidate and attract Iranians. The indigenous Tudeh party disavowed its Communist coloration, betraying a Soviet fondness for early moderation aimed at later radicalization—a growing into socialism *(Perestanie)*.[37] The military arm operated under strict control and was deployed in a nondecisive manner; that is, the Soviet military never committed itself to hostilities or to a stance from which it could not easily retreat. Though Moscow encountered superior force and had to retreat, it has since refined its operations throughout the third world. Moscow's postwar success in different areas owes much to its ceaseless quest for the right way to promote foreign revolutions and its ceaseless study of past exercises like those in Iran. We ignore them at our peril, as the Soviet takeover in Afghanistan so conclusively demonstrates.

A recent article asserts that as the 1945–46 crisis was heating up, reports of an imminent takeover plan by the Tudeh reached the chief of staff of the Iranian army. The reports claimed that Tehran would be attacked simultaneously from Tudeh and Soviet strongholds in the west and north. At the same time, trained partisan units would disrupt communications inside Tehran and on neighboring roads. Soviet armored troops would provide logistical and moral support. The Iranian army restrained the Tudeh in early 1946, provoking the Soviets to launch what appeared to be an invasion in March; but they retreated soon after.[38]

The Afghanistan Invasion

Afghanistan seems to have been a classic example of backwardness as measured by socioeconomic indicators. Economically and socially, it was dominated by what the Soviets call "feudal" landlord-peasant relations. The quite small modern elite was essentially a military-professional elite formed by close ties to the ruling house and its associated cliques. Until the 1970s, its sign was education and its professions military, politics, education, and medicine.

A bewildering plethora of ethnic and tribal groups inhabit the land, commanding primary and primordial loyalties. Until recently, and perhaps even now, there has been little sense of an Afghan nation; rather, the primary kinship affiliation is clannic and familial. Afghanistan is rife with traditions of feuds, and there is a prevailing fierce individualism. Over and above these diverse affiliations is Islam, the unifying universalist "ideology" and the functional embodiment of a consciousness of fate, belief, morals, and

51

so forth.[39] The functional nationalist role of Islam was probably lost on the Soviets, who tended to see Islam as purely a reactionary threat.

Had the Soviets pondered the lessons of their past encounters in Iran and Central Asia more deeply, they might not have acted so rashly after 1978. After all, Afghanistan had served since 1860 as the pivot of the "Great Game" between Russia and the Anglo-American alliance for domination of Central and Southern Asia. Indeed, the Soviets had intervened four times between 1924 and 1930 to threaten the "privileged sanctuary" of the Basmachi. And in 1929, they intervened to restore King Amanullah and a pro-Soviet government.

Thus, information about Afghanistan was not lacking to Soviet leaders. And in Afghanistan, their opportunities revolved around ethnic issues—not internal socioeconomic differentiation and class struggles. The opportunities are, however, many; and skillful long-term political tactics might well have succeeded—and still might if the fighting is stopped.

These opportunities have come about because the boundaries between Iran, Afghanistan, Pakistan, and the USSR do not correspond with the pattern of ethnic settlement in the region. Large numbers of ethnic communities in Afghanistan could be used for irredentist purposes, either to annex parts of Afghanistan to the USSR or to detach parts of Iran and Pakistan and unite them with Afghanistan. In 1925, Soviet forces had tried to annex territories of Afghanistan to Uzbekistan; and the creation of the Tadzhik SSR in 1929 may well have been a similarly motivated effort pending victory in the invasion of that year.[40] And there have been charges that the Soviet regime seriously contemplated an analogous course in 1981–82. Though strenuously denied in Kabul, the reports are based on claims by a defecting secret police (KHAD) senior official, Lt Gen Saddiq Ghulam Miraki. He claimed that Moscow had proposed to annex the eight northern Afghan provinces adjacent to Soviet Central Asia as part of a future settlement of the war. These provinces would become an irredentist Soviet republic and Afghan Communist homeland while the rest of the country would become an "independent" buffer state.[41] The plan encountered fierce Afghan opposition and was shelved after March 1982.

Afghan sentiment for the Pathans (or Pushtuns or Pashtuns) living in Pakistan as a result of the Durand Line settlement in 1893 has inflamed relations with Pakistan, and there has been strong support for a Pathan irredentism by successive Afghan regimes since the British departure from India in 1947. Soviet support for such irredentist movements constitutes the continuing main threat not just to Pakistan, but to Iran and to China. The Baluchi community could be used to destabilize either Iran or Pakistan.[42]

Soviet practice has been to reserve judgment and commitment while constructing a capability to make the irredentist case and deploy these movements. For instance, Selig S. Harrison believes that the movement led by Bizenjo in Baluchistan was Moscow's main card there. At the same time, Bizenjo aspired to use the Soviets to his own ends; that is, a national-democratic government with Communist participation that granted autonomy with an ultimate right of secession to the provinces.[43] Other leaders, such as Murad Khan, looked toward the post-1978 regime in Kabul for support.[44] Seeking to maintain good relations with Pakistan and Iran, Moscow has neither embraced nor repudiated Baluchi nationalism. While acknowledging the integrity of the relevant states, Moscow has hedged, making reservations that their ethnic questions have not been satisfactorily resolved, thus preserving an open door.[45] But the Afghan Communists veered away from Taraki's initial sympathy for the Baluchi and Pathan peoples and toward Amin's increasingly strident rhetoric of a greater Afghanistan with Baluchi autonomy.[46] In 1981, Harrison discerned a Soviet pattern of building up cadre and organization against the time when the ethnic Baluchi card may be worth playing; yet it still refrains from open encouragement of these groups.[47]

The Pushtunistan issue graphically demonstrates how the USSR capitalized on ethnic grievances to gain entrée into Afghanistan. Afghan regimes have claimed Pushtunistan on both historic grounds and national affinities,[48] and have made support for Pathan irredentism a major plank of their foreign policies despite the Durand Line. The intensity with which the irredentist dream has been voiced has always been a barometer of relations with Pakistan. And its continuing validity for Kabul is reflected in Babrak Karmal's statement, "no international border exists between Pakistan and Afghanistan."[49] The recent bombings of the refugee camps by Afghan and Soviet forces attest to the disdain for international borders characteristic of both sides in this war. But Kabul failed to realize that polarizing intraregional disputes was the surest way of perpetuating them and reducing the regional states to dependency on outside great powers.[50]

Afghan overtures to Washington in the first postwar decade were rebuffed precisely because it was feared that the aid would be used against our ally Pakistan. Others argued that Afghanistan was of no strategic value to us or that it was too close to the USSR, that personalities in Kabul were too unstable or even "immoral," and that aid policies they wished to conduct were misconceived large-ticket programs.[51] The deputy chief of mission there in 1950–53 admitted that the State Department "showed absolutely no interest in Afghanistan."[52] US policy saw Kabul through the wrong end of the telescope; that is, its relations with the two superpowers rather than as a regional anchor of neutrality. The entry of Pakistan into CENTO and SEATO only reinforced our pro-Pakistani proclivities and made our rebuffs to Kabul more aggravating. And as Kabul inflamed the Pushtunistan issue, our rebuffs left it increasingly isolated precisely when it started to consider modernization in depth. This conjuncture allowed Moscow, not committed to any status quo there, to intervene with offers of political, military, and economic aid to Kabul.

In 1950, the *Great Soviet Encyclopaedia* characterized Afghanistan as a bourgeois nation where the Pathan majority oppressed the minority tribes or at least held them back from self-determination. But as irredentist agitation in Kabul grew during 1950–51, Soviet diplomats began expressing a cautious sympathy for the campaign and stressed the racial affinities of Pushtunistan with Afghanistan. In 1951, a Soviet journal hinted that Moscow envisaged an Afghan takeover of those areas of Pakistan while the USSR would annex the Tazhik, Uzbek, and Turkmen areas and clean up the debris of British colonialism.[53] Moscow attacked Pakistan for denying Pathan self-determination and said that the Afghan calls for support for the Pathans in the midfifties demonstrated the great affinity between them. Moscow also claimed that a bourgeois nationalist ideology grew up around this movement, which, increasingly linked with anti-imperialism, was in Soviet eyes a progressive, supportable movement.[54] An Afghanistan disenchanted with American support for Pakistan and eager for foreign aid was receptive to a Soviet ambition to penetrate Afghanistan and circumvent CENTO, thereby neutralizing American policy and gaining entrée to the third world. Soviet aid increased steadily from 1950 to 1955, and it was clinched by large assistance agreements in economic and military aid in 1955–56. In return, Bulganin and Nikita Khrushchev displayed open but noncommittal support for Kabul's Pathan policy. This issue worked to deflect Mohammad Daoud's regime to Moscow to such a degree that virtually all post-1956 military training and aid was exclusively Soviet.

The real Soviet attitude toward the Afghanis, both elites and commoners, was not nearly so benevolent. J. Bruce Amstutz's recent book is replete with numerous instances of Soviet Union's colonialist contempt for Afghanistan as it has taken over more and more of the country and its resources.[55] The following citation clearly exhibits such contempt, and it fits in with Soviet belief that the war is Western inspired and has no internal basis in Afghanistan.

> Ever since hostile acts against the Afghan republic began, Western information agencies have tried to suggest that subversive activities against the new authorities were arranged by Afghan feudal lords. In fact, the local feudal lords have at all times been incapable of concerted action, being disorganized and insulated from one another. From the outset subversive activities against Afghanistan were well organized, centralized, and excellently supplied [I believe all three charges are grossly untrue—S.B.], in a way quite uncommon to the local feudal class. Whatever "standard bearers" were advanced here from among the scions of eminent Afghan families, it was immediately evident that they were mere tools or "servants" of an obviously foreign master.[56]

Kabul conceived of the aid package not just as support for Pathan irredentism. The turn to Moscow apparently came about in the belief that

Soviet objectives were not expansionary, that the state could handle any threat, and that neutrality would not be impaired. This outlook was short-sighted, but at least one observer believes that Daoud raised the Pathan issue because he knew it was the only way he could get his colleagues to accept Soviet aid. His main motive was to create a strong national army and a state administration capable of solidifying central authority over the tribes. And the modernized army was able to suppress riots in 1959.[57] The government then opened up army recruitment, allowing the military academies to recruit cadets from all ethnic and linguistic groups as well as all classes, making military education the road to upward social mobility. Also, conscripts were taken from tribal areas hitherto considered to be "exempt."[58]

Aid from the USSR intensified until the entire regime became increasingly dependent on it. Modernization, irredentism, and military integration by means of a Russian-trained, -educated, -supplied, and -dependent elite became the main lines of Daoud's policies; and Moscow steadily improved its position by exploiting the Afghans' dependence. Afghanistan's international situation interacted with internal socioeconomic developments in such a way as to preclude any viable opposition to a Communist coup in 1978.

Reliance on Moscow as trainer, teacher, and supplier of the Afghan army gave the Soviets a veto over any effort to use the army to settle the Pathan party and the basis for an independent Afghan foreign policy steadily eroded. Soviet demands in culture and information were always heeded. No competitors were allowed, and Soviet pressure coerced Afghanistan into declaring the northern part of the country, which adjoins Soviet Russia, closed to foreigners for economic development purposes. Daoud's reluctance to purge many known pro-Soviet Marxists from the military and the administration reflected a deep fear of antagonizing Moscow. By 1978, Afghanistan had long been a virtual satellite state.[59] The scope and scale of the Soviets' growing presence also enabled them to exploit Afghan's wealth while imposing exploitative terms of trade and enhancing Afghan economic dependence on Moscow. Much of the outline of imperial control had already been put into place by 1970, and internal developments produced an almost classic case of third world crisis for Moscow to exploit.[60] The Afghans disregarded American warnings, believing that it was too expensive economically for Moscow to control them, that it would alienate third world opinion too much if Moscow did so, and that such a move would injure Moscow's own interests too much to make it worth the trouble.[61] Thus, complacency was added to fear. Indeed, the Afghans' complacency, and our own, were such that nobody could believe the success previously attained by the People's Democratic Party of Afghanistan (PDPA) when the coup came in 1978.[62]

In the military sphere, the Soviets' aid program quickly started to pay dividends. Approximately 7,000 officers were trained by Moscow from 1954 to 1978, and the Soviet program of logistical support was equally substantial.[63] Thus, the Afghan army quickly fell into dependence on Moscow. The transportation networks built by the Soviets were designed for Soviet military use, pointing to an integrated, coherent plan to build up an infrastructure capable of supporting Soviet strategic objectives.[64]

Moscow saw Afghanistan as a new colony by 1961. That fall, the Pathan issue was revived again. Pakistan, borrowing from Moscow's tactics, offered to hold a plebiscite there if Kabul did so in Afghanistan. Moscow rushed aid to Kabul and denounced this as a CENTO plot, warning Pakistan that it could not expect Moscow's indifference to the provocation—typical pretext for intervention by Moscow. Marshal Sokolovskii and a large retinue secretly visited Afghanistan. According to Oleg Penkovskii:

> The purposes of the trip were to study the combat readiness of the Afghan armed forces, so that we might draw up plans to improve the military skill of these forces and increase their fire power. Plans are being made, also, for extensive training of Afghan military officers in Soviet military schools as well as the dispatch of large numbers of Soviet military instructors to Afghanistan. Under discussion is the possibility of sending Soviet troops into Afghanistan at the appropriate time for joint operations against Pakistan. Sokolovskii also had orders to reconnoiter certain specific areas of Afghanistan for selection as possible missile sites.[65]

Afghanistan developed into Moscow's model third world country during the 1960s. Either by their exposure to socialism and Leninism or by means of other forms of KGB recruitment, the officer corps and the educated elite became steadily more amenable to Soviet influence and ideology.

Facilitating this tendency toward Sovietization from within were a number of internal consequences of the aid program and Daoud's subsequent policies. Moscow's traditional policy of capturing the elite and the state from within dovetailed neatly with internal evolutionary trends. Large-scale educational development opened the door to many newcomers and commoners after 1955; but economic and political stagnation transformed them into a blocked "intellectual proletariat." This frustrated elite of professionals, civil servants, and officers made a perfect target for the Soviets.

The PDPA, formed in 1965, fit perfectly with Moscow's strategy. Indeed, among its founders were men suspected of being KGB agents (Taraki and Karmal). It recruited from all sections of the ethnically and socially fragmented elite—a strategy that was perfectly congruent with that of the Soviets.[66]

The post-1955 elite constituted a decultured base in Afghan society. These officers and educated, who came from diverse and rival sectors of society, had lost their anchor in the old cultural traditions by virtue of their modern education (particularly true of those educated in the USSR). Attracted to modernization and their own advancement, they were susceptible to both the KGB and the PDPA. The PDPA concentrated on teachers and students targeted for future civil service posts. The returning military officers, generally recruited from lower social strata, were distrusted and blocked in their careers, generating great resentment.[67]

Complicating these processes was the breakup of the PDPA into Khalqi and Parcham factions after 1967. Personal rivalries between Karmal and Taraki played a role, but social and political differences were probably more decisive. When originally formed, the PDPA had amalgamated two incompatible social patterns. They finally broke down into Karmal's Parchamis and Taraki's Khalqi factions. Karmal and his faction came from Afghanistan's supreme elite. They favored the Soviet strategy of elite co-optation and recommended working with "progressive" left-wing non-Communists to take over from within while moving only gradually to revolutionize Afghanistan. The Khalqi came from a more modest social stratum, generally outside of Kabul, and they were more responsive to the idea of a radical social revolution coinciding with political power.[68] The Khalqi also possessed a more third world, less overtly pro-Soviet, outlook. Khalqi socialism championed a nationalistic radical revolution that would move directly from feudalism to socialism. The army would be the revolutionary class. Oliver Roy depicts this view, which also was radically anti-Islamic, as being partly inspired by the ideas of the Muslim Soviet heretic Sultangaliev.[69]

Neither faction has been able to dispense with tribalism and clientilism. The Parchamis brought along their clients and conferees; the Khalqis brought their tribal and familial connections. This made it impossible for them to overcome traditional social patterns. But the Afghans' tribalism and clientilism have also made it impossible for Moscow to attain a real mastery over Afghanistan. The 20-year civil war within the PDPA is only an interior mirror of the larger civil war it has spawned. After the 1967 split, the Khalqi continued recruiting students and teachers while the Parchamis continued to recruit officers.

Though this rivalry undoubtedly set back Moscow's plans, the loyalty of both wings enabled Moscow to sponsor a two-track recruitment policy while increasing its foreign policy pressures on Kabul. Soviet concerns with blocking China, with US neglect after the Vietnam War began, and with the progress of Soviet satellization, all emboldened Moscow to adopt a higher profile in South Asia after 1965. Rightly banking on India during 1965–71, it twice engineered defeats of Pakistan; and it pressured Pakistan to join its proposed Asian collective security system.[70] Alternatively, Moscow proposed an economic grouping of Iran, India, Pakistan, and Afghanistan, which Pakistan also turned down.[71] Afghanistan, too, found itself subjected to greater pressures. King Zahir Shah's talks with Aleksey Kosygin in 1972 left him with the distinct impression that *Pax Sovietica* for the region was the new Soviet goal. Kosygin called for Kabul to join the Asian collective security system proposed by Brezhnev in 1972, which would have placed

57

Kabul within Moscow's security perimeter.[72] Zahir Shah's demurral clearly implied to Moscow that the Afghan regime was unreliable.

At home, Daoud, now in political retirement, plotted with his radical allies in the military, among whom were open Parchami members. When the king took the mud-bath cure in Ischia in 1973, he struck, launching a coup d'état. He brought many Parchamis and Khalqi into sensitive positions, and he allowed further penetration of the economy by the Soviets. Soon after this, Soviet-Afghan relations resumed their amicable course, and the Pathan issue again became a rallying cry against Pakistan. Under Daoud, the Khalqi, largely Pathan in affiliation, expected both reforms and favorable settlement of that issue. At the same time, 160 leftists, many of whom were Parchamis, were given provincial appointments. Parchamis also found positions on his revolutionary council and cabinet.[73] The extent of PDPA penetration of Daoud's regime is visible in the following statements culled by Amstutz from interviews and newspapers: a senior Education Ministry official noted that the Communists "were everywhere"; G. A. Ayeen recalled that in 1978 the provincial police chief and provincial education chiefs were Communists, as were an estimated 10 percent of the teachers; a Ministry of Water and Power official estimated that Communists comprised 10 percent of his ministry; a senior official in the Ministry of Planning gave the PDPA proportion as 5 percent at least, with many being camouflaged members; and in the Ministry of Information and Culture, a PDPA leader was paid for nothing. When efforts were made to stop this, those involved were told, from the minister's office, "Don't push the Communists."[74]

As Daoud's rule became more dictatorial, American neglect deeper, and PDPA infiltration and Soviet pressure greater, the right-wing and center parties evaporated. There was no political power outside of Daoud's retinue, the army, and the rival PDPA factions. After 1975, when Daoud's autocratic proclivities and his decision to revert to genuine nonalignment manifested themselves, his isolation deepened and his situation became more precarious. He seemed to envisage a transition to something more democratic—certainly not communism. He started moving Parchamis back to the provinces, where they encountered total frustration. Many resigned, others were put under surveillance. The remainder were steadily removed from power as Daoud relied more and more on kinsmen and others personally loyal to him. By 1977, he was putting together a new constitution that would have enshrined his position and frozen out the Parchamis. He evinced a clear preference for genuine nonalignment, shelved the Pushtunistan issue and considerably improved relations with Pakistan, approached Tehran and Riyadh for aid, and publicly indicated his suspicion of Cuba's "nonalignment." He allegedly upbraided Leonid Brezhnev in a 1977 meeting when the latter told him to remove all non-Soviet foreign advisers. Finally, in March 1978, he indicated to Indian diplomats that he wanted to end Afghan dependence on the Soviets. One month later, he was deposed.

Foreign affairs played an important role in Moscow's decision to reunify the PDPA and abet the coup. Karmal later noted that Daoud was becoming more and more like Anwar Sadat in that he had demonstrated the reversibility of the subversive Sovietization process. While Moscow was harvesting its gains in Angola, the Ogaden, and Iran, which had begun to disintegrate, Daoud had the nerve to assert Afghanistan's mastery of its destiny. But by 1978, Afghan nonalignment had long since outworn its charm for Moscow, which now demanded satellization. Diplomatic actions had converged with the domestic imperatives of the now imperiled PDPA and the two factions of the latter reunified under Moscow and the Indian Communist party's auspices to launch a revolution in Kabul.

This reunification of the Khalqi and Parcham factions was a difficult one. Daoud's defeat of the Parchami after his 1973 coup, outside pressure, and the revised Khalqi tactics of Taraki and Hafizullah Amin comprised the steps leading to this reunification. Parcham, threatened with expulsion and exclusion, had to concede the bankruptcy of its tactic of working through a front organization. Daoud's grand design imparted a growing sense of urgency to the quest for a broader base and new tactics. Time was running out for the Parchamis. Moscow's external pressure also was due to such considerations. The shift to nonalignment, initiatives toward real sovereignty, dispensing with Soviet aid, and Daoud's contemplated trip to Washington all threatened to undermine a generation of gains there. For Moscow, too, time was running out. Planning for a coup began no later than 1976 and waited only on PDPA unity and the right moment to strike.

The Khalqi also learned some important lessons from the 1973 coup and is aftermath—lessons mainly related to the utility of the army, which it now baptized as the revolutionary class. It switched emphasis in its recruitment policy to include officers and soldiers because it now grasped the centrality of the army in any contemplated seizure of power. These changed tactics demonstrated the growing attraction of imposing their drastic revolution following an armed *putsch,* not a genuine political revolution. Naively, they expected mass support.[75] The major change in their thinking related to the idea of a coup, seizing the state from within and above. The Khalqi now believed it was possible to wrest the military's loyalty from the upper class for such purposes.[76] And Daoud's betrayal of the king in 1973 encouraged them. Thus, the unraveling of Afghanistan's traditional value structure and code of conduct was accelerated. Parchami military assets now became valuable in the Khalqi effort to recruit officers. And all the while, Moscow and the CPI were pushing for unity. Thus a tenuous agreement came to pass in 1977.[77] This accord became more urgent because the proposed new constitution would subordinate the army to Daoud through his chairing a supreme council of the army.[78]

Arnold also suggests that the USSR channeled military recruitment through the Khalqi after 1973 to preserve Parcham's delicate position. Soviet sources imply that Daoud's "reactionary" policies led the officers to organize in secret. Once again, Soviet strategy and domestic factors interacted, with Moscow strengthening the PDPA's role in the USSR and the PDPA strengthening Moscow's role in Afghanistan. At the unity conference of the two factions in July 1977, the removal of Daoud and his system was placed on the agenda.[79] Though no statistics are available, PDPA penetration of the officer corps and the civil administration was substantial.

There is abundant reason to believe that while Moscow did not actually take part in the Saur coup on 27 April 1978, it probably gave sanction to it. Afterwards, the Soviet Union could point to Afghanistan as another military-political success in erecting a mutually supporting collective security system.[80] The Saur revolution was a continuation of Moscow's objective to construct anti-Western and pro-Soviet governments in the third world. Coincidental with the processes at work in Afghanistan was the rearmament of Soviet ideological and military forces so they could project their power outwards in classic imperial fashion.[81] This coup seems to have catapulted Moscow into a position it had fought for a generation to attain. Soon afterwards, however, the unraveling of the new regime began. The Taraki regime's virtually total identification with Moscow estranged mass sentiment from the outset. In its quest for draconian socialist revolution, the regime ruled by unprecedented terror that decapitated the elite and enraged the masses. This started the process of diminishing the already small number of educated people available to govern the country. The regime was sawing off the limbs on which it was insecurely perched but did not see its own folly.

Instead of realizing the thin veneeer of support it commanded, the Taraki government passed directly to the socialist revolution, faithfully replicating every mistake made by the IKP in 1920–21. This largely Khalqi-dominated regime forced reforms with no preparation and struck at major arteries of social life without compensating for what was removed. They proceeded impetuously, without building any infrastructure, disregarding Soviet diplomats' admonitions to go slow.[82] Land reforms, female emancipation, linguistic reform, and even limitations on the clergy were not unknown before; but they were carried out in the most inflammatory ways in 1978–79, visibly repudiating Islam and showing subservience to the Russians, whom the Afghans despised and feared. The Taraki regime found itself confronted with insurrection within months of its accession to power.

Instead of backtracking as the Parchami clearly preferred, the regime consumed its energies in fruitless personality cults. Taraki increasingly stood exposed as an inept political dreamer. In 1978–79, several hundred Parchamis were killed or imprisoned by the Khalqi, with the pattern reversing after the 1979 invasion. Khalqi and Parcham continue to conspire against each other and to kill each other, even in Moscow.[83]

Taraki and his main lieutenant, Amin, had fallen out by the summer of 1979 amidst growing insurrection and with Russian penetration occurring all around. Amin saw himself as being more capable than the inept Taraki and was moving to concentrate power in his own hands. But the Soviets saw him as the evil genius of the revolution because he balked at accepting their advice to moderate it. So, no later than September 1979, Moscow hatched a coup wherein Taraki would bring back Karmal and get rid of Amin.[84]

Amin found out about this and launched his own coup on 14 September. He succeeded in removing Taraki, who was soon killed. Although the Soviet ambassador was recalled at Amin's insistence, Amin had no choice but to preserve Soviet aid and assistance. His field of maneuver had so narrowed that anything other than dependence on Russia was ruled out. But Moscow had decided to unseat him; it continued to extend its control over the military and government while masking its preparations for a coup cum invasion in late December. This invasion turned into a major catastrophe for the Soviets. Why was it undertaken?

Much blame must fall on Moscow for utterly misreading the Afghan situation. It was universally reported that Afghan government agencies were increasingly dominated by Soviet advisers who made the important decisions, and that Soviet advisers in the military were present at the platoon level. Yet, despite the fact that after the Saur revolution the number of Soviet advisers grew by 700 percent (to some 8,000), the DRA seemed consistently to follow policies supposedly not favored by these Russian controllers. Perhaps the traditional Soviet contempt for Afghans led them to act in or sanction a radical overbearing manner toward the people.[85]

What is clear is that the Soviet Union poured in advisers to enroot its position in Afghanistan. Large-scale indoctrination of Afghan youths began, as did the program of selective training in the USSR. This was part of the overall program of Russification in Afghan education. By granting the minorities freedom to use their own languages, as Moscow had done in Central Asia, the regime moved to shatter linguistic unity based on Islamic tongues. By simultaneously mandating the teaching of Russian, it complemented that policy in aiming to establish Russian as the language of Afghanistan.

Soviet advisers reportedly went down to the platoon level in the military, but this was apparently not enough to give effective control. As the insurrections grew and the army's unwillingness to support the regime became visible, Soviet troops increased in number. Before the invasion, they came to number 3,500–4,000 and to fly combat missions against the rebels. Yet, more troops had to be brought in to guard Soviet-built bases and installations.

Kabul's foreign policies also went beyond Moscow's limits of expediency in 1978. Taraki, and especially Amin, conducted inflammatory interviews about Baluchi and Pathan claims, alarming Iran and Pakistan when Moscow was seeking to allay their fears. Why Moscow did not stop this earlier, and stop Amin from asking for cross-border raids, is not clear. What is evident is Soviet eagerness to welcome Afghanistan into its orbit and proclaim it a state of socialist orientation; that is, on the way but not yet a member of the bloc.

Only in the spring of 1979, faced by the insurrection at Herat, did Moscow call Afghanistan a socialist state. This built on the friendship treaty of December 1978 which had granted the Soviets grounds for intervening in language designed to lay the groundwork for any future necessity to invoke the Brezhnev doctrine (which obliged Moscow to protect any threatened with reversion to imperialism). Probably, the Soviets could not and cannot believe in 1987 the Afghans are self-motivated in resisting Sovietization.

In response to a steadily deteriorating situation that bode fair to escape its control, Moscow resorted first to a coup, then to a supposedly brief invasion. The Epishev Marshal Pavlovskii missions were clearly reconnaissance missions; both men had been sent on analogous missions to Prague in 1968, and Pavlovskii had no specific military appointment in 1979. Thus, his month-long mission, just before the September 1979 coup, seems particularly ominous. The buildup to the December invasion commenced right after his return.

The factors as to why the Soviets invaded include their ambition in the direction of the Gulf, their fear of Islamic revivalism on their southern border, validation of the Brezhnev doctrine, and a particularly trying conjuncture in world affairs. Validation of the Brezhnev doctrine seems a particularly compelling motive to this author.

Afghanistan had been both a model and a geographic pivot point; if it fell, the whole regional scaffolding would be imperiled.[86] Brezhnev admitted it had been a difficult decision; it soon became clear that it had also been a serious miscalculation.

The Politburo made the fundamental error of misunderstanding the nature of the war it would face. It brought in troops who were unsuited for guerrilla warfare, and the same held true for replacement Russian troops for several years. Moscow evidently assumed that controlling cities, roads, and major strongpoints would mute ethnic resistance and, combined with wise policies of moderation and reconciliation, reduce if not terminate the rebellion without undue complications abroad. Thus, Moscow not only misread the international scene, although those costs were by no means as high as they should have been, but also the domestic Afghan scene—its political and strategic climate. Soviet troops did not command the operational or tactical art or the mass support needed to fight guerrilla war.

The Soviet government's Muslim troops were apparently rapidly demoralized when they found themselves fighting their kinsmen. Morale, through 1984 at least, has been steadily low, with soldiers deserting and bartering their weapons for drugs. This points to not only strategic mal-adjustments to Afghan reality but to organizational and tactical ones as well.[87] The Soviets eventually learned appropriate operational and tactical skills for combat in Afghanistan, but the rebels have been able to keep up with these changes.[88]

Lacking mass support, Soviet intelligence has not been able to function as it did in Iran in 1941–46. Indeed, the shoe is on the other foot; by all accounts, the mujahidin's intelligence has alerted them to Soviet offensives, enabling them to mount their own operations in Kabul, in other cities, and even in the vicinity of Soviet bases. The violent rivalry between Parcham and Khalqi had encouraged both to conspire with the resistance against each other and the Russians as Amstutz observes;[89] and the Soviet contempt for Afghanistan and Islam, and Moscow's myopia, chauvinism, and rigidity in foreign policy blind the Soviets to Afghan realities.[90]

Moscow fell victim to what has been seen as a quintessentially American vice: believing in military solutions to political problems. Thus, all their innovations have been to little or no avail. Khalqi-Parcham feuds are incessant; corruption, intrigue, conspiracy, and inefficiency are sovereign; and demoralization is rampant. Not even people's militias or the belated limited success in co-opting some tribes seems to have ameliorated Moscow's situation.

Muscovite chauvinism, militarism, ideological blindness, rigidity, arrogance, myopia, and paranoia held it back from harvesting the fruits of its formerly sophisticated policies in Kabul. It failed to learn from its own history that indigenous leftists will, once in power, launch a drastic revolution of their own, motivated by their own fanaticism and nationalism, and that failure to control it inevitably puts pressure on Moscow to rescue the endangered revolution by force of arms. As Zalmay Khalizad has noted, inviting Moscow in triggers a profoundly disequilibrizing condition whereby only added Soviet presence can remedy the defects of its own original presence, with this spiraling presence ascending ever higher in scope and intensity. This destructive and addictive process often ends by destruction of the "host body."[91] Such destruction could yet occur in Afghanistan, but the indigenous "healthy forces" are fighting gamely and, all things considered, with amazing success. The Afghan war may be a low-intensity conflict; but it is a life-and-death battle fought in deadly earnest.

It is extremely difficult, if not impossible, to obtain accurate assessments of the Afghan war as of spring 1987. For every report of Soviet and DRA progress, there is an equal and opposite one about the mujahidin's growing prowess and strength. What remains evident, however, is that Moscow has no intention of renouncing its investment in Sovietizing Afghanistan. Moscow undertook the invasion to aid a progressive country threatened by "imperialism." This line of thought actually served as rationalization for a much more sinister commitment to military force. The Soviet Union's ambassador to Paris announced in 1980 that the Brezhnev doctrine had global application; that is, Moscow considered itself totally at liberty to support "social progress" anywhere. Moscow could "not permit" another "Chile"; any country had the full right to choose its allies and friends; and "if it becomes necessary, the Soviets will repel with them the threat of a counterrevolution or foreign intervention."[92] Still more ominous was the February 1979 article in *Kommunist* that ascribed to the takeovers of the Baltic states in 1940 the character of "peaceful" support given to the revolutionary masses.

> Soviet forces did not interfere in the domestic affairs of the Baltic countries, strictly observing the stipulations of the mutual aid pacts concluded between them and the USSR. Meanwhile the presence of Soviet troops on Lithuanian, Latvian, and Estonian territory protected the Baltic from the interference of foreign imperialists. This demoralized the forces of the bourgeoisie and inspired the revolutionary masses to the struggle for the overthrow of the Fascist dictatorship.[93]

It is highly unlikely that Gorbachev has revised this mentality. The Soviets' goal in mid-1987 remains the implantation of an irreversibly Communist trend in the Afghan regime. Their economic policies are becoming steadily more exploitative, and they are geared to permanent Afghan dependence on Soviet resources.[94] The most recent example of this was the agreement to supply Kabul with high-capacity relay centers to introduce television in all the republic's provincial centers. Soviet specialists have built a space communications net there to provide international communication facilities, and agreements have been reached on a series of trade, economic, and cultural links.[95] This means total subordination of the Afghan economy to Moscow.[96]

In the cultural sphere, this takes the form of the well-known program that removes Afghan youth to Russia for education and indoctrination. It has enlisted thousands of Afghanistan's future leaders, and its significance is unmistakable. Not only is Moscow seeking to dissolve traditional family, tribal, and religious loyalties; it also aims to enroot a solidly trained, Sovietized cadre. And while the Afghan claim of 165,000 party members is inflated, the real number must consist of several thousands of people who are too compromised ever to hope for anything but strong Soviet influence.[97]

In March 1987, the press reported a drastic increase in arms shipments to the Philippine Communist insurgents, use of Soviet fishing trawlers as intelligence gatherers there, communications and intelligence construction there, the expansion of consulates with Tagalog-speaking Soviets in Mindanao and Cebu, and the proliferation of diplomats, tourists, businessmen, gold panners, and agents in the Philippines. And Moscow has offered unlimited arms and money to the Communist New People's Army.[98] In Angola, Soviet arms are flooding the country as the government, supported by Soviet advisers and Cuban troops, prepares to strike at the Savimbi forces.[99] In a recent analysis that favors the retrenchment theory of Soviet policy in the third world, the authors admit that in areas where major established commitments are in place, the Soviets are likely to assume risks to preserve that position. In Angola and Afghanistan, and probably Ethiopia, Soviet support shows no sign of retrenchment.

In Afghanistan, all the elements of Moscow's third world policy are in evidence. And the confluence of factors that led to the invasion are precisely those that preclude any settlement which translates into a diminution of Soviet influence in Afghanistan.[100] Indeed, the recent escalation of the fighting into parts of Pakistan, Iran, and the Soviet Union indicates a disinclination to leave the scene. So, too, does the rising Russophillic tone of Mikhail Gorbachev's Russia signify the deep lure imperialism presently holds for the Soviet political mind.[101]

The Soviets have steadily endeavored to retain their preeminent position in Afghanistan in both domestic politics and foreign affairs. It is unlikely they will ever concede a genuinely neutral regime or voluntarily relinquish the large investment in bases and infrastructure they have made. (The former still is the case as of March 1988.) They have resorted to the Baltic analogy—the brutal conflict against the resistance—in Afghanistan. They seek to build a cadre from the careerist, opportunist, and irrevocably compromised elements of the population while terrorizing the rest into submission. To date, it has not worked—but not for lack of trying.

They have convened sham Loya Jirgas (tribal leaders' assemblies), and they have made myriad "concessions" to the sanctity of Islam—all to no avail. More recently, the new Najibullah regime proclaimed an amnesty and issued a call for "patriots" to return "with impunity" and take part in a new government. Its aim is to weaken the rebellion by splitting it up and wearing down the insurgents, just like in the Baltic case after 1945.

These proposals have had a limited success. On 19 March 1987, Najibullah announced the return of 35,000 refugees since January, the crossing over of 10,000 members of antiregime formations, and negotiations with 90,000 others.[102] These figures, particularly those relating to fighters, are probably inflated; but it is part of Najibullah and Moscow's strategy to split the rebels.[103] In this connection, they have formed 690 reconciliation commissions with the participation of elders, clergymen, and tribal chiefs throughout Afghanistan.[104] This program is also intended to restrain the fence sitters from leaving the government, thus diminishing rebel recruitment.[105] This offensive is intended to split the mujahidin and the refugees in Pakistan, weakening them while military pressure intimidates both the refugees and the Pakistanis. Mujahidin attacks over the borders hamper both reconciliation and the attempt to recruit border tribesmen, primarily Pathans, to the regime's side.[106] Border troops are also to be reinforced from KHAD, the DRA army, and the Ministry of Interior.[107]

65

Soviet news broadcasts report that the Wazir tribe supports the government and has established a 500-man force to help the regime.[108] Najibullah has labeled work among the tribes the key for solving most of the problems facing the regime, and he has demanded that his colleagues wrest this sphere's initiative from the rebels. He attacked those who want to work only in Kabul and not out in the provinces or those who wish to work only with their own tribes. He also forcefully attacked the policy of pitting one nationality against another because such policies weaken his regime. Divide and rule will still be a major tactic, but it will be coupled with new policies, to be announced, which will likely serve the goal of deracinating Afghans from these roots to a supra-ethnic loyalty to Communist party and state.[109] Najibullah has also affirmed his intention to have government and Soviet grants go directly to the people rather than be siphoned off by corrupt officials—another move designed to bind the people more closely to Soviet "largesse."[110] Finally, the regime has reaffirmed its military policy to summon all able-bodied men from 18 to 40, recall of those who have served, and call-ups twice a year.[111] The objective is to monopolize these men for the regime, deny them to the mujahidin, and, through rewards for those possessing higher education, create a loyal cadre of educated elite.

The DRA is probably still unable or unwilling to carry out ambitious policies. Both Moscow and Karmal utterly failed to root out the corruption of persons and parties, ethnic rivalry, staggering incompetence, and the Khalqi-Parcham conflict, which continues unabated.[112] Karmal's failures here very likely led to his replacement by the head of the secret service, Najibullah, in 1986. But Najibullah's efforts, too, have not been crowned with success. Khalqi-Parcham rivalry continues as before, with reports of battles between them in the army and reports of betrayal in the mujahidin.[113]

Domestic political antagonisms among Afghans are quite strong. On 18 January 1987, the *Observer* reported that the followers of Karmal had staged a coup against Najibullah which was foiled only by strong Soviet action. This hardly allayed Soviet suspicions and has probably led to even deeper Soviet controls over the regime, though it is hard to imagine any controls deeper than those cited by Amstutz.[114] All this belies the show of deep-rooted popular support for the regime and undoubtedly has prompted Moscow to make such gestures as the reconciliation plan, hints of desire to withdraw, tolerance for Islamic education, and Loya Jirgas. The linguistic policies that give freedom to each group to use its language, a blatant show of divide and rule tactics, serve as another example of the regime's concessions to "ethnic rights."[115]

The insubstantiality of the Soviets' reconciliation policy is evident from the framework in which Moscow and Kabul have posed the issues of withdrawal and future governments. According to Soviet commentators, the reconciliation process calls for the opposing sides to set up a coalition government wherein the contenders will have the opportunity to participate in actual policymaking.[116] Reconciliation also means abandonment by outside supporters of the rebels, after which the Soviet "limited contingent" will supposedly return home.[117] This has been a long-standing Soviet line under Gorbachev.[118] However, the record of such coalition regimes, dating back to World War II, holds out little hope of a quick withdrawal: characteristically, Moscow insists that others cease their aid for freedom fighters before taking 18 months, at least, to wind up its invasion.

The Economist's Foreign Report says that Moscow hints at a government dominated by the PDPA.[119] Afghan officials also insist that the returning and amnestied rebels would have to accept the dominance of the present ruling party.[120] Najibullah insists that the PDPA would retain an important mobilizing and organizing political role, but he refuses to give guarantees that it would facilitate an egalitarian distribution of political power.[121] He also argues that whenever the Red Army leaves, the DRA army could deal with the domestic situation on its own.[122]

This can hardly be the case. Rather his troops, the dreaded KHAD, who are the mainstay of the regime due to its incompetence, will play that role on an expanded scale. It is the only comparatively efficient government agency, and it has in some cases penetrated the rebels. With Najibullah atop the regime, its star has clearly been rising since 1985. At the same time, the army remains unreliable and demoralized. It does not want to fight, and it has been penetrated by the mujahidin.[123] The facades of domestic support erected by Kabul remain just that—facades. The Loya Jirga of 1985 was all too evidently a fraud. Many participants were state functionaries or members of KHAD. It was rushed into action in April 1985, with delegates being paid for their presence or coerced into making television statements. Tribal and local council elections in August–September 1985 were neither secret nor marked by the usual practices of bribery.[124] The emphasis in all these developments was targeted at Pathan tribes to elicit their assent to closing the borders to the mujahidin and at playing the irredentist card against either Iran or Pakistan.[125] Having failed to win support through these means, the regime has resorted to domestic crackdowns such as the new conscription law.[126]

The local equivalent of these political tactics has been the campaign, ongoing since 1985, to win over local tribes, to co-opt them by permitting the formation of local militias to guard their territory, and to win them away from the mujahidin. While the evidence is fragmentary and inconclusive, the Orkand Corporation reported in 1986 that the regime is making visible, if limited, progress toward easing the pressure on the Soviet and DRA armies.[127] These moves point toward establishing a permanently Sovietized Afghanistan. It is clear that while Gorbachev and Najibullah talk vaguely of a sovereign and neutral Afghanistan and of reconciliation, actual Soviet policy as announced at the 27th Party Congress of 1986 concedes nothing. The Soviets still see the problem as outside intervention which must cease before they leave, and they will create a facade of a national reconciliation government under their protégés. They still cling to the retrospective legalization of the invasion by a so-called limited contingent at Afghan request while affirming that Soviet hegemony over Afghanistan remains a vital interest of the USSR.[128] At the same time, Najibullah is moving to consolidate his regime in law by promulgating a new Afghan constitution, modeled on Soviet statutes, which will provide the legal scaffolding for the PDPA's primacy at home.[129]

If the future is clouded, the danger posed by the Soviets is not. The latest round of bombings and attacks in Pakistan (February–April 1987) presage increased pressure on Pakistan in the form of bombing raids, flooding Pakistani markets with cheap Soviet goods, student and Baluchi unrest, border raids, and so forth. Its aim is to test Pakistani resolve to continue support for the resistance and to induce unrest in Islamabad among forces opposed to the Zia regime there.[130] The pressure also aims at Tehran and was one of the factors that brought Tehran and Washington toward ill-fated rapprochement in 1985–86.[131] Soviet pressures aim to unhinge Islamabad at home until it "understands" Kabul's position in its peace offers.[132] Thus, one can already see the Soviets using the strategic advantages garnered by the invasion in their implicit offering to trade stability in Pakistan for peace in Kabul and recognition of their hegemony.

Such Soviet maneuvers support the warnings of numerous observers that Moscow threatens the entire Indian Ocean and Gulf littoral, and that this position constitutes the ultimate strategic rationale of the invasion. The institutionalized presence of air bases in Afghanistan provides an air threat of enormous strategic significance. Several observers believe that the regional geopolitical momentum of the war will inevitably drive the Soviets to widen the war to Pakistan and perhaps Iran.[133] The recent bombing raids seem to bear out Ziring's contention that the Afghan war will involve Pakistan as the next Soviet target.[134] Recent reports also say that Baluchi guerrillas, commanded by Shia Afghan commanders, some of whom have been trained in the USSR, have staged raids, which are paralleled by the Tudeh party's calls for Baluchi autonomy, against Iran. Moscow seems to aim at inducing Iran to abandon the mujahidin and to support a Soviet plan for an international conference on Afghanistan.[135]

By far the most sinister manifestations of this drive are Moscow's annexation of the Wakhan corridor of Afghanistan and the garrisoning there of Soviet Tajiks. These actions have raised fears of future manipulation of the Afghan border and of political moves in conjunction with the Geneva talks.[136] *The Economist* recently reported a spectacular offer by Secretary Gorbachev to both the Iranian and Pakistani foreign ministers in their trips to Moscow. Pakistan was told that if it indicated willingness to sign a nonaggression pact with India, Moscow would guarantee the pact and encourage India to sign as well. It also offered a security guarantee and economic aid. All this would be in return for Pakistan's abandoning support of the mujahidin and supporting a cosmetically reorganized regime in Kabul. For its part, Iran is interested in obtaining a lessening of Soviet support for Iraq—a point Moscow could use as a quid pro quo.[137]

This would not only terminate the Afghan war on terms of a virtual Soviet victory, it would also propel Moscow into the role of guarantor of regional security in South Asia. It would place the Soviet Union in a position to aim constantly at India and Iran. It is already evident that Soviet pressure on Pakistan has restrained Islamabad from all-out support of the mujahidin.[138] The enhancement of the Soviet position that would result from acceptance of these offers would constitute a major Soviet strategic victory with profound implications. In view of the enormously divisive pressures that threaten Pakistan at home and abroad, it might become the Poland of the twenty-first century—a country torn apart by irreconcilable neighbors, in this case India and Afghanistan acting for Moscow.[139]

The similarity between Afghanistan and Baltic states is particularly visible in military operations. Shtromas and Prados have observed that in the Baltic, Soviet forces sometimes resorted to sweeps of the territory but mainly emphasized destruction of the civilian environment in which guerrillas could flourish. This involved mass deportation of refugees, relatives of fighters and so-called kulaks. This also involved collectivization of the land, which pauperized the peasants as it bound them to the land. And Communist troops were ordered to burn all habitats suspected of harboring insurgents. Thus, the rebels were deprived of support in villages.

The Soviets mobilized the formerly dispossessed and the upwardly mobile opportunities and careerists to create a mass basis for their rule. Prominent in such tactics were the Sovietization of education institutions and the rapid promotion of pro-Moscow Lithuanians. Russified Baltic Communists were repatriated to provide a fig leaf of legitimacy. Isolated from Western support, the rebels ultimately surrendered out of weariness and fear for their people, who faced a real threat of genocide.[140]

All these correspond to present events in Afghanistan. So does the use of amnesties (for resistance fighters) that were later revoked. The aim of such operations is to drive out the rebels, deprive them of resources and support, deprive the masses and rebels of any independent economic basis of life, divide the masses internally, and split the masses off from the rebels. In the end, the Afghan population will be reduced to total dependence on Moscow and Kabul. Such tactics entail holding onto urban centers, reinforcing logistical strongpoints, and steadily pushing the war to the borders of Pakistan.

This strategy has punished the rebels, but whether it has brought the Soviets closer to victory is not clear. There are many continuing negatives in the Soviets' military performance. The widespread reports about poor morale appear to be true. Much has been written of the need to upgrade morale through positive indoctrination and patriotic education. There are many reports of poor morale due to lack of hygiene and health care supplies and the exposure of raw recruits to the falsity of Soviet propaganda; and the reaction of local minorities is very negative. There are draft evasions on a massive scale, complaints that officials' children do not get drafted, difficult adjustments for ex-servicemen, homosexuality among troops, and rising levels of resort to drugs.[141] Amstutz corroborates all these reports from his own evidence, citing appalling examples of medical insufficiency, that recall the most gruesome accounts of the Crimean War of 1854–56, lack of drugs, falsity of propaganda, and black-market sale of munitions by Soviet servicemen.[142]

Amstutz maintains that calling up the troops it would take to subdue the revolt (approximately 345,000) would shake Soviet domestic and military morale considerably.[143] And rebel acquisition of Stinger antiaircraft missiles will exacerbate this; morale will probably plummet. Brig Muhammed Sirwar Shinwari, who defected to the rebels, reported that Soviet troops are weary; and he said all reports going to the Kremlin paint a "distressing" picture of the war and propose its termination.[144]

Soviet disaffection with the struggle in Afghanistan has contributed to the rising fear of Soviet authorities about the growing strength of Islam in Central Asia.[145] Demoralization and frustration may also be found in their policies of terrorism and chemical bombing, which are typical reactions to a totally unexpected military environment. Training, command, tactics, and weapon deployments have had to be learned on the job; and there has been a corresponding increase in lethality and violence. Chemical weapons and weapons of purely terroristic significance have been used.

The Soviets utilized airborne, Spetsnaz, tank, and fast-moving mobile infantry troops to seize Afghan C^3 assets initially. A brilliant tactical operation, it was based on similar actions in Prague in 1968 and Budapest in 1956. But it soon became clear that Soviet troops could not fight on Afghanistan's terrain or on its terms. They were unprepared for the intensity of opposition, and they were wedded to conventional warfare strategies. Depending on large tank formations, armored sweeps, and bombers, they could not deal effectively with hit-and-run attacks. That they were unable to retain the initiative or to break enemy morale became evident very quickly. Criticism percolated up Soviet literature in 1980; and 1981, we saw the first instances of revised training and weapons deployment in Afghanistan. Since then, the Soviets have increasingly resorted to physically hardened and trained formations that have been adapted to mountain warfare, and they have encouraged pursuit tactics against the mujahidin.[146]

While individually successful, these tactical deployments have not been large enough to win a victory; but they have enabled the Soviets to retain control of Kabul, large installations, and key roads while expanding their operations. In 1982, they returned to sweeps and got nowhere, though they combined them increasingly with bombing and helicopter airborne assaults. Thus began *migratory genocide* (rendering the land uninhabitable through bombing); and these assaults have increased in frequency and magnitude, shading over to bombing raids on Pakistan early in 1987.[147] Their failure to use paratroop and heliborne assault forces and their lack of nighttime counterinsurgency capability had held the Soviets back earlier.[148] The Soviet air force has taken the lead in publicizing the lessons of Afghanistan while the army has screened such discussion from public view.[149]

Michael Yardley reports that the Soviets now rely heavily of heliborne operations by Spetsnaz and other elite mountain units. Conscripts do little fighting, and they move from base to base only with massive ground and air support.[150] Spetsnaz forces have risen from 4,000 to 5,000 troops. These tough, experienced, well-trained troops are used in small unit operations, ambushes, and nighttime operations. Rockets, artillery, Su–26 ground fighters, and helicopters have been shipped in. Wheeled armored vehicles are being replaced by newer models or by tracked vehicles, and self-propelled artillery is supplanting towed artillery. All this suggests that the Soviets now recognize the need for speed, mobility, initiative, nighttime fighting, guerrilla tactics, and suitable weapons.[151] These tactics were largely unopposed until the rebels acquired Stinger missiles. The success of the Stinger has now led Soviet fliers to resort to more evasive and higher altitude tactics. This has eased the mujahidin's situation, but there have been air raids on Pakistan's "privileged sanctuary." One reason for the attacks on Pakistan is that the rebels have conducted demoralizing attacks on Soviet territory and villages. Since tank formations in the mountains have long since been deemphasized by the Soviets,[152] it is not clear what else the Soviets might do.

Adaptation of the Hind-24 helicopter, and of heliborne as well as Spetsnaz troops, has substantial significance not just for Afghanistan, but for other potential theaters as well. Motorized infantry and helicopters that give ground support to Spetsnaz and mobile troops as well as bombers represent a new wrinkle in Soviet doctrine. The new emphasis on speed, mobility, surprise, and combined arms at the small unit level has resulted in a devastating conjunction of weapons with enormous destructive firepower.[153]

The Soviets have thus enhanced the role of the air force in small unit operations, particularly in mountainous areas.[154] This has obvious importance for further developments at the theater level. The introduction of the combined arms reinforced battalion and the strengthened role of helicopters in operation with such battalions presages such deployments in theater tactics. The Soviets can inflict massive damage on the civilian infrastructure in both Afghanistan and Pakistan, carry out ambushes and deep raids, and increase both troop mobility and support.[155] No long logistical tail is needed for such an operation, which can embrace multiple targets and missions. The suddenness and destructive capability of these Soviet forces have accelerated the depopulation of Afghanistan and the diminution of mujahidin mobility.[156]

These new weapons and units also fit in with the structural reforms of the Soviet military since 1978. They have encouraged decentralized operational command and control, individual unit and commander (or NCO) initiative, speed, and surprise. This Afghan war will play a considerable role in helping to shape the ongoing reconstruction of Soviet command structures, doctrine, training, force structures, and operational art.[157]

The Afghan conflict seems to be escalating. On 27 April, Kabul announced the failure of its cease-fire and reconciliation policies and blamed it on the United States. But the policies were a sham, anyway—fighting has escalated even into Pakistan, which is asking for US sharing of radar planes to create defense against the new air raids.[158] Despite Kabul's claims of 40,000 returnees, 100,000 engaged in talks, and 17,000 rebels returning, it is clear that the policy has failed to blunt the resistance and that regional tension is growing.[159] The Soviets are strengthening Afghan dependence on Moscow, and Tass has stated that Moscow will take all necessary measures to prevent infringements on its frontiers. The Soviets have reaffirmed their intention to support Kabul, and they have threatened those providing support to the rebels from the outside.[160]

There has been no change in Moscow's position. Tass reported this in a sharply and bluntly worded commentary on Secretary of State George Shultz's 13–16 April 1987 negotiations in Moscow.

> The Soviet Union is convinced that the American approach is the main brake on normalization and political settlement in the most acute issue today—the situation around Afghanistan. This was stressed in no uncertain terms at the talks with United States Secretary of State George Shultz. We believe that this evaluation of the American approach is the more correct [in] that the DRA Government's programme of national reconciliation creates a real basis for stabilising the situation and stopping the bloodshed in the country, while the Afghan-Pakistani talks in Geneva have reached the level when the drawing closer of positions becomes real. .... George Shultz was told that the Americans would not succeed either in overthrowing the lawful government in Kabul nor in "exhausting" the USSR by means of the Afghan conflict.[161]

And Moscow feels justified in threatening both Washington and Islamabad with "the most serious consequences" if this military option continues.[162] At the same time, Marshal Kulikov admits that Afghanistan is very strange as a theater of war and that it is difficult to transfer its lessons to Europe. While it is possible to win a victory in such a country in military terms, it is another thing to rule it; and defeating guerrillas determined to defend themselves is a difficult task.[163]

The military has taken over civil aviation,[164] and the Soviets show no sign of willingness to leave behind a neutral and sovereign state. By moving their air defense into the Pamirs, by annexing the Wakhan corridor, and by importing lots of expensive and not easily portable equipment, Moscow gives every indication of aiming to stay.[165] It remains faithful to its imperial heritage and to the pattern of involvement in local wars postulated by Amnon Sella. First comes the providing of advisers, technicians, and high-quality military assets. The second stage is comprised of sealift and airlift on a massive scale. The third stage is the introduction of Soviet combat units, led by airborne troops whose capacity for power projection is increasingly formidable.[166]

Some have opined that Soviet victory in Afghanistan not only threatens South Asia and the Gulf but bodes fair to materially accomplish a strategic encirclement of the Middle East. It would also be a large step forward in the creation and consolidation of a Soviet collective security system.[167] In view of the Soviet assets invested in Afghanistan, the new Asian offensive that has revived Moscow's call for an Asian Helsinki conference, and the changes in Soviet military doctrine and postures, the strategic consequences of a Soviet victory in Afghanistan would be enormous indeed. A fully Sovietized Afghanistan would have more than purely regional significance, profound as that would be. It would encourage future adventures in such low-intensity conflicts by the Soviets or their proxies, who would have learned that it can be done with relative impunity and external apathy.

In January 1982, Abdul Qadir, acting minister of defense, told a Yugoslav interviewer that when Afghanistan is subdued, its Soviet-controlled army will play a significant role throughout the region.[168] And the 1985 political offensive of Karmal provides ample confirmation of the persistence of such ambitions in Pashtunistan and Baluchistan. It is not farfetched to see a Soviet victory unhinging the entire regional, and perhaps global, status quo.

Because much change can be generated through low-intensity conflict, the study of such wars with a view to proper policy responses is crucial. Given the relationship between domestic Soviet imperialism and its projection abroad, blocking that projection should provide substantial benefits. Moscow also grasps this, and it is determined to make a nonaligned Afghanistan a thing of the past. They still seek to contrive a victory that would leave them in control of the field which they have yet to win militarily.

Despite the conventional wisdom that the economic and domestic pressures of Gorbachev's reforms impose a limiting pressure on third world expansion, and that the costs of Afghanistan are deterring Moscow, the evidence points to the contrary. Moscow shows no sign of willingness to cash in its chips. The specter of an Asiatic empire still grips the Soviet political mind, even as it converts Afghanistan into a human crater for military-political experimentation. The success of this experiment could only lead to more of the same. And the laboratory subjects on the USSR's expanded borders for future low-intensity conflicts would become more numerous and more vulnerable.

NOTES

1. *Direktivy Gavnogo Kommandovaniia Krasnoi Armii 1917–1920: Sbornik Dokumentov* (Moscow: Ministervo Oborona SSSR, 1969), 179.

2. A. I. Ishanov, *Bukharskaia Narodnaia Sovetskaia Respublika* (Tashkent: Uzbekistan, 1969), 164–65.

3. *Inostrannaia voennaia Interventsiia i Grazhdanskaia Viona v Srednei Azii Kazakhstana* (Alma-Ata: Izdatel'stov Akademii Nauk Kazakhskovi SSR, 1963–1964), II, 564–65.

4. Mikhail Heller and Aleksandr M. Nekrich, *Utopia in Power: The History of the Soviet Union From 1917 to the Present*, trans. Phyllis Carlos (New York: Simon & Schuster, 1986), 102–5.

5. Ibid., 105.

6. Col Gen M. A. Gareev, *M. V. Frunze Voyennyi Teoretik*, trans. Joint Publications Research Service (Washington, D.C.: Government Printing Office, 1985), 37–38.

7. Ibid., 167.

8. Alexandre Bennigsen and Chantal Lemercier-Quelquejay, "Soviet Experience of Muslim Guerilla Warfare and the War in Afghanistan," in *The USSR and the Muslim World: Issues in Domestic and Foreign Policy*, ed. Yaacov Ro'i (London: Allen & Unwin, 1984), 206–14; Alexandre Bennigsen, *The Soviet Union and Muslim Guerilla Wars, 1920–1981: Lessons for Afghanistan*, Rand Report N–1707/1 (Santa Monica, Calif.: Rand Corp., 1981), passim; Martha Brill Olcott, "The Basmachi or Freedmen's Revolt in Turkestan 1918–1924," *Soviet Studies* 33, no. 3 (July 1981): 352–69; William S. Ritter, "The Final Phase in the Liquidation of the Anti-Soviet Resistance in Tadzhikistan: Ibrahim Bek and the Basmachi, 1924–1931," *Soviet Studies* 37, no. 4 (October 1985): 484–93.

9. Olcott, 352–69; Ritter, 484–93.

10. Bennigsen, passim; Bennigsen and Lemercier-Quelquejay, 206–14.

11. Stephen Blank, "Soviet Politics and the Iranian Revolution of 1919–1921," *Cahiers du Monde Russe et Sovietique* 21, no. 2 (April–June 1980): 173–94; Miron Rezun, *The Soviet Union and Iran: Soviet Policy in Iran From the Beginnings of the Pahlavi Dynasty to the Soviet Invasion of 1941* (Alphen an den Rijn: Sijthoff and Noordhoff International, 1981), 17; John Lenczowski, *Russia and the West in Iran, 1918–1948* (Ithaca, N.Y.: Cornell University Press, 1949), 52–64; Harish Kapur, *Soviet Russia and Asia 1917–1927: A Study of Soviet Policy Towards Turkey, Iran and Afghanistan* (New York: Humanities Press, 1967), 166–84.

12. Blank, 173–80; Kapur, 166.

13. Blank, 173–94.

14. Ibid.; Kapur, 166–84; Lenczowski, 52–64; Rezun, 17; Ervand Abrahamian, *Iran Between Two Revolutions* (Princeton, N.J.: Princeton University Press, 1982), 115–16.

15. Blank, 189–91.

16. Ibid., 184–85, 190.

17. Charles Gati, *Hungary and the Soviet Bloc* (Durham, N.C.: Duke University Press, 1986), 1–100.

18. Georges Agabekov, *OGPU: The Russian Secret Terror*, trans. Henry Bunn (New York: Brentano, 1931); Agabekov, *Zapiski Chekista* (Berlin: Izdatel'stvo Strela, 1931), passim; Kapur, 166–84; Rezun, 17; Lenczowski, 52–64.

19. Kapur, 184; Rezun, 17.

20. Lenczowski, 92–102.

21. Gerold Guensberg, *Soviet Command Study of Iran (Moscow 1941): Draft Translation*

74

and Brief Analysis (Arlington, Va.: SRI International, January 1980), passim.

22. Ibid., 3.

23. Ibid., Intro., 12.

24. Ibid., 89.

25. Ibid., 53.

26. Ibid., 70.

27. Ibid., 113.

28. Ibid., Abrahamian, 169, 173–76.

29. Faramaz S. Fatemi, *The USSR in Iran* (South Brunswick and New York: A. S. Barnes and Co., 1980), 38–39; Bruse Robellet Kuniholm, *The Origins of the Cold War in the Near East: Great Power Conflict and Diplomacy in Iran, Turkey, and Greece* (Princeton, N.J.: Princeton University Press, 1980), 145–49.

30. Kuniholm, 145–49.

31. Ibid., 151–54; Lenczowski, 194–95.

32. Ibid., 197–99.

33. Abrahamian, 291–305.

34. Ibid., 304–5; Fatemi, 47.

35. Fatemi, 47.

36. Kuniholm, 201.

37. Abrahamian, 384–413.

38. Marshall Lee Miller, "How the Soviets Invaded Iran," *Armed Forces Journal International*, February 1987, 30–34.

39. Kuniholm, 296–97.

40. Oliver Roy, *Islam and Resistance in Afghanistan* (Cambridge: Cambridge University Press, 1986), passim; M. Nazif Shahrani, "Introduction," in *Revolutions & Rebellions in Afghanistan: Anthropological Perspectives*, ed. M. Nazif Shahrani and Robert Canfield (Berkeley, Calif.: Institute of International Studies, University of California, 1984), 3–51.

41. J. Bruce Amstutz, *Afghanistan: The First Five Years of Soviet Occupation* (Washington, D.C.: National Defense University, 1986), 297.

42. Agabekov, *OGPU*, 160–70.

43. Selig S. Harrison, *In Afghanistan's Shadow: Baluch Nationalism and Soviet Temptations* (New York: Carnegie Endowment for International Peace, 1981), passim.

44. Ibid., 60.

45. Ibid., 80.

46. Ibid., 127–48.

47. Ibid.

48. Ibid., 196 99.

49. Thomas T. Hammond, *Red Flag Over Afghanistan* (Boulder, Colo.: Westview Press, 1984), 24.

50. G. S. Bhargava, *South Asian Security After Afghanistan* (Lexington, Mass.: D. C. Heath & Co., 1983), 21, 25.

51. Amstutz, 20–21; Hammond, 23–27; Henry Bradsher, *Afghanistan and the Soviet Union, New and Expanded Edition* (Durham, N.C.: Duke University Press, 1985), 19–22; Leon Poullada, "Afghanistan and the United States: The Crucial Years," *Middle East Review* 35, no. 2 (Spring 1981): 178–90.

52. Amstutz, 20–21.

53. Bradsher, *Afghanistan and the Soviet Union*, 22.

54. V. Baskatov, trans. *A History of Afghanistan* (Moscow: Progress Publishers, 1985), 249–54.

55. Amstutz, passim.

56. Boris Petkov, *Afghanistan Today: Impressions of a Journalist* (New Delhi: Sterling Publishers Private Ltd., 1983), 11.

57. Leon Poullada, "The Search for National Unity," in *Afghanistan in the 1970's*, ed. Louis Dupree and Linette Albert (New York: Praeger Publishers, 1974), 43–44.

58. Shahrani, 36.

59. Amstutz, 22–28; Hammond, 27; Alvin Z. Rubinstein, *Soviet Policy Toward Turkey, Iran and Afghanistan* (New York: Praeger Publishers, 1982), 135.

60. Abdul Tawab Assifi, "The Russian Rope: Soviet Economic Motives and the Subversion of Afghanistan," *World Affairs* 145, no. 3 (Winter 1982–1983): 253–66.

61. Amstutz, 28–30.

62. Ibid., 28–30, 49, 87–88.

63. Patrick J. Garrity, "The Soviet Military Sales in Afghanistan: 1956–1979," *RUSI* 125, no. 3 (September 1980): 31–36.

64. David Chaffetz, "Afghanistan in Turmoil, International Failure of American Diplomacy in Afghanistan," *World Affairs* 145, no. 3 (Winter 1982–1983): 230–52.

65. Joseph J. Collins, *The Soviet Invasion of Afghanistan* (Lexington, Mass.: Lexington Books, 1986), 23.

66. Poullada, "The Search for National Unity," 34–49; Muhammad R. Azmi, "Soviet Politico-Military Penetration in Afghanistan (1955–1979)" (Unpublished paper, Miami University of Ohio, Dept of History, 1985); Olivier Roy, "Le Double Code Afghan: Marxisme et Tribalisme," *Revue Francaise de Science Politique* 36, no. 6 (December 1986): 846–61; Ralph Magnus, "The Military and Politics in Afghanistan: Before and After the Revolution," in *The Armed Forces in Contemporary Asian Societies*, ed. Edward A. Olsen and Stephen Jurika, Jr. (Boulder, Colo.: Westview Press, 1986), 334–36.

67. Ibid.

68. Roy, "Le Double Code," 846–61; Anthony Arnold, *Afghanistan's Two-Party Communism: Parcham and Khalq* (Stanford, Calif.: Hoover Institution Press, 1983), 23–51.

69. Ibid.

70. Ibid.; Zalmay Khalizad, *The Return of the Great Game: Superpower Rivalry and Domestic Turmoil in Afghanistan, Iran, Pakistan, and Turkey* (Santa Monica, Calif.: California Seminar on International Security and Foreign Policy, September 1980), 19–20; G. W. Choudhury, *India, Pakistan, Bangladesh and the Major Powers* (Glencoe, Ill.: The Free Press, 1975), 63–69.

71. Choudhury, 63–69.

72. Lawrence E. Grinter, "The Soviet Invasion of Afghanistan: Its Inevitability and Its Consequence," *Parameters* 12, no. 4 (December 1982): 55.

73. Amstutz, 35.

74. Ibid., 35–36.

75. Arnold, 31, 48.

76. Ibid.

77. Bradsher, *Afghanistan and the Soviet Union*, 69–71.

78. Baskator, 302–3.

79. Azmi, 15; Arnold, 52–56; Bradsher, *Afghanistan and the Soviet Union*, 56.

80. Avigdor Haselkorn, *The Evolution of Soviet Security Strategy 1965–1975* (New York: Crane, Russak & Co., Inc., 1977), passim; John Erickson, "The Soviet Strategic Emplacement in Asia," *Asian Affairs* 27, no. 1 (January 1981): 1–19.

81. Hannah Negran, "The Afghan Coup of April 1978: Revolution and International Security," *Orbis* 33, no. 1 (Spring 1979): 93.

82. Shahrani, passim.

83. Amstutz, 54, 79–80.

84. Arnold, 52–56; Bradsher, *Afghanistan and the Soviet Union*, 19–22; Hammond, 24.

85. Rubinstein, *Soviet Policy*, 161–62.

86. Hammond, 132–44.

87. Amstutz, 161, 177–78, 381–82.

88. Henry Bradsher, McLean, Va., October 1986, interview, *U.S. News and World Report*, 19 January 1987.

89. Amstutz, passim.

90. Ronald R. Pope, "Miscalculation in Soviet Foreign Policy (with Special Reference to Afghanistan)," *Crossroads*, Winter–Spring 1982, 107–24.

91. Zalmay Khalizad, "Soviet-Occupied Afghanistan," *Problems of Communism* 29, no. 6 (November–December 1980): 40.

92. Keith Payne, *Nuclear Deterrence in U.S.–Soviet Relations* (Boulder, Colo.: Westview Press, 1982), 110.

93. Ibid., 90–91.

94. Zalmay Khalizad, "Moscow's Afghan War," *Problems of Communism* 35, no. 1 (January–February 1986): 9; *Washington Post*, 20 October 1986, 1, 16.

95. *Foreign Broadcast Information Service (USSR)*, 17 March 1987, D9 (hereafter cited as *FBIS* with the appropriate country shown in parentheses).

96. Ibid., 20 February 1987, D3.

97. Ibid., 16 December 1986, CC1.

98. *Washington Times*, 24 March 1987, 1A, 6A.

99. *Christian Science Monitor*, 7 April 1987, 1, 8.

100. Robert S. Litwak and S. Neil Macfarland, "Soviet Activism in the Third World," *Survival* 29, no. 1 (January–February 1987): 33.

101. Alvin Z. Rubinstein, "Speculations on a National Tragedy," *Orbis* 30, no. 4 (Winter 1987): 597–99.

102. *FBIS (USSR)*, 20 March 1987, D1.

103. *FBIS (South Asia)*, 9 February 1987, C1.

104. *FBIS (USSR)*, 27 February 1987, D3–4.

105. Ibid., 17 March 1987, D2.

106. *FBIS (South Asia)*, 20 March 1987, C1.

107. Ibid.

108. *FBIS (USSR)*, 16 March 1987, CC3.

109. *FBIS (South Asia)*, 9 February 1987, C2.

110. Ibid.

111. *FBIS (USSR)*, 24 February 1987, D4.

112. Henry Bradsher, "Stagnation and Change in Afghanistan," *Journal of South Asian and Middle Eastern Studies* 10, no. 1 (Fall 1986): 5–12.

113. Khalizad, "Moscow's Afghan War," 8.

114. Amstutz, 54 et seq.; Zalmay Khalizad, "The War in Afghanistan," *International Journal* 41, no. 1 (Spring 1986): 281.

115. Eden Naby, "The Ethnic Factor in Soviet-Afghan Relations," *Asian Survey* 20, no. 3 (March 1980): 237–56; Department of State, *Soviet Influence on Afghan Youth* (Washington, D.C.: Government Printing Office, 1986), 1–7.

116. *FBIS (USSR)*, 31 March 1987, CC9.

117. Ibid., 5 March 1987, CC7; 5 February 1987, D2.

118. Rubinstein, "Speculation," 595.

119. *Foreign Report*, 12 March 1987, 5.

120. *The Economist*, 27 March–3 April 1987, 40.

121. *FBIS (South Asia)*, 14 February 1987, C2.

122. Ibid., C1.

123. *Washington Times*, 30 October 1986, 1.

124. Khalizad, "Moscow's Afghan War," passim; Khalizad, "The War in Afghanistan," passim; Department of State, *Afghanistan: Six Years of Soviet Occupation* (Washington, D.C.: Government Printing Office, December 1985).

125 Ibid.

126. *FBIS (South Asia)*, 9 February 1987, CC2; *U.S. News and World Report*, 28 July 1986 and 9 February 1987, 44.

127. *The Soviet in Afghanistan: Adapting, Reappraising, and Settling In* (Washington, D.C.: Orkand Corporation, 1986), 10–13.

128. *Foreign Report*, 19 April 1987, 1–2; *The Economist*, 7 February 1987, 40–41.

129. *FBIS (South Asia)*, 19 April 1987, C1.

130. *New York Times*, 6 April 1987, 1.

131. Ibid.

132. *FBIS (South Asia)*, 26 March 1987, C1.

133. Alvin Z. Rubinstein, "A Third World Policy Waits for Gorbachev," *Orbis*, 30, no. 2 (Summer 1986): 356; Lawrence Ziring, ed., *The Subcontinent in World Affairs* (New York: Praeger Publishers, 1982).

134. Ziring, 130.

135. *Foreign Report*, 29 January 1987, 4.

136. Ziring, 136–38.

137. *Foreign Report*, 19 February 1987, 1–2.

138. *Newsweek*, 23 March 1987, 33.

139. *U.S. News and World Report*, 28 July 1986, 29.

140. Alexsandr' Shtromas, "The Baltic States," in *The Last Empire*, ed. Robert Conquest (Stanford, Calif.: Hoover Institution Press, 1986), 193–97; John Prados, *Presidents' Secret Wars* (New York: William Morrow & Co., 1987), 38–44.

141. *Foreign Report*, 12 February 1987, 6.

142. Amstutz, 161, 177–78; *New York Times*, 18 February 1987, 7.

143. Amstutz, 198.

144. *FBIS (USSR)*, 31 March 1987, D3.

145. Ibid., 13 February 1987, R7.

146. Thomas M. Cynkin, "Aftermath of the Saur Coup: Insurgency and Counterinsurgency in Afghanistan," *The Fletcher Forum* 6, no. 2 (Summer 1982): 295.

147. Edward Girardet, *Afghanistan: The Soviet War* (New York: St. Martin's Press, 1985), 36–40; *Washington Post*, 13 February 1983; James B. Curren and Phillip A. Karber, "Afghanistan's Ordeal Puts a Region at Risk," *Armed Forces Journal International*, March 1985, 78–80.

148. Cynkin, 295; David Isby, *Russia's War in Afghanistan* (London: Osprey Publishing Co. Ltd., 1986), 8.

149. William P. Baxter, "Ground Forces," in *Soviet Armed Forces Review Annual*, ed. David Jones (Gulf Breeze, Fla: Academic International Press, 1982), 6:127.

150. Michael Yardley, "Afghanistan: A First Hand View," *International Defense Review*, March 1987, 275–77.

151. Department of State, *Afghanistan: Seven Years of Soviet Occupation* (Washington, D.C.: Government Printing Office, February 1987), 11.

152. Capt Anthony A. Cardoza, "Soviet Aviation in Afghanistan," *Proceedings*, February 1987, 85–89; Curren and Karber, 82–87; Lt Col Denny R. Nelson, "Soviet Air Power: Tactics and Weapons Used in Afghanistan," *Air University Review* 36, no. 2 (January–February 1985): 30–45.

153. Alfred L. Monks, *The Soviet Intervention in Afghanistan* (Washington, D.C.: American Enterprise Institute, 1981), 40–48.

154. Yossef Bodansky, "Afghanistan: The Soviet Air War," *Defense & Foreign Affairs*, September 1985, 13.

155. Ibid., 14.

156. Ibid.

157. Douglas M. Hart, "Low-Intensity Conflict in Afghanistan: The Soviet View," *Survival* 24, no. 2 (March–April 1982): 61–68.

158. *New York Times*, 28 April 1987, 1, 4.

159. *FBIS (USSR)*, 22 April 1987, CC1.

160. Ibid., 20 April 1987, D1–2.

161. Ibid., 24 April 1987, CC3.

162. Ibid.

163. Ibid., 21 April 1987, AA11.

164. *FBIS (Eastern Europe)*, 20 April 1987, D6.

165. Isby, 9; Nelson, 30–45; Maj John M. Hutcheson, "Scorched-Earth Policy: Soviets in Afghanistan," *Military Review*, April 1982, 33; Yossef Bodansky, "The Bear on the Chessboard: Soviet Military Gains in Afghanistan," *World Affairs* 145, no. 3 (Winter 1982–1983): 273–86.

166. Amnon Sella, "Patterns of Soviet Involvement in a Local War," *RUSI* 124, no. 2 (June 1979): 53–55.

167. Bodansky, "Bear on the Chessboard," 273–86; Erickson, 1–19; Haselkorn, passim.

168. Testimony of Roseanne Klass, Senate, *The Situation in Afghanistan: Hearings before Foreign Relations Committee*, 97th Cong., 1st sess., 1982, 73.

Factors Affecting the Emergence of Low-Intensity Conflict in Latin America

Dr Bynum E. Weathers

Latin America possesses certain inherent and acquired characteristics associated with the development and proliferation of low-intensity conflict (LIC). This chapter reviews the basic ingredients, derived from the colonial experience and accentuated during the independence era, that have laid the foundation for and enhanced the likelihood of LIC throughout the region. Latin America, so vital to our national security interests, is truly the "soft underbelly" of the United States.

Historically, Latin America has figured heavily in US foreign policy—from the days of encroachment by European colonial powers to the contemporary era of Cuban-Soviet intervention. A major third world region, Latin America encompasses nearly three dozen independent countries spread out over an area of some eight million square miles (comparable to the size of the USSR) inhabited by approximately 390 million people. And with the highest birth rate of any region in the world, it may well double its present population in the early part of the twenty-first century. Ethnic diversity is a major characteristic of the region, with white, black, Indian, mestizo, and mulatto classifications predominating. This heterogeneous pattern of ethnic composition distinguishes Latin America from other regions of the world.

The apogee of US–Latin American relations occurred during the Franklin D. Roosevelt administration's "Good Neighbor Policy." World War II and the concept of Western Hemisphere defense paved the way for the emergence of the inter-American system. The ink had hardly dried on the legal framework binding the colossus of the North to the American republics of the South when the cold war began deflecting US attention to defending Europe and Asia against Communist aggression.

As the World War II Grand Alliance crumbled and globalism took precedence over regionalism in American policy considerations, the southern republics' prewar fear and distrust of the United States returned in the wake of apparent US disinterest in the region. And cold war intensification led to further deterioration of US–Latin American relations, as the Guatemalan intervention of 1954 and the violence directed toward Vice President Richard Nixon during his 1958 tour of South America dramatically demonstrated. But the most significant postwar event occurred in 1959 with the victory of Fidel Castro and the subsequent emergence of Cuba as a satellite of the Soviet Union. Until this event, Soviet interest in and attention to Latin America had been minimal. Now the gateway to Latin America was open; and the Cuban-Soviet axis lost little time in securing a Communist beachhead in the Americas.

Castro's victory at the Bay of Pigs bolstered his image throughout Latin America and solidified the Cuban-Soviet alliance. Shipments of Soviet military equipment increased, highlighted by the dispatching of offensive missiles and bombers to Cuba in the fall of 1962. The Cuban missile crisis brought a direct confrontation between the two superpowers. Despite the crisis resolution, the buildup of Soviet "defensive" weapons continued as increasing numbers of Soviet troops and civilian technicians were assigned to Cuba.

Soon after seizing power, Castro pledged his support for insurrectionary activities throughout Latin America; and many such activities were orchestrated by the guerrilla strategist Ernesto "Che" Guevara until his death in Bolivia in 1967. But Castro's exportation of revolutionary warfare was not successful during the decade of the 1960s, as shown by his failures in Panama, Venezuela, and Bolivia. At the same time, Cuba steadily drifted inexorably into the role of a Soviet surrogate. By 1968, in the wake of the Soviet suppression of the Czechoslovakian uprising, Castro had accepted without qualification the Brezhnev Doctrine.

The Cuban revolution had a major impact on the reorientation of US policy toward Latin America. John F. Kennedy's Alliance for Progress was presented as a revolutionary program to ameliorate the social and economic ills of the region. As a matter of fact, however, the Alliance could be categorized more accurately as reformist and gradualist rather than revolutionary. It offered the Latin American republics the opportunity to achieve modernization and development through peaceful democratic efforts rather than through violent Marxist-Leninist initiatives. In essence, these alternative routes to modernization provided a linkage between the cold war and the developmental problem in Latin America; and East-West competition gained a foothold.

As a means of understanding the emergence and development of LIC in Latin America, it appears logical at this point to examine the colonial background and heritage of the region. Such an effort should illuminate the political, economic, and social characteristics that have had, and will continue to have, an impact on US-Latin American relations.

From the earliest days of colonization, popular participation in government was a rarity; and the concept of the strong leader and a submissive populace was carried over into the independence era. Instead of checks and balances among the branches of government, the executive emerged as the dominant force. The legislative and judicial branches have yet to attain parity. Military intervention and the coup d'état were accepted alternatives to popular election; and the tenure of office depended on the will of individuals instead of the populace as a whole.

Since independence, the Latin American republics have depended heavily on agricultural and mining products to accumulate foreign exchange and to purchase manufactured goods and services. But monoculture has subjected the region to unpredictable fluctuations in the world market, which has resulted in miserable living conditions for a majority of the inhabitants. In terms of land tenure, Latin America has been plagued by the twin evils of latifundia and minifundia—the former consisting of the ownership of large estates by a small percentage of the population; the latter representing the division of landholdings into small, submarginal units barely capable of sustaining life. Economic progress has been stifled by the absence of a viable middle class with entreprenurial propensities. A dynamic trade union movement to monitor the laborers' wages and working conditions has been conspicuously absent. The lack of an industrial infrastructure can be attributed to the emphasis given agriculture and mining in the colonial period.

During the colonial era, a rigid social stratification existed. In the Spanish holdings, for example, the peninsular (Spanish born) and the creole (Spanish born in America) were at the top of the societal ladder. They were followed in descending order by the mestizo (mixture of Spaniard and Indian), the Indian, and the black. Following independence, this class distinction remained; and cleavages between the elite and the masses grew deeper. To this day, in those republics with large indigenous populations, the Indians retain their language and customs; and for all practical purposes, they live outside the effective control of the central governments. Because of the low levels and poor quality of education provided the majority of the inhabitants, a high degree of illiteracy exists in Latin America. Intense poverty and social unrest are basic characteristics of the region.

Having achieved independence by the sword in a struggle lasting nearly two decades, the military either directly or in the shadows of the throne guided the destinies of foundling republics in the postcolonial era. Instead of a government of laws, it was one of men. Personalism and dictatorship were its most enduring manifestations. Authoritarianism was justified as an alternative to anarchy and social disintegration. The military assumed the role of state guardian; it determined the point in time when intervention was necessary. Continuismo (prolongation of a government's tenure), state of siege (emergency powers for a stipulated period), and imposition (determination of the choice of a political successor) were some of the devices employed to retain control. Formal constitutions seldom corresponded completely with the real and operative ones.[1]

Having reviewed the basic characteristics of the Latin American environment that have an important bearing on the development and proliferation of low-intensity conflict, it is appropriate at this time to develop an analytical survey of three representative republics in the region—Nicaragua, Chile, and Peru—that have experienced or are experiencing LIC in their territories. An analytical survey of the societal and political configurations of these three countries will be presented in order to identify and classify those characteristics that serve or have served to attract foreign intervention, manipulation, and control, thereby providing the groundwork for the launching, direction, and intensification of revolutionary conflicts.

From an ideological standpoint, Castrosim was a major force in low-intensity conflicts that occurred in Nicaragua, Chile, and Peru. The success of the Cuban revolution and the exploits of Che Guevara were significant factors. Although the Guevara model that was tried initially in Peru failed, its failure resulted in the formation of an indigenous movement based on a divergent ideology derived from a mixture of Maoism, Marxism, Leninism, and cultural ingredients rooted in the Peruvian historical experience. The asymmetries existing in a region so large and diverse as Latin America would appear to require multiple models to explain LIC potential. In reality, a single model appears capable of providing guidance for decisionmakers in the formulation of policy and strategy to combat LIC in the region.

In the search for factors that provide the environment for the emergence of low-intensity conflict in Latin America, a study of sociopolitical conditions in Nicaragua, Chile, and Peru is both appropriate and representative. These countries have experienced similar cultural and political incursions by foreign forces; and these incursions have had a significant impact on the ensuing LIC environment as manifested in the contemporary era.

During their early years, Nicaragua, Chile, and Peru were Hispaniolized with slight regard for the existing Indian cultures. Warfare, intermarriage, and disease drastically reduced the Indian population and, except for Peru, left an enduring legacy of mestizo/ladino predominance in these countries. Tribal organizations were supplanted by governments acting in response to dictates emanating from the Spanish court. Authoritarianism, exploitation, and discrimination were the rule rather than the exception. Class stratification ensured that the workings of colonial society would benefit the peninsulars and creoles at the detriment of the mestizos, the Indians, and the blacks. Unfortunately, this colonial legacy did not disappear with the coming of the independence movement. Following the wars for independence, Nicaragua, Chile, and Peru emerged as states dominated by caudillos (strong ad hoc rulers), large landowners, and the Church.[2]

Nicaragua

In Nicaragua, independence emerged as a backwash of the Mexican revolt against Spain. Mexico moved into the dominant power position. A few years later, however, Nicaragua joined the other Central American states in a federative arrangement that survived for a decade and a half, after which Nicaragua attained full sovereignty. But dissension continued to run rampant throughout the new republic: conservative versus liberal, centralist versus federalist, procleric versus anticleric, large landowner versus small farmer, and propertied versus landless. Local concerns overrode national interests as private armies sought to impose their will in the absence of a unified armed force. Personalities rather than issues dominated the national scene, and bullets rather than ballot boxes determined the nature and direction of public policy.

In addition to the conflictive domestic environment, Nicaragua experienced foreign interventions—first by Great Britain and the United States in the nineteenth and early twentieth centuries, then by the Cuban-Soviet axis in the 1970s and 1980s. The second US intervention (1927–33) provided the raison d'être for the Somoza dynasty. For more than four decades, the Somoza regime maintained power, with the backing of the national guard, by granting special favors to supporters, withholding rights or privileges from opponents, and violating human rights at will. Neither democratic elections nor effective opposition parties were permitted on the political scene. The absence of accountability, which made it possible to deny the expression of a popular mandate, contributed to an atmosphere of frustration and futility. Violence, employed as an instrument of power by the ruling elite, ultimately became the weapon used to unseat them.[3]

Organized in the early 1960s, the Sandinista Front of National Liberation (Frente Sandinista de Liberación Nacional or FSLN) represented itself as the champion of the dispossessed and maltreated Nicaraguan majority. In its campaign to gain broad-based mass support, the FSLN made a concerted effort to recruit adherents from universities, labor unions, the professions in the cities, and peasant organizations in the rural areas. Yet, the guerrilla movement received its greatest boost internally from the corrupt and repressive practices of the Somoza regime. A major earthquake in 1972 that virtually leveled the capital brought in large amounts of relief funds and materials from abroad for the victims—but much of this humanitarian assistance went into the Somoza coffers. This uncontrolled personal aggrandizement was revealed in other areas as well. Interlocking business and land interests (some 8,000 square miles of choice real estate) gave the Somoza family effective control of the national economy.

While internal factors worked to the advantage of the FSLN cause, the support provided the guerrilla movement by the Cuban-Soviet axis was the most decisive. The FSLN cadre received schooling and training at the Patrice Lumumba People's Friendship University in Moscow, in the Soviet–satellite countries of eastern Europe, and in Cuba. By the mid–1970s, the FSLN had split into three factions—the Prolonged Popular War, the

Proletarian, and the Insurrectionists (terceristas); but under pressure from Havana, the three factions had merged by the end of 1978. Such a merger appears to have been a prerequisite decreed by Castro in return for substantial military assistance to the FSLN, which was subsequently provided. In early 1979, the FSLN confirmed its unity pact and announced the establishment of a nine-member directorate to oversee and coordinate its campaign against the Somoza government. On 23 June, the Organization of American States passed a resolution calling for the immediate replacement of the Somoza regime by a government that would permit opposition elements, reflect the will of the populace, hold free elections, and respect human rights. In return, humanitarian assistance for the reconstruction and rehabilitation of Nicaragua would be provided by the member states. On 12 July, the FSLN notified the regional organization of its acceptance of these conditions and, eight days later, the victory of the Sandinistas was achieved.[4]

During the eight years that have intervened since the acceptance of the Organization of American States resolution, the Sandinista government has refused to abide by its pledge. Opponents of the Marxist regime have been harassed and suppressed. The major opposition newspaper, *La Prensa,* was heavily censored and eventually closed by the government. This action deprived the Nicaraguan people of their only significant source of news outside the ideological constraints imposed by the Sandinistas. Antipathy toward the Church, as witnessed by the expulsion of the Roman Catholic priests who spoke out against the actions of the Marxist government, and interference in the activities of independent labor unions and private business organizations are examples of the government's efforts to prevent the emergence of opposition groups and deny the validity of pluralism and voluntarism. Under these conditions, the will of the people cannot be expressed.

In addition to insistence on conformity, the Sandinistas have refused to hold free and open elections. Although a new constitution has been promulgated and presidential elections have been held, opposition parties were not permitted to campaign freely or to promote alternative governmental proposals. Continued Sandinistas tenure of office was assured by state control over the media and other facets of Nicaraguan society.

In regard to human rights, the Sandinista government has a consistent pattern of violations and abuses. Basic civil liberties are restricted or denied as the government establishes uniformity in, and conformity to, Marxist standards. Dissenters face arrest, imprisonment, torture, and deprivations; and thousands of Nicaraguans have fled to neighboring countries for refuge. Neighborhood block committees relay information to Managua on individuals suspected of counterrevolutionist behavior or who criticize governmental actions. Forced relocation of the Miskito Indians, living along the Caribbean coast, by the Sandinista authorities resulted in a massive flight of the Indians across the border to Honduras. In sum, the Nicaraguan government has failed to implement any of the provisions of the Organization of American States resolution that were accepted by the Sandinistas before they came to power.[5]

US support of the anti-Sandinistas (contras) began, during the Reagan administration, as a covert operation. But in 1983, the US Congress approved $24 million in aid for the contras; and by 1986, that appropriation had grown to $100 million ($70 million in military aid and $30 million for humanitarian purposes). Organized as the United Nicaraguan Opposition (UNO), the contras claim to have a fighting force of 20,000, consisting of anti-Sandinistas, former Somoza national guardsmen, and dissidents who became disenchanted with the Marxist regime.

Despite US backing, the contras' success against the Sandinista regime has been limited. There are several reasons for this. First, substantial arms shipments by the Soviet Union and Cuba have bolstered the Sandinista military capabilities to a significant degree. Second, the efficiency of the contra forces has been affected adversely by low funding, insufficient training, and disagreements among the contra leaders. Third, the absence of a supportive popular insurrection has tended to isolate the contras from the Nicaraguan people. Finally, the failure of the contra leadership to present a viable alternative plan of government to replace the Marxist system has hindered the rebel effort.[6]

In addition to the threat of insurgency, Nicaragua is faced with a critical economic situation requiring the government to implement severe austerity measures. A serious shortage of foreign exchange exists, and indebtedness to lenders abroad is increasing. Financial stress has been compounded by the US embargo on trade and by a credit freeze on the part of the World Bank. The fight against the contras has absorbed funds that might otherwise have been used for productive economic purposes. Inflation continues to climb at a high rate; living standards are steadily declining; widespread shortages in consumer goods have brought about a surge in black-market operations; wages of the workers are low while prices of goods and services are high; and the agricultural sector has been hit hard by the contra incursions, resulting in a notable decline in farm production.

The deteriorating economic situation is of major concern to the Sandinistas, who face a mounting conflict with the contras. The potential for disruptive effects is great. That the Marxist government will be able to overcome these formidable obstacles in the near term appears doubtful.[7]

Having completed an examination of the political, social, and economic factors that have an important bearing on the emergence and proliferation of LIC in Nicaragua, it is appropriate at this point to undertake a similar analysis of Chile.

Chile

Similarities between the Nicaraguan and Chilean experiences in the colonial and early independence periods gave way to discernible differences
as the nineteenth century progressed. These differences would have a significant impact on the development and proliferation of LIC. Conservatives
and liberals debated incessantly over the issues of constitutional monarchy
versus republicanism and centralism versus federalism. In 1829, after efforts to settle the issues through the election process failed, a civil war
broke out. It was to have a profound influence on Chilean society for the
remainder of the nineteenth century. The victorious conservative forces
controlled Chile for the succeeding three decades. During this time, they
consolidated national power, improved the quality of the armed forces
(achieving victory in the war against the Peruvian-Bolivian Confedera-
tion—1836–39), and made significant economic progress.[8]

The presidential elections of 1861, tolling the death knell for the conservative forces, ushered in liberal control for the next 30 years. During
this period, Chile was victorious in the war with Spain (1864–70), in the
War of the Pacific against Peru and Bolivia (1879–83), and in the pacification of the Indians (1883)—a struggle that had continued for nearly 350
years. Military reforms bolstered by economic recovery, largely through the
sale of nitrates abroad, were followed by improvements in social services,
public administration, and civic responsibilities. At the same time, unequal
distribution of wealth produced middle class unrest and labor strikes, the
first in Chilean history.[9]

In 1891, a second civil war broke out. Chile was split over the issues of
presidential versus parliamentary supremacy and economic nationalism
versus laissez-faire capitalism. President José Manuel Balmaceda, who was
supported by the regular army, was defeated by the congressional forces,
composed of army irregulars and the navy. In a scenario remarkably akin
to that of Allende in 1973, President Balmaceda took his own life rather
than face the consequences. The leader of the victorious congressional
forces became the first president of the parliamentary-dominated republic.

Instability and indecisiveness characterized the Chilean government for
the next 30 years, until the end of World War I. There were some 120
cabinet changes involving approximately 530 different ministers. It was
during this period that conflictive elements in the societal structure that
would later contribute to LIC were most observable. Population increases
in the urban areas led to the emergence of a well-defined middle class,
heterogeneous in composition and reformist oriented. The lower classes—
including peasants, laborers, and miners—felt deprived of their fair share
in the face of agricultural, business, and mine owner domination. The
emergence of a proletariat class was evident in the larger cities—such as

Santiago, Valparaíso, Concepción, Antofagasta, and Tarapaća. Discontentment among the workers was reflected in the growth of the labor movement in the decade before 1920, during which time there were some 300 strikes by approximately 150,000 laborers.[10]

Chile's policy of neutrality during World War I was due primarily to strong German sentiment there, coupled with its remoteness from the combat zone. A sizable German community resided in the republic, and the Chilean military forces earlier had engaged Prussian officers to train and modernize the army. Anti-US feelings also played a role, however. Chileans were displeased with Gen John Joseph Pershing's Punitive Expedition into Mexico, the Veracruz incident, and US interventions in Central America and the Caribbean. Closer to home, Chileans were apprehensive about the US involvement in the Tacna-Arica dispute between Chile and Peru, arising from the War of the Pacific. Nor had they forgotten their humiliation at the hands of the United States in the celebrated Baltimore Affair of 1891.

In the immediate postwar period, Chile was plagued with a deepening recession, spiraling inflation, massive unemployment, and the plummeting of nitrate prices on the world market (nearly 40,000 workers in the nitrate industry alone were jobless). Labor unions increasingly came under the control of Socialists and Communists. Domestic instability and social inequities pointed to three possible alternatives in the political sphere: the replacement of parliamentary control by a strong executive through popular elections, an illegal takeover of the government by the Socialists, or the imposition of rule by the military. During the interwar years, all of these alternatives came to pass as political unrest, social disarray, and economic upheaval engulfed the republic.

President Arturo Alessandri, popularly elected in 1920, replaced the constitution with one that institutionalized the presidential form of government. His administration was interrupted first by a military dictatorship and later by a short-lived Socialist Republic. By the end of Alessandri's second term in office (1932–38), Chile had returned to the democratic fold. During World War II, Chilean support of hemispheric defense was both hesitant and limited. Not until 1943 did Chile break relations with the Axis powers.

From the viewpoint of socioeconomic development, the war years were significant for the republic. The economy was bolstered by heavy US purchase of copper, nitrates, and other raw materials. Chile also had access to loans and lend-lease benefits. At the same time, the strength of the Communist party increased, particularly in the national labor unions, and Salvador Allende gained control of the Socialist party. The impact of these developments, seemingly nonthreatening at the time, would be felt in the postwar years.[11]

Between 1946 and 1964, the factors creating a conflictive environment conducive to the outbreak of LIC can be more clearly discerned. Important changes were taking place in the Chilean political party system that would have profound implications for the future. A new political grouping, the Popular Action Front (Frente de Acción Popular or FRAP), emerged in 1956. Led by Allende, it included both Socialists and Communists. A second new organization was the Christian Democratic party, which resulted from the fusion in 1957 of two other factions. Under the leadership of Eduardo Frei, the Christian Democratic party had become the nation's largest political organization by 1963. Campaigning on the theme of a "Revolution in Liberty" rather than one engendered by Castroism, Frei defeated Allende in the 1964 national elections, chalking up the first presidential victory for the Christian Democrats in the Western Hemisphere.[12]

Despite conscientious efforts to alleviate problems in housing, education, land distribution, agricultural production, and other socioeconomic areas, Frei's administration was confronted with numerous labor strikes, public works stoppages, negative national growth rate, and high inflation. In 1965, a guerrilla group, the Revolutionary Left Movement (Movimiento Revolucionario Izquierdo or MIR) linked to Castro, began a campaign of violence in the countryside. Founded by some 100 Socialist students at the University of Concepción, MIR sought to establish a Marxist-Leninist government in Chile through subversion and violent actions rather than follow the nonviolent program of the Chilean Socialist party.

Looking to Che Guevara as its revolutionary mentor, MIR depended on five-man cells, called political-military groups, to carry out combat actions. A central committee, whose members were selected by regional organizations, established a national executive body to oversee the activities of the political-military groups and to coordinate their actions against the Chilean government. Working under the assumption that a Socialist government would never be permitted to attain power in Chile through popular elections, MIR prepared for the inevitable civil war by organizing armed cadres among the workers, the peasants, and industrial laborers. These cadres were directed to seize private holdings before Frei's administration could get the government's machinery for systematic land distribution under way.

MIR expanded its operations in 1967–68. It now covered the entire nation and included urban terrorist actions in its operations. It also came under the control of more radical leaders, known as the "Young Turks," whose membership included Pascall Allende (nephew of Salvador Allende). An MIR splinter group, known as the Vanguard Organization of the People (Vanguarda Organización del Pueblo or VOP), joined in the insurrectionary activities against the Frei administration. President Frei had failed to make inroads toward quelling the guerrilla violence by the end of his term, and only a small number of the estimated 300 members had been imprisoned.[13]

In the presidential elections of 1970, Salvador Allende of the Popular Unity coalition received 36.3 percent of the votes. The coalition had been formed in 1969 by a merger of Socialists, Communists, Radicals, Social

Democrats, the Movement for Unitary Popular Action, and the Popular Independent Action groups. This compared to 34.98 percent for the independent candidate and 27.84 percent for the Christian Democrats. In accordance with their constitution, Congress made the selection because no candidate received a majority. On 24 October, Congress informed Allende that he had been chosen for the highest office. President Allende took office on 3 November with the distinction of being the world's first freely elected Marxist ruler.[14]

In office for less than three years, Allende attempted without success to achieve his Socialist goals. Rapid nationalization of industries and agricultural establishments coupled with radical income redistribution efforts and land expropriations led to social unrest and economic chaos. Spiraling inflation, production declines, food shortages, and decreases in consumer goods dominated the national scene. Foreign exchange reserves of some $400 million in 1970 dwindled to a minus $28 million by the end of the Allende years. Protests by consumers, prolonged strikes by shopkeepers and truck drivers, and mounting violence plagued the government.[15]

In addition to social unrest and economic stress, the Allende administration was faced with terrorist actions by the MIR guerrillas, also called the miristas. Although most of the miristas had boycotted the presidential elections, President Allende, in order to appease the Communists and radical leftists in his Popular Unity coalition, had dismissed all existing criminal charges against MIR guerrillas and freed those still held in prison. Furthermore, he included miristas in his presidential bodyguard. Despite these conciliatory actions, MIR intensified its campaign of violence, labeled "insurrection or death." Its main thrust was seizing private landholdings and turning them over to landless peasants and Indians. Efforts on the part of the landowners to regain their lands through appeals to the Chilean authorities were not successful. The landowners' organizing vigilance committees, such as the White Guard (Guardia Blanca), only led to more bloodletting. The MIR refused to recognize the extent of land expropriation carried out by the government even though, in 18 months, these expropriations were almost double the number accomplished by Frei during his six-year term.[16]

Cuban interest in the new administration was revealed by Fidel Castro's extended visit to Chile in November 1971. Originally planned as a ten-day visit, Castro's speaking tour throughout the nation comprised three and one-half weeks, enabling him to witness the housewives' "March of the Empty Pots," which he labeled "fascism in action." In his messages to students, labor unions, peasants, and workers, he emphasized the need for supporting the Allende government and championing the cause of revolutionary unity. In an interesting display of odd bedfellows, the miristas cooperated with government security forces in quelling anti-Castro demonstrations.[17]

The MIR acquired large stockpiles of armaments and munitions, possibly from Cuba but also on the black market and in thefts from local sources. Shortly before the end of the Allende administration, the miristas were making preparations for the takeover of the Chilean government. The plan provided for coordinated action involving three simultaneous events: the calling of a general strike to immobilize the urban areas; the initiation of attacks by so-called popular militias, which had been armed and posited in the larger cities; and he unleashing of a major guerrilla offensive in the rural areas of the populous south.[18]

The military coup of September 1973 put an end to these plans. Within a period of slightly more than a year, the military junta, headed by Gen Augusto Pinochet, succeeded in suppressing the mirista threat.

As perceived by the Pinochet forces, the coup was predicated on several factors: the republic had to be rescued from the most devastating political-social-economic crisis encountered in modern times; Allende's plan to establish a Marxist state had to be blocked; opposition elements in the legislative, judicial, and trade union sectors indicated a sincere popular mandate for military intervention; and the actions of the MIR and other extreme leftists represented a direct challenge to the military's monopoly of forces and arms.[19]

Since his seizure of power, General Pinochet has maintained a tight grip on all aspects of Chilean society. In the first years following the military coup, he carried out a widespread purge of pro-Allende officials, supporters, and followers. Improvised prisons were required to hold the thousands arrested; and thousands of others fled to sanctuaries abroad or sought protection in foreign embassies. A clandestine intelligence organization, known as the National Intelligence Directorate (Dirección de Inteligencia Nacional or DINA), gathered voluminous information on subversives and their activities, much of it obtained from prisoners through coercion or torture. Primary targets of the purge were Communists, Socialists, and extreme leftists. Major supporters of Pinochet's government in the early period came from members of the upper and middle classes who had been most adversely affected by the Allende administration. Least supportive of the military regime were the working class and the peasants.[20]

Despite concentrated efforts, Pinochet was unable to liquidate the Chilean Communist party. One of the largest and oldest in Latin America, it had gone underground following the military coup. In 1980, the party abandoned its traditional political practices and embraced violence as a means of achieving victory. Soon thereafter, a guerrilla organization, the Manuel Rodriguez Patriotic Front (Frente Patriotico Manuel Rodriguez or FPMR), was organized. Its combat actions against the Pinochet government, begun in 1983, have continued to the present time. In addition to the Moscow-directed FPMR, the Castroite MIR guerrillas continue to conduct urban terrorist operations against such strategic targets as electric pylons and security installations. It is estimated that some 6,000 Communist guerrillas are operating in the republic.[21]

During 1986, the Soviet-Cuban axis increased its support of guerrilla actions against the Pinochet regime. In August, Chilean security forces uncovered the largest arsenal of Soviet-Cuban origin yet found in the Western Hemisphere. In the following month, urban terrorists made an unsuccessful attempt to assassinate the president. The increase in Soviet-Cuban support of insurgency represents a major factor that accentuates and accelerates LIC in Chile.[22]

Having completed the analysis of the LIC environments in Nicaragua and Chile, attention is now directed toward an examination of those conflictive forces in Peru.

Peru

While Peruvian society contains the elements of the colonial heritage (political authoritarianism, economic exploitation, social inequalities, and military predominance) found in Nicaragua and Chile, it is nevertheless necessary to make distinctions in terms of extent and magnitude. One distinction is the large Indian population, approximately one-half of the total, which lives outside the effective control of the nation. These Indians retain many of the ancient customs of the Incas, and they speak the Quechua language.

Another difference from Nicaragua and Chile is the extent of large land-holdings by the mestizos, called cholos in Peru, and the lack of land ownership by the peones, who make up a majority of the population. Also, in contrast to these two countries, Peru has a longer history of precious metal and mineral exploitation. The resultant severe economic repercussions have persisted to the present time. Authoritarian governments have been the rule rather than the exception throughout Peruvian history. Only since 1980 have Peruvians been given the opportunity to choose their president through popular elections. The military has been, and continues to be, a major force in the government structure; and it plays a large role in Peruvian society.[23]

During the nineteenth and early twentieth centuries, opposition to "colonialism, traditionalism, and clericalism" became the rallying cry of the liberal publicist, Manuel Gonzalez Prada, the grandfather of reformism in Peru. Two of his students at the University of San Marcos, who became disciples of reformism, have had a major impact on the modernization of Peruvian society. One of these, Juan Carlos Mariategui, chose the route of Marxism; he extolled the communal life of the Incas as the answer to the unequal distribution of landholdings. The other, Victor Raul Haya de la Torre, repudiated Marxism; he sought change through the existing political system by means of a left-of-center party, the American Popular Revolutionary Alliance (Alianza Popular Revolucionaria Americana or APRA, founded in 1924). Sixty-one years passed before APRA succeeded in placing its candidate in the presidential chair. (Although winning the presidential elections of 1931 and 1962, Haya de la Torre was denied the office by military intervention.) Mariategui's contributions bolstered the strength of the Peruvian Communist party and provided ideological support to leftist guerrillas who have plagued Peru since the late 1950s.[24]

At the present time, the Shining Path (Sendero Luminoso) guerrilla organization is presenting a grave threat to the Peruvian government. Since the Shining Path made its appearance on the national scene in 1980, the guerrillas have accounted for the deaths of some 8,000 persons and the destruction of public and private properties valued at more than $1 billion. The magnitude of the threat is revealed by the government's imposition of a state of emergency in one-third of the nation's territory, including the capital. The nucleus of the Shining Path movement is in the remote departmental capital of Ayacucho, some 250 miles southeast of Lima. The region is heavily populated by Indians.[25]

The roots of the Shining Path movement are imbedded in the earlier guerrilla outbreaks of the 1960s. Under the banner of the Revolutionary Workers' Party (Partido Obrero Revolucionario or POR), Hugo Blanco concentrated his efforts from 1958 until his arrest and imprisonment in 1963 to ameliorating the plight of the Indian campesinos in his native department of Cuzco, once the capital of the Inca Empire. Organizing peasant unions, he first sought redress of grievances—low wages, poor working conditions, ill treatment by hacienda owners, and so forth—through strikes and work stoppages. Later, under the slogan "Land or Death," Blanco led the campesinos as they seized several haciendas in the Cuzco area. In the final phase, Blanco and his followers attacked security garrisons in a quest for arms. This escalation in violence set off a major army counterinsurgency campaign that eventually resulted in the campesinos' downfall.[26]

From 1963–65, three urban leftist intellectuals carried out rural guerrilla actions modeled after Che Guevara's "foco" theory in the heavily Indian-populated Andean region east of Lima. According to the "foco" theory (also called foquismo), guerrilla warfare relies on an established base or bases in the countryside from which revolutionary actions are carried out; it rejects reliance on such bases in the cities to spread the revolution.[27] The principal strategist and most important leader of the trio, Luis de la Puente Uceda, had been trained in Cuba during his exile there in 1959. He returned to Peru and formed the cadre of the MIR-Pachacutec Front. It operated north of Cuzco and south of the Valley of La Convención, an area formerly controlled by Hugo Blanco.

The second leader, Guillermo Lobaton, headed the MIR-Tupac Amaru

Front. It carried out guerrilla actions in the Andamarca River valley directly east of Lima. The last of the trio, Hector Bejar, led the Javier Heraud Front of the National Liberation Army (Ejército de Liberación Nacional or ELN), which operated in an area between the other two (in Ayacucho Department). The failure of the movements, leading to the deaths of de la Puente and Lobaton and the capture of Bejar by the Peruvian army, can be attributed to several factors: impractical application of the Cuban "foco" theory to the Peruvian revolutionary scene; irreconcilable differences between the urban intellectuals and the Indian campesinos; inability of the ELN leaders to speak the Quechua language; traditional distrust of Spanish-speaking newcomers by the Indians; and insistence of the Indian on tangible, immediate returns.[28]

The beginnings of the Sendero Luminoso can be traced to the formation of the ELN-Huamanga Command in 1962. Its mentor was Abimael Guzman Reynoso, a philosophy professor at the National University of San Cristobal de Huamanga in Ayacucho, who sent his most promising students to Cuba for study and for social work in neighboring Indian villages. Prominent leaders of Sendero Luminoso were drawn from this student pool.

In 1966, Professor Guzman led the ELN-Huamanga Command into the Maoist Communist party of Peru-Red Flag (Partido Communista del Peru-Bandera Roja or PCP-BR). By 1970, Guzman and his followers had designated their movement the "Communist Party of Peru in the Shining Path of Mariategui" (Partido Comunista del Peru en el Sendero Luminoso de Mariategui). The two major prophets of the Shining Path organization were Mao Zedong, who gained international notoriety along with the Gang of Four during the Chinese Cultural Revolution, and Juan Carlos Mariategui. The name of the guerrilla movement is derived from Mariategui's "Seven Essays of the Peruvian Reality," which includes the statement that "Marxism-Leninism will open the shining path to revolution."[29]

During the decade of the 1970s, Guzman continued to construct his eclectic theory of revolution, which consisted of Marxist, Leninist, Maoist, Christian, and Incan concepts, and to indoctrinate his associates in the new ideology. He also made a concerted effort to spread the influence of the Shining Path movement from Ayacucho into the surrounding countryside.

By the late 1970s, Professor Guzman, under the nom de guerre of "Comrade Gonzalo," had gone underground. He and the leadership cadre were making preparations for implementing the revolutionary strategy. The revolution was to be accomplished in five stages: (1) transforming underdeveloped regions into advanced and solid bases of revolutionary support; (2) attacking the symbols of both the burgeois state and revisionist elements; (3) spreading violence and conducting guerrilla warfare; (4) developing and expanding support bases; and (5) laying siege to the cities and bringing about the total collapse of the state.

The incubation period of the Shining Path occurred during the 12-year rule of the Peruvian military junta (1968–80). Beginning in mid-1980, as presidential elections were being held that would bring civilian Fernando Belaúnde Terry to power, the Shining Path committed its first acts of insurgency by attacking voting polls and destroying ballot boxes in remote Andean villages. During the intervening seven years, the Sendero guerrillas have become a major threat to the survival of democratic government and capitalism in Peru.[30]

In addition to spiraling insurgency, Peru is confronted with another conflictive element that is conducive to LIC—a major economic crisis. Following President Belaúnde's tenure (1963–68), Peru was ruled for 12 years by the military. When he returned to the presidency in 1980 for a five-year term, Belaúnde inherited from the military regime a multitude of economic problems which could have caused a collapse of the new democratic government. Peru had experienced its worst recession since the Great Depression of 1929. Service on the foreign debt wiped out more than one-half of the earnings derived from exports. Double-digit inflation, a high unemployment rate, depressed wages and salaries, and stagnated industrial production characterized the Peruvian economic profile.[31]

Belaúnde replaced the statist policy of the military regime with that of private enterprise and the interplay of the free market. While retaining control of basic industries, the government sought to sell more than 150 state-owned companies to private capitalists. Export subsidies on traditional products such as fish meal, minerals, and farm goods were removed; and tariff fares were reduced to enable domestic industry to compete with foreign shipments, thereby reducing inflation. The greatest opposition to these changes came from those who were beneficiaries of the old system and from the overstaffed government bureaucracy.

Despite Belaúnde's determined efforts to improve the Peruvian economy, the situation went from bad to worse. The demand for Peruvian exports fell and the price of her most marketable goods dropped significantly. A severe drought followed by torrential rains played havoc with the agricultural sector and reduced the productivity of the fishing industry by one-half. Large imbalances occurred in the nation's foreign trade activities. Unemployment increased as domestic enterprises failed in their attempts to compete with foreign suppliers. The process of moving from state-owned to private industry was hindered by a lack of domestic investment capital and the refusal of investors to take risks. Soaring costs of living resulted in triple-digit inflation. Government revenues dwindled as the economy declined. Large financial outlays (some $4 billion) were made for the purchase of military equipment and sophisticated weapon systems. To meet financial deficits, Belaúnde found it necessary to obtain additional foreign loans that by the end of his term amounted to nearly $14 billion.

In regard to the counterinsurgency operations against the Shining Path guerrillas, Belaúnde's accomplishments during his term of office were no

96

better than those associated with overcoming the Peruvian economic dilemma. In the latter part of 1981, a state of emergency was declared in the Ayacucho region. The police were given additional powers but were unable to contain the violence. By 1982, the government had found it necessary to decree the Ayacucho region a military zone and send in the armed forces. Guerrilla violence had spread to Lima and other cities. By the end of his term, Belaúnde faced accusations of human rights abuses in his counterinsurgency campaign. He had also witnessed the growth and intensification of the guerrilla challenge to the newfound democracy.[32]

The July 1985 inauguration of Alan García as president of Peru was significant for several reasons: It was the first victory for APRA; it was the first time in 40 years that a popularly elected president had turned over control to another popularly elected president; and it was the first time that an orderly succession of power had been completed from an incumbent to an opposition party.[33]

Soon after coming to office, García began the implementation of a 42-point program aimed at stemming the tide of economic erosion. Emphasis was placed on reducing inflation, instituting an emergency development program for the neglected remote regions around Ayacucho, implementing austerity measures in government operations, seeking foreign investments, and freezing wages, prices, and rents. These emergency measures have not yet resuscitated the weak economy, however. Hanging like the sword of Damocles over the domestic economy is the foreign debt of more than $15 billion. García has rejected the financial plan instituted by the International Monetary Fund (IMF) and has stated that Peru will pay no more than an amount equal to 10 percent of its export earnings for debt servicing. As a consequence, the IMF has removed Peru from the list of countries eligible for future loans. The implications of Peru's action for foreign creditors, including US banks, could be serious insofar as US-Peruvian relations are concerned.[34]

President García took a fresh approach to the Shining Path insurgency. Whereas the previous administration relied primarily on military force to overcome the guerrilla threat, García followed a variegated strategy that included major attention to the socioeconomic plight of the Andean Indians, the formation of a peace commission to open a dialogue with the guerrillas, and increased concern for human rights abuses by the military. More recently, the president has come to realize the necessity for increasing counterinsurgency actions in view of more frequent attacks in Lima and the expansion of the Shining Path movement southeast into Puno and northeast into Cuzco.[35]

The basic problem faced by García (and by all popularly elected governments involved in counterinsurgency operations) is how to defeat the insurgents without eroding the democratic process. As García has stated:

I don't want to convert Peru into a police state but [terrorism] is hurting the life of our citizens and the development of our economy.[36]

After a vicious three-week guerrilla offensive that began in mid-January 1987, the largest since the emergence of the Shining Path movement, García announced the establishment of a hot line for citizens to use in reporting any suspicious behavior. One quarter of Peru's departments containing one-third of her population are presently controlled by the military, and a state of emergency has been in effect in Lima for more than a year. In sum, the government's efforts toward curtailing the Shining Path guerrillas have not succeeded; and there are no prospects for success in the near term.[37]

Completion of the analysis of the LIC environment in Peru, along with that of Nicaragua and Chile, now focuses attention on the application of the results to Latin America as a whole.

Conclusion

Mario Vargas Llosa, a distinguished Peruvian novelist and member of a government commission investigating guerrilla atrocities, has offered an explanation of the rationale for guerrilla warfare in Latin America:

> These guerrilla movements are not "peasant movements." They are born in the cities, among intellectuals and middle class militants. . . . Put simply, the peasants are coerced by those who think they are the masters of history and absolute truth. The fact is that the struggle between the guerrillas and the armed forces is really a settling of accounts between privileged sectors of society, and the peasant masses are used cynically and brutally by those who say they want to "liberate" them. The peasants always suffer the greatest number of victims. . . .[38]

Insurgent movements in Latin America now number 27. They involve 25,000-odd members in nine countries, encompassing 25 percent of the Latin American republics.[39] If past performance is any guide, insurgency is more likely to increase than subside, and to make these countries more susceptible to Soviet-Cuban intervention. The removal of those conflictive elements which lead to the outbreak of LIC becomes critical for US–Latin American relations in the decades ahead.

An examination of the LIC environments in Nicaragua, Chile, and Peru reveals the conflictive factors that may be applied to Latin America in general and that adversely affect US relations with the region.

One factor is political authoritarianism. In Nicaragua, from the founding of the republic to the present, the people have had little opportunity to guide their own destiny through popular participation in the political process. Caudillismo (strong-man rule) has been the rule rather than the exception. In recent times, Cuban-Soviet incursions have sought to implant governments favorable to their interests. After enduring more than four decades of the Somoza dynasty, Nicaraguans discovered belatedly that the democratic promises had been betrayed by the Marxist Sandinista regime.

In the case of Chile, caudillismo has been the exception rather than the rule. Except for short periods of political aberrations, the governments of Chile have come to power through popular elections that are held regularly and are open to opposition parties. During the late 1960s, the Frei administration was confronted with an insurgency movement, and a deterioration of the socioeconomic environment, that had an important bearing on the outcome of the 1970 presidential election.

For the first time in history, a Marxist government came to power by way of the democratic process; however, a combination of factors led to Allende's overthrow in 1973. Possibly the most important factors were usurpation of power by the executive, spiraling economic deterioration, and the arming of workers who challenged the monopoly of force by the military. During his 14 years of authoritarian rule, General Pinochet has attempted to purge the country of Communist and extreme leftist elements and to make structural changes in the Chilean political system to support his ideological aspirations. Beginning in 1983, Soviet- and Cuban-backed guerrillas have aimed combat actions against the Pinochet government. The ability of Pinochet's rightist regime to remain in power beyond the decade of the 1980s is highly questionable.

The traditional political style of Peru is more akin to Nicaragua than to Chile in the sense that caudillismo has been a persistent factor in the history of the republic. Only in the contemporary period has Peru been subjected to changes in political styles representing opposite poles of the ideological spectrum. After more than a decade of military rule, Belaúnde gained the presidency by popular election in 1980. In the same year, the Shining Path guerrillas made their appearance on the national scene. They instituted a campaign of violence that has steadily escalated until the present time. Despite the humane efforts of President García since 1985, the threat to the maintenance of democratic government in the republic has become even more critical. Unless the conflictive factors in the LIC environment are subdued, Peru could revert to an authoritarian regime in the near term.

Economic exploitation and social injustice have produced a turbulent atmosphere that enhances the prospects for LIC. In Nicaragua, Chile, and Peru, there exists a marked degree of economic disparity between the elite and the lower classes. This disparity is most evident in Peru where the so-called forty families of affluence have rigorously opposed significant socioeconomic reforms. Furthermore, Peru has by far the larger Indian population, which continues to suffer from economic deprivations and social injustices. The same applies to the smaller Indian population of Nicaragua, however, and it has become more accentuated during the Sandinista regime.

Other factors of economic instability and social injustice in each of the three countries under review are monoculture, population growth in excess of food supply, maldistribution of land and wealth, foreign trade imbalance, and dependence on foreign loans and capital. Reliance on single commodity exports, such as coffee (Nicaragua), copper (Chile), and fish products (Peru), has resulted in costly importations of manufactured goods. Furthermore, trade imbalances have contributed to economic and social dislocations as well as to increasing foreign exchange shortages. Unequal distributions of land and wealth are evident, and there is a vast gap between the incomes of the upper and lower classes. Although the countries under review have primarily agricultural economies, Nicaragua and Peru rely heavily on foreign sources for food supplies. High rates of population growth and inefficient agricultural practices have served to create domestic food shortages. In regard to foreign indebtedness, Peru faces the most severe crisis; but Nicaragua and Chile also are afflicted with large debts owed to foreign creditors. The socioeconomic stress on these three countries represents a major factor contributing to LIC.

The predominance of the military in the societies of Nicaragua, Chile, and Peru constitutes another conflictive element that contributes to the development and growth of LIC. In contrast to the United States, where civilian supremacy over the military has been an honored tradition for more than 200 years, armed forces in Latin America do not hesitate to take over governments when national security appears to be in jeopardy. At the present time, Nicaragua and Chile are ruled by the military; Peru was governed by a military junta from 1968 to 1980.

Since coming to power, the Marxist regime of Nicaragua has more than quadrupled the strength of its armed forces through substantial aid and assistance from the Cuban-Soviet connection. And despite several years of armed opposition by the anti-Sandinista contra forces, it appears unlikely that the well-entrenched Marxist government will be overthrown soon. In Chile, the rightist Pinochet dictatorship has successfully defended against opposition for nearly a decade and a half; but there has been an unsuccessful assassination attempt on the president and a substantial increase in Cuban-Soviet support of guerrilla activities. Although General Pinochet has indicated a transfer of political power to civilian government in the 1990s, it seems probable that a change in government will occur earlier. And in Peru, the inability of the civilian government to stem the tide of the Shining Path guerrillas could bring about the return of military rule. As a significant aspect of the LIC environment, the predominance of the military in Latin American societies cannot be overlooked.

The conflictive factors in the three selected countries have a commonality that makes them applicable to Latin America in general. Since the region is so vital to our national security interests, US foreign policy toward Latin America should incorporate constructive and realistic measures to reduce and eventually overcome the LIC threat. In the past, US-Latin American policy has been cyclical, reactive, and piecemeal. Now there is a critical need for a policy that is unswerving, innovative, and comprehensive; the United States must cope with Cuban-Soviet support of insurgency and anti-US propaganda campaigns throughout Latin America. For example, the Soviet Union seeks to broaden its appeal in Latin America through a visit to Mexico and several South American countries in the summer of 1987—the first visit of a Soviet premier to the mainland of the region. It should be noted that, except for Chile and Paraguay, the Soviet Union has established diplomatic relations with all the Latin American republics.[40]

In order to overcome the LIC threat, it is necessary for US policymakers to concentrate on the development of long-range measures in five major policy areas. First, the United States should capitalize more effectively on democratic openings in the Latin American governments. Second, once democratic governments come to power in the region, the United States should continue active support of those governments and their leaders to ensure their tenure in power. Third, the United States should develop an innovative yet realistic economic assistance program for Latin America—one which ensures that the dispossessed majority actually receive the benefits. Fourth, the United States should remain sensitive to human rights violations in the region; and a more reliable and credible verification of serious abuses should be developed jointly with Latin American counterparts. Fifth, the United States should encourage the development of truly professional armed forces in the Latin American republics—forces that are well schooled in democratic concepts and processes, that are fully accountable to civilian authority, and that are guaranteed a monopoly of force in their respective countries.

Finally, if verbiage and complexity appear to becloud US policy toward Latin America, the view of Dr Federico Gil, Latin American scholar and Kenan Professor of Political Science, Emeritus, University of North Carolina, should be considered:

> Perhaps we should adopt a policy that simply says one thing: we are prepared to maintain normal bilateral relations with any Latin American government, so long as it does not threaten our security or engage in gross violations of rights.[41]

NOTES

1. Hubert Herring, *A History of Latin America: From the Beginnings to the Present* (New York: Alfred A. Knopf, 1968); Federico G. Gil, *Latin American–United States Relations* (New York: Harcourt Brace Jovanovich, 1971); Bynum E. Weathers, *Strategic Appraisal of Latin America* (Maxwell AFB, Ala.: Air University Center for Aerospace Doctrine, Research, and Education, December 1984); James L. Busey, *Prospects for the Social Transformation of Latin America* (London: Economic and Social Science Research Association, 1985).

2. Ibid.

3. Thomas W. Walker, ed., *Nicaragua: The First Five Years* (New York: Praeger Publishers, 1985), 1–26; Shirley Christian, *Nicaragua: Revolution in the Family* (New York: Random House, 1985), 1–27; Bernard Diederich, *Somoza and the Legacy of U.S. Involvement in Central America* (New York: E. P. Dutton, 1981).

4. Bynum E. Weathers, *Guerrilla Warfare in Nicaragua, 1975–1979* (Maxwell AFB, Ala.: Air University Center for Aerospace Doctrine, Research, and Education, November 1983); Elliott Abrams, "Development of U.S.–Nicaragua Policy," *Current Policy* 915, Bureau of Public Affairs, Department of State, 5 February 1987.

5. "Nicaragua: A Betrayed Revolution," *The Soviet-Cuban Connection in Central America and the Caribbean* (Washington, D.C.: Government Printing Office, March 1985), 19–36; Violeta Barrios de Chamorro, "The Death of La Prensa," *Foreign Affairs*, Winter 1986–1987, 383–86; Nina H. Shea, "Human Rights in Nicaragua," *New Republic*, 1 September 1986, 21–23.

6. Edward Gonzalez, *Central America: U.S. Policy and Its Critics* (Santa Monica, Calif.: Rand Corp., April 1986), 19–23; James P. Wootten, *The Nicaraguan Military Buildup: Implications for U.S. Interests in Central America* (Washington, D.C.: Congressional Research Service, Library of Congress, 18 December 1985), 15–24; James LeMoyne, "The Guerrilla Network," *New York Times Magazine*, 6 April 1986, 14–20; Peter Ford, "Vying for Allegiance of Nicaragua's Indians," *Christian Science Monitor*, 26 January 1987, 9, 12.

7. Jorge I. Dominguez, *Central America: Current Crisis and Future Prospects* (New York: Foreign Policy Association, 1985, 15–24; Thomas G. Weiss, "Nicaragua: The Real War Is Now Economic," *Christian Science Monitor*, 14 January 1987, 14.

8. Bynum E. Weathers, *The Role of the Military in Chilean Politics, 1810–1980* (Maxwell AFB, Ala.: Documentary Research Division, Air University Library, February 1980), 1–25; Herring, 645–52.

9. Ibid., 26–38, 652–56.

10. Ibid., 42–48, 657–60.

11. Ibid., 64–107, 660–69.

12. Ibid., 108–24, 669–76.

13. Raymond Estep, *Guerrilla Warfare in Latin America, 1963–1975* (Maxwell AFB, Ala.: Documentary Research Directorate, Air University, June 1975), 82–86; Weathers, *The Role of the Military in Chilean Politics, 1810–1980*, 133–42.

14. Robert Moss, *Chile's Marxist Experiment* (New York: John Wiley & Sons, 1973), 25–51; Weathers, *The Role of the Military in Chilean Politics, 1810–1980*, 142–46.

15. Ibid., 23, 161–65, 167–69, 171–75.

16. Estep, 86–89; Weathers, *The Role of the Military in Chilean Politics, 1810–1980*, 159–61; Moss, 99–122.

17. Moss, 123; Weathers, *The Role of the Military in Chilean Politics, 1810–1980*, 158–59.

18. Estep, 89.

19. Ibid., 89–90; Moss, i–v.

20. David Brock, "Communists Raise the Stakes in Chile," *Insight*, 15 December 1986, 8–13; Lake Sagaris, "General Who Will Not Relax His Grip," *Times* (London), 9 September 1986, 5.

21. Ibid.

22. Pamela Constable, "Pinochet's Grip on Chile," *Current History*, January 1987, 17–20; Mimi Whitefield, "Pinochet Gets Stronger As Opposition Splinters," *Miami Herald*, 2 November 1986, A30; Paul Glickman, "Critics Say US Is Easing Pressure on Chile for Political Reform," *Christian Science Monitor*, 22 January 1987, 5; Philip Jacobson, "Violent Ambush for Reagan's Hopes in Chile," *Times* (London), 9 September 1986, 14.

23. Herring, 593–95; David Scott Palmer, "Rebellion in Rural Peru: The Origins and Evolution of Sendero Luminoso," *Comparative Politics*, January 1986, 130–33.

24. Miguel Jorrin and John D. Martz, *Latin-American Political Thought and Ideology* (Chapel

Hill: University of North Carolina Press, 1970), 328–58; David P. Werlich, "Debt, Democracy and Terrorism in Peru," *Current History*, January 1987, 30.

25. Kathryn Leger, "Garcia Enlists Each Peruvian in Battle against Terrorism," *Christian Science Monitor*, 11 February 1987, 9; Alan Riding, "Peru Cracks Down Again on Rebels of the Shining Path," *New York Times*, 16 November 1986, E3; Alan Riding, "Cuzco Journal: In the Incas' Land, A War for the People's Hearts," *New York Times*, 18 November 1986, A4.

26. Estep, 6–10.

27. Ernest E. Rossi and Jack C. Plano, *The Latin American Political Dictionary* (Santa Barbara, Calif.: ABC-Clio, 1980), 87–88.

28. Estep, 10–14.

29. David Scott Palmer, "The Sendero Luminoso Rebellion in Rural Peru," in *Latin American Insurgencies*, ed. Georges Fauriol (Washington, D.C.: Georgetown University Center for Strategic and International Studies, 1985), 67–70; Jorrin and Martz, 277–80; David P. Werlich, "Peru: The Shadow of the Shining Path," *Current History*, February 1984, 81–82, 90; Cynthia McClintock, "Sendero Luminoso: Peru's Maoist Guerrillas," *Problems of Communism*, September-October 1983, 20–23.

30. Ibid.

31. Werlich, "Peru: The Shadow of the Shining Path," 78–80; Jackson Diehl, "Mysterious Rebel Band Threatens Political Stability of Peru," *Washington Post*, 1 November 1982, A17; William D. Montalbano, "Terror-by-Night Haunts the Andes," *Miami Herald*, 15 December 1982, Al; Edward Schumacher, "Suddenly, Little-Known Rebels Force Grim Choices for Peru," *New York Times*, 5 June 1983, E3; James Nelson Goodsell, "Peru Rebel Fights to 'Tear Down Corrupt Society'—Interview," *Christian Science Monitor*, 15 September 1983, 7.

32. Ibid.

33. Werlich, "Debt, Democracy and Terrorism in Peru," 30.

34. Ibid., 29–32; Riding, "Cuzco Journal," A4.

35. Ibid.

36. Leger, 9.

37. Ibid.; Riding, "Peru Cracks Down Again on Rebels of the Shining Path," E3; Werlich, "Debt, Democracy and Terrorism in Peru," 32, 36–37.

38. Mario Vargas Llosa, "Inquest in the Andes," *New York Times Magazine*, 31 July 1983, 56.

39. Richard Halloran, "Latin Guerrillas Joining Forces, U.S. Officers Say," *New York Times*, 3 March 1987, 8.

40. Carl J. Migdail, "Gorbachev: He Sees Opportunity in Latin America," *Christian Science Monitor*, 30 March 1987, 16.

41. Federico G. Gil, "United States and Latin American Relations: The More Things Change," *SECOLAS ANNALS*, March 1986, 14.

Low-Intensity Conflict in Southern Africa

Dr Thomas P. Ofcansky

Since the early 1960s, low-intensity conflicts have occurred with increasing frequency throughout sub-Saharan Africa. Sadly, untold millions of Africans have suffered or died because of this warfare. At the 1986 Organization of African Unity (OAU) summit meeting in Addis Ababa, Ethiopia, for example, Yoweri Museveni, president of Uganda, revealed that at least 750,000 people had died in his country as a result of nearly 20 years of fighting. To make matters worse, on occasion, such as during the 1960–64 Congo crisis, the superpowers have become involved—usually because they have perceived hostilities between Africans as yet another manifestation of the East-West struggle. At other times, so-called surrogates—presumably acting on behalf of, or in concert with, the Soviet Union or the United States—have intervened in Africa to stop or prolong a particular conflict. A typical case involved the Cuban deployment of approximately 50,000 combatants and civilians to Angola and Ethiopia in the 1970s.

Despite this activity, very little has been written about the causes of low-intensity conflicts in sub-Saharan Africa. Reasons for the lack of literature include the tendency of some scholars to focus on African militaries as political actors or agents of social change, or on explaining African warfare in white-versus-black or East-West terms. Still others have maintained that economic backwardness or social instability have precipitated sub-Saharan Africa's low-intensity conflicts.[1] Although each approach undoubtedly provides the policymaker with valuable insights, all fail to consider the role ethnicism has played in these wars. Appreciating this factor could help the policymaker avert situations in which local hostilities pull the superpowers into unwanted confrontations.

Since time immemorial, diversity has existed among the peoples of sub-Saharan Africa. This heterogeneity stems from a variety of causes, including the growth of small, close-knit groups for protection and mutual support; linguistic and cultural differences; the proliferation of political, economic, and religious rivalries that produced factions and subdivisions throughout African society; constant migration to new areas in search of food and security; and the gradual spread of non-African peoples throughout the continent. As a result of these processes, sub-Saharan Africa's human population coalesced into more than 1,000 ethnic groups, most of which have a unique language, religion, and culture. What this means in political terms is that most African countries are as culturally diverse as India and as socially fragmented as Lebanon.[2]

Until the advent of European colonial rule in the mid-1850s, Africa was socially organized and politically divided along ethnic lines. Then, in the aftermath of the 1884–85 Berlin Conference—which convened to settle territorial disputes in the Congo basin—the major European powers partitioned the continent and grouped its peoples into modern nation-states. As long as these countries remained under European colonial rule, this system however imperfect, worked fairly well.[3] After the wave of African independence began in the late 1950s, however, old ethnic tensions gradually resurfaced and, in many cases, degenerated into low-intensity conflicts. Nowhere is this phenomenon more in evidence than in the nations of Zimbabwe, Angola, Mozambique, Namibia, and South Africa.

By offering an alternate interpretation and showing how ethnic rivalries—many of which were exacerbated by superpower competition, racial conflict, social instability, and economic dislocation—have contributed to the spread of violence, we may be able to help policymakers better understand the causes of low-intensity conflicts. This analysis also will serve as a model for understanding the causes of low-intensity conflicts elsewhere in sub-Saharan Africa.

Zimbabwe

Zimbabwe represents a classic case of how ethnic rivalries influenced the course of a low-intensity conflict. The country's two most important ethnic groups are the Shona (about 75 percent of total black Zimbabweans) and the Ndebele (approximately 16 percent of total black Zimbabweans). A small but politically important European population is unofficially estimated at roughly 170,000. Difficulties between the Shona and Ndebele began in 1822, when an African military leader by the name of Mzilikazi led 5,000 of his followers (known collectively as the Ndebele, the people with long shields) into what became western Zimbabwe. This force slowly extended its hegemony over western and southern parts of Shonaland and forced the inhabitants to pay tribute.[4]

After Mzilikazi died in 1868, one of his sons, Lobengula, became the Ndebele's *ikosi* (leader). The latter's career coincided with the arrival of European settlers from South Africa. Twenty years later, Lobengula concluded the Moffat Agreement with a British representative from Cape Town. On the basis of this accord, Great Britain claimed that vast stretches of Zimbabwe fell within its sphere of influence. Shortly thereafter, the industrialist Cecil Rhodes created the British South Africa Company (BSAC) to exploit mining and land concessions in Zimbabwe. In 1889, the British government granted a royal charter to the BSAC that authorized land development by European settlers.[5]

Within four years of their arrival, the Europeans became involved in an ethnic controversy that eventually led to war. In late 1893, an Ndebele raiding party traveled to Fort Victoria to punish some Shona people who had defaulted in their tribute payment. During the ensuing fracas, the Ndebele disrupted mining operations and killed a few Shona who worked for the BSAC. After Lobengula learned that Europeans had shot some members of an Ndebele peace delegation, he declared war on the settler community. Encouraged by the initial success of Ndebele resistance, about a third of the Shona people also rose up against the British. Given the superiority of European technology, however, it was only a matter of time before the British defeated the Ndebele and extended their rule throughout Zimbabwe. Indeed, by 1895, British authorities had all but completed the pacification and colonialization of the country.[6] For the next 70 years, the British government, initially working through the BSAC and then the Colonial Office, ruled Zimbabwe as part of the British Empire.[7]

Although many African chiefs retained considerable power under this system, ultimate local authority rested with British administrators known as Native Commissioners. With varying degrees of success, this corps—backed by colonial soldiers when necessary—maintained peace between the Ndebele and Shona peoples.[8] In the early 1960s, however, as colonialism became more and more unpopular with Africans and the international community, friction between these two groups reemerged as they sought to end European rule.[9] Indeed, the ensuing struggle between various African liberation groups and the Ian Smith regime intensified interethnic rivalry for control of the country's political system and brought about a low-intensity conflict that has lasted to this very day.[10]

Understanding the evolution of this process and its impact on current events requires an appreciation of the development of African nationalist opposition in Zimbabwe. In December 1961, to reduce urban unrest, European authorities banned the National Democratic party (NDP) and arrested most of its leaders. Within days, however, black Ndebele political activist Joshua Nkomo established the Zimbabwe African People's Union (ZAPU). Questions about his leadership abilities caused some ZAPU executive committee members to plot his overthrow. Upon discovering this scheme in mid-1963, Nkomo immediately expelled several dissidents—including Robert Mugabe—from ZAPU. In response, these individuals formed a more militant party known as the Zimbabwe African National Union (ZANU). Within months of this split, it became clear to most Zimbabweans that ZAPU was primarily an Ndebele organization while ZANU gained its support from the Shona people.[11]

Despite the efforts of President Julius Nyerere of Tanzania, President Kenneth Kaunda of Zambia, and the Organization of African Unity to forge an alliance between ZANU and ZAPU, both groups devoted most of their energies to fighting one another rather than the country's European regime. Subsequent attempts by neighboring African leaders to persuade Nkomo and Mugabe as well as other black nationalist leaders to use an umbrella organization to further their political aims also failed to eliminate tribal tensions. When nationwide elections finally were held in early 1980, ethnic support enabled Mugabe to win a commanding majority that assured his leadership in the new government of Zimbabwe.[12] Sadly, since independence, Zimbabwe has continued to suffer from the ongoing Ndebele-Shona rivalry.

The first major postindependence clash between these two peoples occurred in February 1981, among soldiers from three supposedly integrated battalions. Apparently, a barroom disagreement led to a brawl; over the next few days, violence spread to other battalions and assembly camps. The situation finally returned to normal after the intervention of two battalions of European-led government troops and pleas for a cease-fire from Nkomo and threats of retaliation from Mugabe. The fracas resulted in approximately 300 deaths and countless injuries. In addition, Mugabe issued orders to disarm about 6,500 soldiers and dissolve three battalions.[13]

Six months later, Mugabe announced that 106 North Koreans, with $16 million worth of military equipment, had arrived in Zimbabwe to train the 5,000-man Fifth Brigade in the Eastern Highlands' remote Inyanga Mountains.[14] Almost immediately, ZAPU complained that the North Koreans were molding the brigade into a special praetorian guard to impose a one-party state dominated by the Shona. In January 1983, Mugabe finally deployed the Fifth Brigade to Matabeleland to crush dissident elements loyal to Nkomo. In the ensuing battles, the brigade, which was comprised mainly of troops belonging to the Shona tribe, showed no mercy toward the Ndebele, who initially received military assistance from the Soviet Union and then from South Africa.[15] According to the Roman Catholic Bishops Conference and international press reports, the unit slaughtered 1,000 to 2,000 innocent civilians. Nkomo, on the other hand, believed the actual number was "3,000 or more."[16] To this day, the government of Zimbabwe has refused to acknowledge or investigate these allegations.[17] Since 1983, Mugabe has sent troops, police, and intelligence operatives into Matabeleland each year to carry on similar operations. Repeated appeals by Nkomo to his Ndebele followers to "cooperate" with the security forces have failed to reduce the growing number of human rights violations. Those Ndebele opposed to Nkomo's apparent attempts to effect a reconciliation with Mugabe claimed they had to keep fighting to save the Ndebele people from genocide.[18]

The ongoing, tribally based low-intensity conflict between the Shona and

Ndebele caused a dilemma for a succession of American administrations, all of which perceived Zimbabwe's problems in white-versus-black or East-versus-West terms. To promote racial equality, democracy, and stability, the United States helped to bring about black majority rule; and to reduce the possibility of an east-west conflict, it became the largest aid donor to the government of Prime Minister Robert Mugabe, an acknowledged Marxist who had relied on aid from the People's Republic of China during the struggle against the Ian Smith regime.[19] The country's independence and subsequent general elections, however, failed to ensure domestic tranquility; on the contrary, these events only intensified existing tribal tensions. As a result, the disputants secured military assistance from a variety of sources which, in turn, guaranteed a continuation of the violence that slowly continues to tear Zimbabwe apart.[20]

Namibia

Like the other countries in southern Africa, Namibia (South-West Africa) is an agglomeration of many different ethnic groups. The heterogeneous population includes seven African tribes: Ovambo (600,000), Kavango (100,000), Caprivi (40,000), Kaokovelder (11,000), Herero (76,000), Tswana (9,000), and Damara (83,000); five non-African groups: San (35,000), Nama (45,000), Baster (25,000), and Coloured (40,000); and three European groups: English (10,000), German (25,000), and Dutch (35,000). In 1915, South African forces, after defeating German imperial forces, administered this territory under military occupation. Five years later, the League of Nations granted a mandate over South-West Africa and conferred it upon Great Britain "for and on behalf of the government of the Union of South Africa."[21]

Although the United Nations General Assembly terminated the mandate in 1966, the South African government, claiming this action was an illegal intrusion into its domestic affairs, refused to withdraw from the country. Five years later, the International Court of Justice declared that South African rule over Namibia was illegitimate, a decision also rejected by Pretoria.[22] Since then, the international community has been unable to resolve this problem.

Meanwhile, opposition to South Africa's continued presence in Namibia began in 1958, when Herman Toivo-ja-Toivo, a university student then studying in Cape Town, formed the Ovamboland People's Congress, which later became the Ovamboland People's Organization (OPO). Initially, the OPO represented Ovambo workers who believed the existing contract-labor system was a form of slavery. To gain support among the country's other ethnic groups, the Ovamboland People's Organization changed its name in 1960 to the South-West Africa People's Organization (SWAPO). The group's goals include majority rule, freedom of speech and organization, an end to South African administration of Namibia, and the abolition of racial discrimination.[23] Although SWAPO's attempts to become a national liberation movement have been somewhat successful, it has continued to be dominated largely by the Ovambo people. To gain the country's independence, SWAPO launched a low-intensity conflict against South Africa on 26 August 1966, infiltrating a small number of troops into north-central Namibia. As hostilities intensified, SWAPO became increasingly dependent on the Soviet Union for military and economic support while South Africa remained committed to the organization's destruction.[24]

For the United States—which has tended to perceive the Namibia problem as a manifestation of the superpower rivalry or as a white-versus-black struggle—this dilemma has been a continuing source of frustration, largely because all attempts to effect a negotiated settlement have been unsuccessful.[25] This ineffectiveness stems from America's inability to control or alter the course of events in Namibia. More important, however, until the 1980s, America's Namibia policy ignored the political ramifications of that country's ethnic diversity. Even after adopting a negotiating strategy to provide constitutional safeguards and guarantees for all ethnic groups, the Reagan administration undercut its limited influence by concentrating its efforts on linking Namibia's independence to the withdrawal of Cuban troops from neighboring Angola. Although this tactic succeeded in quelling South Africa's fears about its future military security, it also helped prolong Namibia's low-intensity conflict and create a situation in which many of the country's ethnic groups preferred a political stalemate to a negotiated settlement. In addition, this deadlock afforded South Africa the opportunity to build a national alternative to SWAPO among those peoples fearful of an Ovambo-dominated government.[26]

The first attempt to devise another viable national political force occurred in 1977 when 11 parties (one of each ethnic group) formed the Democratic Turnhalle Alliance (DTA) and won 80 percent of the election vote the following year. SWAPO boycotted the election, charging that DTA was nothing more than an arm of the South African government. To make matters worse, the lack of international recognition and the slow pace of independence negotiations eventually reduced DTA to five ethnic parties. After the resignation of DTA leader Dirk Mudge in January 1983, Namibian authorities authorized the establishment of a new alliance known as the Multi-Conference party (MPC). Once again, however, SWAPO refused to recognize or join what it believed was "yet another puppet government."[27]

To end this impasse, MPC and SWAPO representatives met in mid-1984 in Lusaka, Zambia, to work out a new independence plan. Unfortunately, the talks broke down following divisions within MPC and rumors of Soviet pressure on SWAPO to avoid a compromise agreement. In view of this development, the South African government announced the formation of a "Transitional Government of National Unity," which was based on earlier MPC proposals. This decision not only served as a warning from Pretoria that it was unwilling to wait indefinitely for SWAPO to abandon its militancy and enter the negotiating process, but also to legitimize and strengthen the MPC.

Sometime in early 1986, Chester Crocker, US assistant secretary of state of African affairs, tried to bridge this widening gulf between Pretoria and SWAPO by resuming efforts to persuade the former to adopt a more conciliatory approach toward the Namibia problem.[28] As far as the United States was concerned, this meant fixing a date for South Africa's withdrawal from Namibia in exchange for a parallel agreement for the departure of Cuban troops from Angola. Obviously, Washington believed this strategy would lessen the possibility of superpower confrontation in southern Africa and, secondarily, allay South Africa's security concerns about an independent Namibia.

Shortly after the Crocker initiative, South African State President P. W. Botha set 1 August 1986 as the date for Namibia's independence, provided the Cubans left Angola before then.[29] From Pretoria's perspective, the American suggestion was a godsend. Indeed, by accepting the linkage concept and the notion that the Namibian dilemma was primarily a pawn in the ongoing superpower rivalry in southern Africa, Botha was able to score several important diplomatic victories. Among other things, he drew the United States further into the Angolan quagmire; legitimized South Africa's repeated cross-border raids into that country; shifted responsibility for a Namibia settlement to Luanda, Moscow, Havana, and Washington; and gave Pretoria more time to erode SWAPO's position and strengthen MPC. More important, however, there was little likelihood that the American proposition would facilitate a settlement.[30]

On the contrary, by overemphasizing regional considerations and ignoring the ethnic nature of Namibia's low-intensity conflict, the Crocker scheme guaranteed a continuation of hostilities in that country. According to an *International Herald Tribune* report, South Africa-supported political parties and leaders displayed rare unity in expressing displeasure about the independence plan.[31] In addition, SWAPO spokesmen condemned Botha's 1 August offer as a preposterous propaganda ploy. As for the Angolan government's response, a statement released by the Angolan Press (ANGOP), the country's official news agency, claimed "the linkage between a Namibian settlement and the Cuban presence in Angola was totally unacceptable."[32]

The failure of America's foreign policy to end the Namibia fighting and bring about a peaceful transition to independence reflects a basic misunderstanding of the nature of this particular low-intensity conflict. The success of any settlement depends mainly on allaying the fears and suspicions of Namibia's ethnic minorities about an Ovambo-dominated government. By adopting a strategy of linking developments in Namibia with those in Angola, the United States not only neglected this issue but also reduced its already limited ability to influence or control the course of events in that country. "Linkage diplomacy" also gave Africa free rein to manipulate and prey on minority fears about an independent Ovambo-dominated government so as to justify its continued presence in Namibia.

Angola

Since its independence on 11 November 1975, Angola has been plagued by a low-intensity conflict that threatens to dismember the country and draw the superpowers into an unwanted confrontation. Understanding the nature of this ongoing warfare requires an appreciation of Angola's ethnic diversity. Indeed, this country, a former Portuguese colony, is home to seven major groups.

The Ovimbundu people, who constitute approximately 37 percent of the population, are located in west-central Angola. The second largest group, the Mbundu (23 percent), live in the same general area just north of the Ovimbundu. The Kongo (14 percent) are situated in the northwestern provinces of Zaire, Uíge, and Cabinda as well as in the neighboring countries of Congo and Zaire. Central Angola contains the Lunda-Chokwe people (8-9 percent) while the southeastern portion of the country is home to the Nganguela (7 percent). Although Mestiços (of Euro-African ancestry) account for only 2–3 percent of the population, they are important because of their long-standing political and economic influence throughout Angola. Estimates of the country's Portuguese population at independence range from 290,000 to 350,000.[33]

The significance of these ethnic divisions was apparent even before Angola's independence. Indeed, throughout the struggle against Portuguese colonial rule, African nationalists were split along ethnic lines. The Popular Movement for the Liberation of Angola (MPLA), which had connections to some elements in the Mestiço, Lunda-Chokwe, and Nganguela communities, enjoyed support primarily among urbanized Mbundu. The Kongo people identified with the goals and aspirations of the National Front for the Liberation of Angola (FNLA). Members from the Lunda-Chokwe and Nganguela groups who opposed MPLA usually joined the Ovimbundu-dominated National Union for the Total Independence of Angola (UNITA).

The inability of these liberation groups to reconcile their differences meant that they often spent as much time fighting one another as they devoted to the conflict with the Portuguese. On the eve of independence, the domestic situation had become so divisive that Portugal recognized all three independence movements, showed neutrality in negotiating with them, and advocated a postcolonial coalition government.[34] Unfortunately, this strategy failed to unite the nationalists. Even after a transitional government came to power on 31 January 1975, relations between the MPLA, FNLA, and UNITA remained so tense and hostile that, by April, Angola found itself in the midst of a civil war.

Over the next several months, the superpowers slowly became involved in this escalating low-intensity conflict. American intelligence reports revealed that the Soviet Union was covertly arming the MPLA.[35] The People's Republic of China initially supplied UNITA with some arms and medical supplies before switching allegiance to FNLA. For its part, the United States adopted a secret military aid program for the FNLA in January 1975.[36] From an African point of view, these associations were merely vehicles to facilitate their own political and military survival.[37]

For the United States, however, Angola was a test of its strength and resolve against Soviet imperialism in Africa. According to William E. Schaufele, Jr., who served as assistant secretary of state for African affairs from 1975 to 1977, senior officials in the Ford administration believed Angola had "the greatest likelihood of Soviet interest penetration in Africa."[38] Schaufele also maintained that Angola was an example of Soviet-sponsored aggression, intended to change the world balance of power.[39]

By perceiving events in Angola solely as a superpower confrontation and ignoring the ethnic dimension of that country's escalating low-intensity conflict, the United States doomed its policy to failure. Indeed, Gerald Bender, a long-time observer of Angolan affairs, maintained that America's "single-minded determination to respond to the Soviet Union" blinded policymakers to Angolan realities and years of accumulated intelligence about the FNLA's questionable battlefield capabilities. Nevertheless, the United States continued underwriting FNLA even after the People's Republic of China had abandoned the organization because of its poor performance. William Colby, then director of Central Intelligence, told a House Select Committee on Intelligence that Washington had supported FNLA only because the Soviet Union backed MPLA.[40]

Unfortunately for the Ford administration, the nation, still suffering from the Vietnam trauma, was unwilling to support a "tit-for-tat" strategy against the Soviet Union in Angola. In late 1975, two democratic senators, Dick Clark of Iowa and John Tunney of California, were instrumental in passing legislation, known as the Clark Amendment, that denied funding for covert operations in Angola. Meanwhile, the Soviet Union had increased aid to MPLA, and Cuban troops had intervened in Angola to prop up the regime. Thus, by the beginning of 1976, America's Angola policy was in shambles and conservatives throughout the country were claiming that the Soviet Union had scored an important victory in Angola.

For the next several years, the question of US military aid to anti-MPLA forces remained dormant. Then, in his presidential election campaign, Ronald Reagan raised the issue again in the context of supporting anti-Marxist guerrillas throughout the third world. According to this policy, which eventually became known as the Reagan Doctrine, American intervention on the side of freedom fighters could contain or even roll back the frontiers of Communist tyranny. During Reagan's first term in office, there was little congressional support for this strategy; but, beginning in 1984, Congress accepted the so-called Reagan Doctrine and agreed to send assistance to rebel forces in Cambodia, Afghanistan, and Nicaragua.[41]

In late 1985, the question of American military aid to UNITA became a matter of national concern. Debate over this issue invariably centered on whether UNITA's leader, Jonas Savimbi, was a genuine "freedom fighter." According to the Congressional Black Caucus, he was a "surrogate for South Africa" and "hostile to the interests of blacks." Worse still, other administration critics such as democratic Senator William Proxmire charged that Savimbi, who had received his early training in Communist China, would readily "exchange one Marxist revolution for another." On the other hand, Secretary of Defense Caspar Weinberger and several other senior government officials believed support of UNITA was necessary because Angola was the "key" to Moscow's strategy in southern Africa.[42] The Reagan administration eventually prevailed and, on 18 February 1986, disclosed that it had decided to furnish military equipment, including Stinger antiaircraft missiles, to UNITA.

The ramifications of this policy shift were immediately apparent. In mid-March, the Angolan government asked United Nations Secretary-General Javier Perez de Cuellar to act as chief mediator in any future southern Africa peace negotiations. Then, on 8 April 1986, leaders of the frontline states (Angola, Zambia, Tanzania, Mozambique, Botswana, and Zimbabwe) issued a joint communiqué condemning the United States for "gross and inadmissible interference" in Angola's internal affairs. Moreover, the document charged that Washington had lost its credibility as a mediator in southern Africa and "forfeited its role as an honest broker" in the Namibian independence talks.[43] Approximately two months later, on 3 June 1986, Angola's foreign minister, Afonso Van Dunen, announced that his government would no longer have any direct contacts with the United States about the southern Africa situation.[44]

At no time since the Angolan civil war began have ethnic factors figured in the formulation and implementation of American policy toward that country. Instead, the United States continues to believe that a favorable peace can be achieved by supplying arms to UNITA while trying to persuade MPLA to negotiate a settlement on the basis of "linkage diplomacy."[45] By allowing superpower politics to determine the course of US actions in Angola, Washington has failed to understand the nature of Angola's low-intensity conflict. Even Jonas Savimbi, who has become a master at portraying himself as the West's man in Africa, has privately rejected the reputation he enjoys among so many American conservatives. According to Savimbi, his was "a pro-Angola fight, a fight for the right of people to choose their own government."[46] Within an African context, this means selecting a government dominated by minority Mbundu, Mestiço, and assimilado elements, or one backed by the Ovimbundu people, the country's largest ethnolinguistic group.

When seen in this light, the Angolan conflict is little more than a classic tribal power struggle. Superpower considerations such as Namibia's independence, South Africa's continued military involvement in Angola, and Havana's relationship to Luanda are pertinent only insofar as they affect access to external aid or have a direct impact on MPLA-UNITA relations. In other words, Savimbi will readily embrace the image of an anti-Marxist "freedom fighter" to get American arms, while his MPLA opponents will laud the benefits of communism to please their Soviet, Cuban, East German, and North Korean benefactors.

Even if the United States government somehow brought about Namibia's independence, convinced South Africa to stop launching cross-border raids against its northern neighbor, and persuaded all foreign troops to leave Angola, the UNITA-MPLA rivalry would still exist. Moreover, given the violent history between these two movements, it is unlikely that either side would be willing to enter into peaceful negotiations. As long as UNITA and MPLA continue to wage an "all-or-nothing" armed conflict against one another, it is naive and unrealistic to believe that the United States can broker a settlement acceptable to all parties.

Mozambique

Like Angola, Mozambique continues to suffer from the ravages of civil war. The cause of this conflict has been the subject of considerable international debate. According to the more traditional interpretation, shortly after the Front for the Liberation of Mozambique (FRELIMO) took power from the Portuguese in mid-1975, white-ruled neighboring Rhodesia established and supplied a small group of Mozambicans who were dissatisfied with the FRELIMO government and its harsh political and economic policies. Operating from bases in southern Rhodesia, these dissidents, known as the Mozambique National Resistance (MNR or RENAMO), started launching hit-and-run raids in 1976 against western Mozambique's rail, road, power, and communications lines as well as isolated villages, state farms, and remote police posts.

When white-ruled Rhodesia became black-ruled Zimbabwe in early 1980, South Africa assumed responsibility for the MNR's continued operation. This was in retaliation for FRELIMO allowing African National Congress (ANC) guerrillas to stage attacks against South Africa from bases in Mozambique. Within three years, the MNR, under the guidance of the South African Defence Force (SADF), had penetrated all of Mozambique's ten provinces and had extended control over vast areas of the country. During this period, FRELIMO estimates indicated that MNR caused nearly $4.5 billion in damage, a figure equal to Mozambique's debt to Western countries.[47]

As Mozambique degenerated into social, political, and economic chaos, FRELIMO sought to save the country by seeking an accommodation with South Africa. On 16 March 1984, the two governments signed a non-aggression pact known as the Nkomati Accord. Under this agreement's terms, Mozambique and South Africa agreed that neither of the "two countries would serve as a base for acts of aggression or violence against the other and that both countries undertook not to use the territory of a third state for this purpose."[48]

In August 1985, however, the Mozambique government revealed that its troops had captured a desk diary and several notebooks with minutes of meetings between MNR officials and South African envoys. These documents indicated that South Africa had furnished guns and other military supplies to MNR long after signing the Nkomati Accord.[49] Critics maintain that, since then, South Africa, despite public protestations to the contrary, has continued sponsoring and orchestrating MNR's destabilization and revolutionary campaigns either directly or via Malawi.[50] Because of these allegations, MNR lacks credibility in the eyes of many African and Western nations. Typical criticisms include charges that MNR is an illegitimate national movement without a coherent program or an adequate political base among the Mozambican people.[51]

Explaining the causes of Mozambique's civil war in terms of MNR's relationship to South Africa ignores the historical ethnic rivalry that generated that conflict. From its formation in 1962, FRELIMO attracted most of its recruits from the Maconde people, a northern minority group comprising only about 2 percent of the country's population. Indeed, the Maconde, along with the Nyanji people, another northern minority (less than 3 percent of the population) provided the bulk of FRELIMO's fighting forces.[52] This alliance caused disunity in northern Mozambique because the Makua (approximately 27 percent of the population) refused to join FRELIMO. In addition, their active opposition initially restricted FRELIMO's military operations to a 100-mile area south of Cabo Delgado.[53]

When a bomb concealed in a book killed FRELIMO's president, Dr Eduardo Mondlane, in 1969, the organization sank into further disarray. After a period of bitter infighting made the appointment of a successor impossible, FRELIMO's central committee replaced the office of president with a three-man council. Within three months of this decision, however, a "strong feeling of sectarianism, regionalism, and tribalism" plagued FRELIMO's ranks.[54] After Samora Machel, a Shangaan from southern Mozambique, became FRELIMO's president on 22 May 1970, the organization started broadening its support by filling leadership posts with southerners, Mestiços, and Portuguese. Nevertheless, many people from northern and central Mozambique still maintained that FRELIMO was fundamentally a minority Maconde movement led by the Shangaan people in collaboration with some whites and Mestiços.[55]

Developments in Mozambique took an unexpected turn in 1974 when a military reformist group staged a coup in Lisbon and then offered self-determination to all Portuguese overseas territories. Colonial authorities in Mozambique proposed an immediate cease-fire and nationwide referendum to determine the country's future and invited FRELIMO and other liberation groups to participate in this democratic process. FRELIMO, however, insisted that Portugal grant independence without a referendum. Moreover, even though it controlled only about one-third of Mozambique, FRELIMO demanded recognition as the people's sole representative and the transfer of all governmental authority to its ranks. Internal strife prevented Portugal from negotiating these issues, thus enabling FRELIMO to achieve its demands and to transform Mozambique into a one-party Marxist state allied to the Soviet Union.

After independence, FRELIMO concentrated much of its efforts on establishing political hegemony over the entire country, assuaging ethnic anxieties, and generating a common national identity. FRELIMO used a multifaceted strategy to achieve these goals. For example, some of those who opposed FRELIMO during the independence struggle admitted their wrongdoing at government-supervised "confession ceremonies," while others repented at reeducation centers. In addition, Samora Machel and other senior party officials made repeated trips to every province to emphasize that "the fulfillment of the giant task that lies ahead of us implies achieving and consolidating unity." Radio broadcasts and newspapers also continually repeated the theme that "we are all Mozambicans." So-called dynamizing groups sprang up in rural communities, factories, and urban neighborhoods to help overcome ethnic stereotypes and to explain the value of national unity.[56] Despite these efforts, Machel was unable to consolidate his hold over Mozambique or convince the country's various ethnic groups that FRELIMO was a national movement.

These failures became the basis of MNR's power. Prior to 1980, MNR confined its activities to central Mozambique's Ndau-Shona people. To gain money and recruits from this group, MNR stressed the fact that FRELIMO's leadership was largely Shangaan; and emphasized FRELIMO's opposition to chiefs, missionaries and other religious persons, and traditional practices such as bride price and polygyny.[57] After 1980, MNR, using many of these same arguments, succeeded in establishing a stronghold among central Mozambique's Sena people.[58] In the mid-1980s, MNR told prospective supporters that Mozambique's drought and associated famine were signs that the country's ancestors were alienated from FRELIMO.[59] Such assertions, coupled with rising civilian dissatisfaction, with draft dodging, army desertions, and FRELIMO's methods in dealing with a faltering economy, made MNR recruitment much easier.[60] After consolidating its support among these ethnic groups, MNR gradually extended its operations throughout the country.[61]

Regional and, to a lesser extent, superpower considerations have been the basis of American policy toward Mozambique's low-intensity conflict. The United States brokered the Nkomati Accord, for example, expecting that, by endorsing the sovereignty of South Africa and Mozambique, the former would stop aiding MNR, thereby bringing about an end to the war. This belief was based on the erroneous assumptions that MNR lacked support in Mozambique and that Pretoria exerted absolute control of the organization. Inded, by early 1985, a variety of Western sources had attested to MNR's continuing strength and had reported that it was getting arms and supplies from many places, including right-wing Portuguese groups, former Portuguese businessmen and industrialists who left Mozambique after independence, several "middle eastern and African" nations, and "certain Islamic countries."[62]

Later in 1985, American concern about Mozambique focused on that country's role in the superpower rivalry. The White House, supported by the State Department, hoped to "wean away" Mozambique from the Soviet Union by arranging a meeting between presidents Machel and Reagan, which occurred on 18 September. In response, many American conservatives spoke out against what they perceived to be "a highly questionable policy."[63] To counter a possible American-Mozambican rapprochement, Senator Malcolm Wallop of Wyoming and Representative Danny L. Burton of Indiana introduced legislation calling for aid to MNR and an end to US economic assistance to Machel.[64] Although this bill failed to pass Congress, the controversy between the Reagan administration and the American right has never ended.

At the end of 1986, two powerful conservative lobby groups, Free the Eagle and Conservative Action Foundation, helped MNR set up two offices in Washington, D.C., to disseminate information about the war in Mozambique.[65] The White House, on the other hand, has repeatedly but unsuccessfully requested military assistance for Mozambique.[66] As far as aid for MNR is concerned, US Assistant Secretary of State for Political Affairs Michael Armacost told a group of reporters in Maputo on 18 December 1986 that the American government did not support this organization.[67] Meanwhile, in the midst of this ongoing debate that has paralyzed US policy, the war in Mozambique continues with no end in sight.[68]

118

South Africa

Despite the excitement, interest, and passion associated with recent events in South Africa, there is little understanding or appreciation of the forces that precipitated this low-intensity conflict. According to that country's many critics, a ruthless white oligarchy has caused this violence by refusing to dismantle apartheid and accommodate the black majority's legitimate demands for social and political equality. Moreover, they say the South African government's refusal to accede to black majority rule makes a racial bloodbath inevitable. Explaining South Africa's troubles solely in terms of a white-versus-black confrontation, however, oversimplifies the problems confronting Pretoria and ignores the wider conflict that undoubtedly would result from black majority rule.

Apart from focusing the world's attention on South Africa, the recent wave of violence, which began in September 1984, has exacerbated ethnic tensions in many parts of the country. Although all leaders and organizations who claim to represent black South Africa publicly denounce tribalism, the fact of the matter is that ethnic factors still play a role in black politics, most significantly among the Zulu and Xhosa people who, together, comprise about half of South Africa's black population. The historical animosity between these two groups is reflected in the fighting that often occurs in mining compounds or black townships like Soweto.[69]

Gatsha Mangosuthu Buthelezi has served as the elected chief minister of KwaZulu, the semiautonomous Zulu homeland within South Africa, since 1970. He also founded KwaZulu's only official political movement, known as Inkatha, which claims a membership of more than one million.[70] During his career, Buthelezi has built an international reputation as an advocate of nonviolent resistance to apartheid. His willingness to work for change within the system, however, has caused many colleagues and opponents to brand him an "Uncle Tom" and a "puppet of Pretoria."[71] Despite such attacks, Buthelezi has continued to reject the use of violence as a vehicle for political change.

Since 1984, the African National Congress, a Soviet-supported organization that advocates the violent overthrow of the South African government, has become increasingly critical of Buthelezi. Almost without exception, the Western press has attributed this hostility to disagreements about strategy and tactics (e.g., whether to support Western economic sanctions against South Africa). A closer examination of the relationship between Buthelezi and the ANC, however, reveals another dimension to their mutual antagonism.

In 1952, Chief Albert Lutuli—a Zulu pacifist and reformer who had started his career in the Training College at Adams, in Natal—became the ANC's president-general. During his tenure in office, he worked for a mul-

119

tiracial society and for passive resistance rather than violent confrontation.[72] Nine years later, however, the more radical ANC members rejected nonviolence, preferring instead to work through the organization's newly formed guerrilla arm, *Umkhonto we Sizwe* (Spear of the Nation). Lutuli, who became more and more estranged from the ANC's radical wing, continued arguing unsuccessfully for negotiations with Pretoria and for nonrevolutionary political changes. After his 1967 death, which marked the decline of Zulu influence within the ANC, Lutuli became a hero to the Zulu people.

Once Buthelezi—who saw Lutuli as his mentor—became chief minister, he not only embraced nonviolence but also launched a series of attacks against the ANC. Among other things, he has accused the ANC of starting a civil war, plotting to assassinate him, and trying to lure away his supporters.[73] By the mid-1980s, Buthelezi was saying that, after failing to launch a successful armed struggle against the South African security forces, the ANC had stepped up its campaign of turning "Black brother against Black brother." In addition, Buthelezi made it clear that he would not "lead Black South Africans to maim, kill and hack other Black South Africans, nor [would he] lead Blacks to maim, kill and hack White South Africans."[74]

Even more important than these disagreements about the role of violence in the liberation struggle was Buthelezi's continual allegations that the ANC was a Xhosa organization. As proof, he has pointed out repeatedly that the Zulu people lack adequate representation in the ANC.[75] Moreover, Buthelezi has called attention to the fact that there are a disproportionate number of Xhosas in the ANC's senior ranks. Such individuals include Oliver Tambo, president-general; Alfred Nzo, secretary-general; Govan Mbeki, former national chairman now imprisoned on Robben Island; Thabo Mbeki, director of information; Walter Sisulu, former secretary-general now in Pollsmoor Prison; and Nelson Mandela, former deputy national president also in Pollsmoor Prison. It is interesting to note that, when confronted with this charge, Tambo responded by claiming he was unaware of his colleague's tribal origins.[76]

Buthelezi has made similar accusations against the United Democratic Front (UDF), an antiapartheid organization formed in 1983 of more than 650 local and community groups. Inkatha spokesmen also maintain that UDF worked "hand-in-hand" with the Xhosa-dominated ANC.[77] While it is true that many prominent Xhosas, including Govan Mbeki, Nelson and Winnie Mandela, and Walter and Albertina Sisulu, are UDF patrons or presidents, there also are some distinguished Zulus in senior UDF positions. Curnick Ndlovu, a Durban Zulu, is national chairman while Archie Gumede, son of Josiah Gumede, the late ANC leader, is a copresident.[78] Nevertheless, Buthelezi and Inkatha have been unswerving in their opposition to UDF, an organization which they believe to be an instrument of Soviet and Xhosa imperialism.

By using the tribalism issue, Buthelezi has been able to mobilize Zulu opposition against the ANC and UDF. This has resulted in the rise of the so-called right-wing vigilantes or what the Western press has termed *black-on-black* conflict. Indeed, the use of large groups of assegai-bearing[79] Zulus has been so effective at quelling ANC/UDF-inspired violence that, until August 1985, the unrest which plagued most of South Africa's larger black townships was absent from areas under KwaZulu authority.

In that month, however, a virtual civil war erupted between Inkatha and the UDF following the funeral of Victoria Mxenge, a Xhosa-speaking UDF lawyer who had been murdered by unknown assailants. Outraged UDF students organized a week-long boycott of classes to protest Mxenge's death. Unfortunately, what had started as peaceful student demonstrations soon degenerated into violence. Groups of UDF supporters, called comrades, set fire to school buses and other targets such as Zulu- or Indian-owned businesses. Criminal elements then became involved in the protest as a cover for their looting and arson activities.

To end this lawlessness, carloads of armed Zulus poured into Umlazi, Mrs Mxenge's hometown, from all over Natal. Local Inkatha officials ordered them to conduct house-to-house searches for looters, stolen goods, and, more important, UDF members and sympathizers. During what has become known as the "bloody eight days of August," 67 people died while hundreds, perhaps thousands, were injured. Since then, Inkatha has not hesitated to take action against ANC/UDF elements anywhere in KwaZulu or Durban. The Centre for Applied Legal Sudies, University of the Witwatersrand, in Johannesburg, has rejected the usual explanation that the country's security forces have incited such attacks. According to their findings, official complicity in right-wing vigilante activities depends on local circumstances and ranges from active support to benign neglect.[80] In any case, Buthelezi has managed to distance himself from this violence while holding out the possibility of more unrestrained hostility against his foes.[81]

The rise of the right-wing vigilante movement has made it possible for the Zulus to stop UDF from operating openly in Durban or anywhere in KwaZulu; but they have been unable to end ANC terrorist attacks altogether. Another consequence was a drop in Indian support for the UDF-affiliated Natal Indian Congress (NIC), a left-wing organization that has sought to establish links with similar black and coloured movements. Many members of Natal's prosperous Indian community suffered losses during the August 1985 violence when criminals, masquerading as political demonstrators, looted their shops and homes. Most blamed the UDF for these assaults. Indeed, an Institute for Black Research poll, taken months after the August 1985 incidents by a pro-UDF University of Natal professor, revealed that Indian support for the NIC and other UDF affiliates was only 5.1 percent while more than 53 percent named President P. W. Botha as their preferred leader. Another 3.7 percent opted for a government led by Nelson Mandela.[82] Since this poll, the UDF has been unable to rees-tablish a meaningful presence in Natal or KwaZulu.

In the long run, the events of 1985–87 suggest that any resolution of the South African imbroglio involving an ANC/UDF takeover of the govern-ment would cause a civil war similar to the one in Zimbabwe. Moreover, Buthelezi and Inkatha are in the same political predicament as Nkomo and ZAPU; namely, they are too weak to rule the entire country but too strong to be left out of any settlement. This dilemma, according to Buthelezi, has only strengthened the Zulu position: "No armed struggle can win without Inkatha participation. There can be no political negotiations without our taking part in them. We are an inexpungible presence in the struggle for liberation."[83]

The United States has failed to incorporate these ethnic factors in its policy toward South Africa (which has, for all intents and purposes, become a domestic civil rights issue). Instead, as far as Washington is concerned, the ultimate question in South Africa is "how blacks, along with whites, can participate equally and meaningfully in the political system and in the economic, social, academic, and cultural life of that country, at both the local and national levels."[84] To help facilitate these changes, the US Con-gress, in October 1986, voted to override a presidential veto of the Com-prehensive Anti-Apartheid Act of 1986; thus, the United States imposed a package of economic sanctions stronger than any yet adopted by any mem-ber of the international community.

Had this policy hastened the advent of drastic reforms and black majority rule, as many Americans believed it would, the United States could very well have provoked a far greater bloodbath than anything that has occurred so far in South Africa. This action has not, however, been translated into political reforms in that country. On the contrary, according to a special commission of the Southern African Catholic Bishops' Conference, Amer-ican sanctions have "clearly had a totally counterproductive effect on gov-ernment thinking . . . [and have] consolidated the government in its retreat from meaningful and, indeed, any reform."[85]

Conclusion

Explaining the causes of southern Africa's low-intensity conflicts largely in terms of ethnic rivalries will undoubtedly provoke much controversy. Critics can point to economic backwardness, social instability, the struggle for democracy and racial equality, South Africa's support of groups like UNITA and MNR, the Soviet Union's backing of SWAPO and ANC, and the continued Cuban troop presence in Angola as more legitimate reasons for the wars engulfing the region. Such reasoning, however, mistakes symp-toms for causes. Obviously, South Africa has aggravated tensions throughout southern Africa; but to suggest that Pretoria has created UNITA in Angola, MNR in Mozambique, the Shona-Ndebele crisis in Zimbabwe, or the alliance against SWAPO in Namibia, to preserve white domination of the area rule, overestimates her power and ignores the ethnic divisions that have plagued these countries for decades—sometimes centuries.

Likewise, the Soviet menace in southern Africa is oftentimes portrayed as the driving force behind ANC, SWAPO, FRELIMO, and MPLA. Indeed, many Western analysts argue that peace in southern Africa depends on thwarting Soviet ambitions throughout the region. This can be accomplished only by defeating Soviet client states like Mozambique and Angola, and by preventing pro-Soviet organizations such as SWAPO and ANC from coming to power.[86] But such an evaluation is also misleading; the Russians and their allies have used local conditions to further their own interest, but it is inaccurate to blame them for the area's low-intensity conflicts. The Soviet Union, like the United States, is used by various African groups as a source of political, economic, and military support.

For the United States, the southern Africa dilemma has been particularly frustrating. Its foreign policy—expressed through concepts such as black majority rule, linkage diplomacy, support of anti-Marxist guerrillas, and an abhorrence of apartheid—has been unable to end any of the region's low-intensity conflicts. This failure has resulted not only from a misunderstanding of these wars' causes but also from America's limited ability to affect or control the course of events in Angola, Mozambique, Namibia, Zimbabwe, or South Africa.

The nature of the American political system has helped create this state of affairs. More often than not, domestic pressures and considerations determine the nature and scope of America's foreign policy. Certainly this has been true with regard to southern Africa. For most Americans, the spectre of white policemen beating blacks—which was a part of most nightly television news programs, newspaper accounts, and magazine articles until the South African government imposed restrictions on foreign reporters—conjured up images of Selma, Alabama, during the 1960s. The perception that South Africa was nothing but a nationally based racial confrontation was an article of faith for many American politicians and private citizens; indeed, by the mid-1980s, apartheid was more of a domestic civil rights issue in the United States than a foreign policy problem.[87] Moreover, any politician questioning this interpretation ran the risk of losing votes or being branded a racist. To drive home this point, Transafrica, an antiapartheid organization based in Washington, D.C., started running full-page advertisements in selected newspapers throughout the United States identifying certain presidential candidates, senators, and congressmen as "one of the faces behind apartheid." According to Randall Robinson, head of Transafrica, the campaign's goal was to make apartheid "an important litmus test" for black voters.[88]

In such a highly charged atmosphere, it was easy, and perhaps necessary, to believe that Pretoria had caused southern Africa's low-intensity conflicts. Once apartheid was dead, peace, prosperity, and racial equality would descend upon the entire region. Unfortunately, these views failed to acknowledge the ethnic divisions that have degenerated into open warfare.

Anticommunism is another characteristic of the American political system. Ever since the immediate post–World War I era, the United States has been committed to stopping the spread of communism. But it was not until the early 1960s, during the so-called Congo crisis, that the Soviet Union became involved in sub-Saharan Africa. Since then, however, Washington, to greater or lesser degrees, has been determined to neutralize, or eliminate altogether, the Soviet presence throughout Africa. Arguments used to support this policy include Moscow's supposed plan to control the continent's resources and dominate the Cape sea route, the South Atlantic, the Persian Gulf, and the Indian Ocean littorals.[89]

Needless to say, southern Africa plays a significant role in this equation. Its minerals—such as chromium, cobalt, manganese, and titanium—are vital to the US defense industry.[90] Moreover, 30 percent of America's oil imports travel via the Cape sea route. Many conservatives believe that, if pro-Soviet governments were allowed to dominate this region, the effect on the United States and its allies would be catastrophic. They therefore argue that support of groups like UNITA and MNR and rejection of ANC, SWAPO, FRELIMO, and MPLA are vital to US national interests.[91]

Thus, the peculiarities and shortcomings of the American political system, more than an appreciation of the forces at work in southern Africa, have shaped US foreign policy. This is especially true with regard to South Africa. To placate the rising number of individuals and organizations who opposed Pretoria on moral grounds, the Congress voted to override a presidential veto and imposed economic sanctions against South Africa to bring about racial and political reforms. Then, a few months later, in early January 1987, Washington exempted ten South African-produced strategic minerals from the sanctions law. John C. Whitehead, deputy secretary of state, defended this decision by saying that the minerals were "essential for the economy or defense of the United States."[92] At the end of that month, Secretary of State George Shultz—hoping to demonstrate to domestic and international critics that the Reagan administration was willing to go the extra mile to bring about a settlement in South Africa—met with ANC president Oliver Tambo.[93] These discussions reversed a long-standing American policy of not dealing with organizations committed to violent political change.[94] Notwithstanding these actions, however, Washington maintained that its "constructive engagement" policy remained unchanged.[95] Despite the increasing number of business, civic, and civil rights leaders who supported corporate disinvestment, the Reverend Leon Sullivan, a black baptist minister, continued arguing that his so-called Sullivan

124

Principles—which urged American companies to stay in South Africa and work for reform—should remain an instrument of US foreign policy.[96]

Given America's democratic heritage, it is understandable that US foreign policy tends to reflect the public emotionalism surrounding the southern Africa issue. As a result, Washington oftentimes finds itself pursuing simplistic (i.e., end apartheid), contradictory (supporting anti-Marxist forces in Angola but not in Mozambique), or unattainable goals (an end to Soviet and Cuban influence). Correcting this imbalance would, of course, require closing the foreign policy process to ordinary citizens, an unacceptable option in a democratic society. Even if such an action were possible, America's limited power in southern Africa would preclude a US-initiated settlement of the low-intensity conflicts that are slowly tearing the region apart. Thus, this paper prescribes no solutions to the southern Africa imbroglio; indeed, to do so would overestimate America's capabilities in the region. Rather, it offers an alternate interpretation of the causes of southern Africa's low-intensity conflicts in the hope of fostering a greater appreciation of the complex forces at work throughout the region.

NOTES

1. Some of the better known literature in this area includes Samuel Decalo, *Coups and Army Rule in Africa: Studies in Military Style* (New Haven and London: Yale University Press, 1976); Henry Bienen, *Armies and Parties in Africa* (New York: Africana Publishing Co., 1978); Henry Bienen, "African Militaries as Foreign Policy Actors," *International Security* 5/2 (Fall 1980): 168–86; and William J. Foltz and Henry S. Bienen, eds., *Arms and the African: Military Influences on Africa's International Relations* (New Haven and London: Yale University Press, 1985).

2. There are a number of works that discuss African ethnicism. Some of the classics in the field include G. P. Murdock, *Africa: Its People and Their Culture History* (New York: McGraw-Hill, 1959); C. G. Seligman, *Races of Africa* (London: Thornton Butterworth Ltd., 1939); and James L. Gibbs, eds., *People of Africa* (New York: Holt, Rinehart and Winston, 1965). For a more current treatment of the subject, see Aristide R. Zolberg, "Tribalism Through Corrective Lenses," *Foreign Affairs* 51/4 (July 1973): 728–39. David Crary, "Tribal Strife Thwarts Dreams of African Nations," *International Herald Tribune*, 20 February 1986, 1–2, argues that Africa's coups, wars, riots, and famines are all linked to "ethnic jealousies."

3. For a survey of this period, see Robin Hallett, *Africa since Eighteen Seventy-Five: A Modern History* (Ann Arbor: University of Michigan Press, 1974).

4. For a discussion of the country's early history, see L. H. Gann, *A History of Southern Rhodesia: Early Days to 1934* (New York: Humanities Press, 1969).

5. Ibid., 74–87.

6. Ibid., 88–139.

7. The post-1934 period is covered in Robert Blake, *A History of Rhodesia* (New York: Alfred A. Knopf, 1978), 217ff.

8. For a sympathetic treatment of British colonial administration, see Joy Maclean, *The Guardians: A Story of Rhodesia's Outposts and of the Men and Women Who Served in Them* (Bulawayo: Books of Rhodesia, 1974).

9. According to Julian Henriques, "The Struggles of the Zimbabweans: Conflicts Between the Nationalists and With the Rhodesian Regime," *African Affairs* 76/305 (October 1977): 495. The African nationalists spent more time fighting one another than the Rhodesian army. For an analysis from the Rhodesian perspective, see J. K. Cilliers, *Counter-Insurgency in Rhodesia* (London: Croom Helm, 1985).

10. The continuing Shona/Ndebele rivalry is covered in David Cante, "Mugabe Turns the Screw," *New Society*, 7 February 1986, 226–27; Tendayi Kumbula, "A Mandate for Mugabe," *Africa Report*, September–October 1986, 70–73; and "Zimbabwe Moves Centre Stage," *South*, November 1985, 29–30. See also, *Manchester Guardian Weekly*, 20 July 1986, 17; *International Herald Tribune*, 12 February 1986, 1–2; *Christian Science Monitor*, 13 August 1985, 12; *The Economist*, 13 July 1985, 18–20; and *Keesing's Record of World Events*, February 1987, 34917–18.

11. Henriques, "The Struggles of the Zimbabweans," 495–96. Two authoritative studies that deal with ethnicity in the Zimbabwean nationalist movements are: W. W. Nyangoni, *African Nationalism in Zimbabwe* (Lanham: University Press of America, 1978); and M. Sithole, *Zimbabwe: Struggles within the Struggle* (Harare: Rujeko, 1979).

12. Xan Smiley, "Zimbabwe, Southern Africa and the Rise of Robert Mugabe," *Foreign Affairs* 58/5 (Summer 1980): 1060–83.

13. For a discussion of Zimbabwe's human rights record, see *Amnesty International Report 1985* (London: Amnesty International Publications, 1985), 115–19. Also see Steve Askin, "Matabeleland Goes Hungry," *New African*, October 1986, 24–25; Edward Girardet, "Zimbabwe: Human Rights under Fire," *Christian Science Monitor*, 22 October 1986, 13; *Times* (London), 28 July 1985, 18; *Manchester Guardian Weekly*, 9 June 1985, 16; and *Africa Research Bulletin*, 15 September 1986, 8199–200.

14. Colin Legum, ed., *Africa Contemporary Record: Annual Survey and Documents 1981–1982* (New York and London: Africana Publishing Co., 1981), B 888.

15. Gregory Copley, "Storms of Change," *Defense and Foreign Affairs*, October 1984, 15; "Zimbabwe: North Koreans Go Home," *Defense and Foreign Affairs*, September 1984, i.

16. Tony Rich, "Zimbabwe: Only Teething Troubles?" *The World Today*, December 1983, 501.

17. On 22 August 1986, Enos Nkala, minister of home affairs whose responsibility includes issuing detention orders, and Emmerson Munangagwa, the minister of state for security, denounced Amnesty International as an "enemy of Zimbabwe." *Africa Research Bulletin*, 15 September 1986, 8199. Early in 1987, he announced in Parliament that he would detain anyone who furnished information to Amnesty International or to the Lawyers Committee for Human Rights, which published a critical report on Zimbabwe. Bill Berkeley, "Zimbabwe's Tortured Path," *New Republic*, 16 February 1987, 23. Ironically, on 18 November 1986, a local editorial blamed South Africa for the continuing problems in Matabeleland. *Herald* (Harare), 18 November 1986, 4.

18. Aida Parker, "Africa in Conflict: The Rise of ZIPRA: Zimbabwe at War," *Journal of Defense and Diplomacy* 1/2 (May 1983): 16. It is interesting to note that, according to Godwin Matatu, "Zimbabwe Rebels Face United Front in Badlands," *Observer*, 8 March 1987, 17, by early 1987, it was the Ndebele dissidents rather than government forces who were harassing the civilian population. Matatu also suggests that the dissidents may have infiltrated into Zimbabwe from South Africa.

19. For a review of US policy toward Zimbabwe, see Edgar Lockwood, "The Case of Zimbabwe," in Rene Lemarchand, ed., *American Policy in Southern Africa*, 2d ed. (Lanham: University Press of America, 1981), 167–92. also see David A. Dickson, *United States Policy towards Sub-Saharan Africa: Change, Continuity and Constraint* (Lanham: University Press of America, 1985), 82–83, 88–89, and 108–9.

20. After David Karimanzira, Zimbabwean minister of youth, sport, and culture, criticized the United States for failing to adopt economic sanctions against South Africa, former Pres-

ident Jimmy Carter walked out of a 4 July 1986 celebration at the American embassy in Harare. Shortly afterwards, the Reagan administration terminated its aid program in that country. Since then, relations between the two governments have remained strained. *International Herald Tribune,* 11 July 1986, 3; *Christian Science Monitor,* 7 July 1986, 14; "Zimbabwe's Independence Not for Sale, Mugabe Warns the White House," *Africa Report,* September–October 1986, 41–42; and *Africa Research Bulletin,* 31 July 1986, 8274. See also *Times* (London), 31 March 1987, 9.

21. Quoted in Irving Kaplan et al., *Area Handbook for the Republic of South Africa* (Washington, D.C.: Government Printing Office, 1971), 758.

22. The mandate dilemma is discussed in numerous publications. Some of the more useful are *Ethiopia and Liberia Versus South Africa: An Official Account of the Contentious Proceedings on South West Africa Before the International Court of Justice at The Hague 1960–1966* (Pretoria: Department of Information, n.d.); Ernest Gross et al., *Ethiopia and Liberia vs South Africa: The South West African Case* (Los Angeles: UCLA African Studies Center, 1968); and John Dugard, *The South West Africa-Namibia Dispute: Documents and Scholarly Writings on the Controversy Between South Africa and the United Nations* (Berkeley: University of California Press, 1973).

23. For background information about SWAPO, see Margaret A. Novicki, "Sam Nujoma: President, South West Africa People's Organization," *Africa Report,* September–October 1986, 57–61; or Randolph Vigue, "SWAPO of Namibia: A Movement in Exile," *Third World Quarterly* 9/1 (January 1987): 85–107.

24. For discussions of the Namibia War, see Gavin Cawthra, *Brutal Force: The Apartheid War Machine* (London: International Defence and Aid Fund for Southern Africa, 1986), 176–214; Robert S. Jaster, *South Africa in Namibia: The Botha Strategy* (Lanham: University Press of America, 1985); or John A. Evenson, "The Question Still Stands," *Africa Report,* September–October 1986, 62–65.

25. US policy toward Namibia is reviewed in William Johnston, "Namibia," in *American Policy in Southern Africa: The Stakes & the Stance,* ed. Rene Lemarchand, 2d ed. (Lanham: University Press of America, 1981), 193–222; Robert I. Rotberg, "Namibia and the Crisis of Constructive Engagement," in *African Crisis Areas and U.S. Foreign Policy,* Gerald J. Bender et al. (Berkeley: University of California Press, 1985), 95–109. See also Pauline H. Baker, "Deadlock in Namibia—And a Shift in U.S. Policy," *Christian Science Monitor,* 8 May 1986, 16.

26. During the Carter administration, the United States worked through the so-called Contact Group, which consisted of the United Kingdom, France, Canada, West Germany, and the United States, to negotiate an agreement for Namibia's independence. Although this group continued functioning during the early years of the Reagan presidency, it gradually fell victim to "linkage diplomacy," which sought to link the withdrawal of Cuban troops from Angola with Namibia's independence. This period is covered in Margaret P. Karns, "Ad Hoc Multilateral Diplomacy: The United States, the Contact Group, and Namibia," *International Organization* 41/1 (Winter 1977): 93–123.

27. *South African Digest,* 26 April 1985, 359.

28. Baker, 16.

29. *South African Digest,* 7 March 1986, 191.

30. Baker, 16.

31. *International Herald Tribune,* 6 March 1986, 2.

32. Foreign Broadcast Information Service, Middle East and Africa, 6 March 1986, U1 (hereafter cited as FBIS-MEA).

33. Irving Kaplan, ed., *Angola: A Country Study* (Washington, D.C.: Government Printing Office, 1979), 65. Up to 300,000 Portuguese left Angola after the country's independence.

34. Ibid., 131.

35. John Ranelagh, *The Agency: The Rise and Decline of the CIA* (New York: Simon and Schuster, 1986), 608.

36. Richard Gibson, *African Liberation Movements: Contemporary Struggles Against White Minority Rule* (London: Oxford University Press, 1972), 238; and Dickson, 86.

37. See, for example, "Savimbi Tells West Why Chinese Support Is Vital," *To the Point*, 7 March 1980, 21.

38. Quoted in Dickson, 85.

39. Ibid.

40. Gerald Bender, "Kissinger in Angola: Anatomy of Failure," in *American Policy in Southern Africa*, ed. Lemarchand, 104–5, 115.

41. Jack Kemp, "The Reagan Doctrine in Angola," *Africa Report*, January–February 1986, 12–14; and William W. Pascoe III, "Angola Tests the Reagan Doctrine," *Backgrounder*, 14 November 1985.

42. Quoted in Peter Worthington, "Can We Trust Savimbi," *National Review*, 9 May 1986, 28. For Weinberger's position, see David B. Ottaway, "Angola Rebel Aid Is Pushed," *Washington Post*, 1 November 1985, A1.

43. Marga Holness, "Washington Arms Rebels," *Africa*, May 1986, 35–36.

44. "Angola Bans Direct Talks With U.S. on Peace Efforts in Southern Africa," *International Herald Tribune*, 3 June 1986, 6.

45. Chester A. Crocker, "The U.S. and Angola," *Current Policy* 796, n.d.; see also Chester A. Crocker, "South Africa: Toward Peace and Stability," *Current Policy* 897 (n.d.), 2–3.

46. Quoted in Fred Bridgland, *Jonas Savimbi: A Key to Africa* (Edinburgh: Mainstream Publishing Co., 1986), 455.

47. Quoted in Mota Lopes, "The MNR: Opponents or Bandits?" *Africa Report*, January–February 1986, 67.

48. Quoted in Horace Campbell, "Nkomati, Before and After: War, Reconstruction and Dependence in Mozambique," *Journal of African Marxists* 6 (1984): 48.

49. Excerpts from these documents appear in *Africa News*, 4 November 1985, 8–12.

50. *New African*, February 1987, 24–26. In late 1986, the leaders of Mozambique, Zambia, and Zimbabwe traveled to Lilongwe, Malawi, and warned that country's government to stop supporting MNR. To emphasize their point, the three frontline states threatened to blockade Malawi and pursue MNR guerrillas into the country while Mozambique claimed it would use its surface-to-surface missiles to destroy MNR bases in southern Malawi. After renouncing MNR, Malawi raised a 300-man contingent to deploy against MNR. As of early 1987, it is unclear whether this action will have any impact on MNR operations. See Godwin Matatu, "Malawi in Sudden Change of Heart," *Observer*, 22 March 1987, 17; and *Star* (Johannesburg), 22 November 1986, 5.

51. Robert Jaster, "Mozambique: The Issues for U.S. Policy," *Christian Science Monitor*, 31 October 1985, 15. For a disccusion of MNR goals, see "Secretary-General Evo Fernades: Mozambican National Resistance," *Journal of Defense and Diplomacy* 3/9 (September 1985): 45–49; and FBIS–MEA, 17 December 1986, 113–114

52. Gibson, 280–99.

53. Ibid., 280.

54. Ibid., 284.

55. Harold D. Nelson, ed., *Mozambique: A Country Study* (Washington, D.C.: Government Printing Office, 1984), 98.

56. *Perspectives on Mozambique* (Washington, D.C.: Government Printing Office, 1978), 37.

57. Nelson, 252.

58. *Foreign Report*, 19 June 1986, 2; and 6 November 1986, 6–8.

59. Allen F. Isaacman, "Mozambique: Tugging at the Chains of Dependency," in *African Crisis Areas*, Bender, 142.

60. *Christian Science Monitor*, 1 April 1986, 13.

61. The most recent study dealing with MNR is Steven Metz, "The Mozambique National Resistance and South African Foreign Policy," *African Affairs* 85/341 (October 1986): 491–507.

62. *Defense and Foreign Affairs Weekly,* 14–20 January 1985, 3; Colin Legum, "Mozambique Suspects Islamic Support for MNR Rebels," *Third World Reports,* 8 March 1985. See also "Rebels Have Samora Machel at Bay," *Insight,* July 1986, 32.

63. Jamime Pinto and Mark Huber, "The White House's Confusing Signals on Mozambique," *Backgrounder,* 19 September 1985, 1.

64. *Africa Research Bulletin,* 15 October 1985, 7803.

65. *Africa News,* 13 October 1986, 1.

66. John Cristman and Winrich Kuhne, "Mozambique: Adrift between the Superpowers," *Journal of Defense and Diplomacy* 4.11 (November 1986): 14.

67. Quoted in *Journal of African Defence,* February 1987, 29.

68. On 19 October 1986, a plane crash took the lives of President Samora Machel and 33 others. Shortly afterwards, Mozambique's minister of foreign affairs, Joaquim Chissano, became the successor head of state. In his first press conference as president, Chissano claimed Mozambique "could not negotiate with terrorists" (i.e., MNR). Since then, the FRELIMO-MNR war has continued unabated with neither side able to gain victory over the other. For a transcript of the Chissano press conference, see FBIS-MEA, 5 December 1986, U1–U3.

69. Graham Leach, *South Africa* (London and New York: Routledge and Kegan Paul, 1986), 111.

70. For a biography of Buthelezi, see Ben Temkin, *Gatsha Buthelezi: Zulu Statesman* (Capetown: Purnell, 1976); or "Buthelezi, Gatsha Mangosuthu," *Current Biography* 47/10 (October 1986): 6–9. Another helpful article is Michael Massing, "The Chief," *New York Review of Books,* 12 February 1987, 15–22. See also Gerhard Maré and Georgina Stevens, *An Appetite for Power: Buthelezi's Inkatha and the Politics of Loyal Resistance* (Braamfontein, South Africa: Ravan Press, February 1988).

71. "Buthelezi, Gatsha Mangosuthu," 6.

72. L. H. Gann and Peter Duignan, *Why South Africa Will Survive: A Historical Analysis* (New York: St. Martin's Press, 1981), 124.

73. *South African Digest,* 4 October 1985, 901.

74. Quoted in ibid., 901.

75. *The Economist,* 14 September 1985, 41; *Africa Confidential,* 11 December 1985, 4.

76. *Africa Confidential,* 11 December 1985, 4.

77. Jo-Anne Collinge, "The United Democratic Front," *South African Review* 3 (1986): 259; also see *Foreign Report,* 30 May 1985, 7.

78. *Africa Confidential,* 11 December 1985, 4.

79. The assegai is a traditional Zulu stabbing spear.

80. Nicholas Haysom, *Mabangalala: The Rise of Right-Wing Vigilantes in South Africa* (Johannesburg: Centre for Applied Legal Studies, 1986), 137–38.

81. Ibid., 99.

82. *Africa Confidential,* 11 December 1985, 4.

83. Quoted in *Manchester Weekly Guardian,* 27 July 1986, 12.

84. Department of State, *A U.S. Policy Toward South Africa: The Report of the Secretary of State's Advisory Committee on South Africa* (Washington, D.C.: Government Printing Office, 1987), 1.

85. Quoted in *Wall Street Journal,* 11 February 1987.

86. For a discussion of this position, see William W. Pascoe III, "Moscow's Strategy in Southern Africa: A Country by Country Review," *Backgrounder,* 21 July 1986.

87. See, for example, Andrew Young, "A Letter to Bishop Tutu: Don't Give Up On Us Yet," *New York Times,* 27 July 1986, 23E; see also Steven Metz, "The Anti-Apartheid Move-

ment and the Populist Instinct in American Politics," *Political Science Quarterly* 101/3 (1986): 379–95.

88. Quoted in *Christian Science Monitor,* 20 April 1987, 7. Senator Robert Dole was one of the first presidential candidates identified as "one of the faces behind apartheid."

89. Henry S. Bienen, "African Strategies of Containment," in *Containment: Concept and Policy,* ed. Terry L. Deibel and John Lewis Gaddis, vol. 2 (Washington, D.C.: National Defense University Press, 1986), 544–45. It is interesting to note that Patrick J. Buchanan, former White House director of communications, lamented the contradictions in US policy toward southern Africa. In particular, he pointed out that, although Washington supported UNITA in Angola, it backed Mozambique's Marxist regime against the anti-Communist MNR. He attributed this state of affairs to "domestic politics." See Patrick J. Buchanan, "A Conservative Makes a Final Plea," *Newsweek,* 30 March 1987, 25.

90. For a discussion of the relationship between South Africa's strategic minerals and the US defense industry, see *Africa Research Bulletin,* 28 February 1987, 8544–45.

91. See, for example, Pascoe, "Moscow's Strategy;" or Warren L. McFerran, "A Meeting of Minds: The U.S. Government and South Africa's Revolutionaries Are Working Hand-in-Hand," *New American,* 2 March 1987, 7–11.

92. Quoted in *Los Angeles Times,* 18 January 1987, 7; *New York Times,* 8 February 1987, 8, and 15 February 1987, 2E. The exempted minerals included andalusite; antimony; chrysotile asbestos; chromium, including ferrochromium; cobalt; natural industrial diamonds; manganese, including ferrosilicomanganese, platinum group metals; rutile, including titanium-bearing slag, and vanadium.

93. For an assessment of this meeting, see *Foreign Report,* 12 February 1987, 5–6. For a biographical sketch of Tambo, see "Tambo, Oliver," *Current Biography,* April 1987, 47–51.

94. According to Department of State, *Misconceptions About U.S. Policy toward South Africa* (Washington, D.C.: Government Printing Office, 1986), 13–14, "The ANC advocates violence and revolution to bring down apartheid; it has claimed responsibility for many acts of violence in South Africa. The United States cannot condone the use of violence by any party in South Africa as a means to achieve its goals."

95. See, for example, *International Herald Tribune,* 12 January 1987, 2.

96. See, for example, "A Conversation with the Rev. Sullivan: Going All-Out against Apartheid," *New York Times,* 27 July 1986, F1, 27.

Low-Intensity Conflict in Southeast Asia: Challenges, Responses, and Implications for the United States

Dr Lawrence E. Grinter

The subregion of East Asia known as Southeast Asia is composed of 10 countries: Burma, Thailand, Vietnam, Laos, Kampuchea, Malaysia, Singapore, Indonesia, Brunei, and the Philippines. Often labeled the "Balkans" of East Asia, Southeast Asia is a polyglot of lingual, sociocultural, and political entities. There are vast differences between these countries; and there is no central cultural or political legacy in Southeast Asia comparable to the Chinese (or "Sinic") legacy in Northeast Asia. China's culture penetrated Vietnam thoroughly and Thailand to some extent; but the rest of Southeast Asia, despite Indian, Christian, and Moslem influences, was never dominated by a single cultural tradition or society. As a result, the many ethnic minorities in these countries have tended to remain outside the mainstream of social, political, and economic life; and secession movements and violence have been frequently resorted to as a means of rectifying grievances. One obvious result has been low-intensity conflicts (LICs). Indeed, low-intensity conflicts have recently occurred, or are occurring, in eight of these Southeast Asian countries; Singapore and Brunei are the exceptions. These LICs exhibit a wide range of ethnic, political, ideological, and socioeconomic dynamics as well as complex patterns of external involvement.

United States and Soviet interests in Southeast Asia are obvious, tending to be derived more from the subregion's location rather than from its intrinsic importance, although the region has nearly 400 million people. Southeast Asia contains the Malacca Straits—arguably the most critical maritime chokepoint in all of East Asia—the key transit point between the Pacific and Indian oceans. Through these straits pass much of the oil, commerce, and military traffic on which the larger East Asian region depends.

Then there are the contributions of the Association of Southeast Asian Nations (ASEAN) to the entire region's economic dynamism. Not surprisingly, the United States and more recently the Soviet Union have poured money and prestige into military facilities in the area; for example, the

131

United States facilities at Subic Bay and Clark Air Base in the Philippines and the Soviet installations at Cam Ranh Bay and Da Nang in Vietnam.

Accordingly, some of the low-intensity conflicts in Southeast Asia are of particular importance to both Washington and Moscow; and several have a potential impact on the whole subregion. Consequently, this investigation concentrates on three critical low-intensity conflict environments—all different, all important to the region's overall stability:

Indonesia—where a quasi-authoritarian regime led by President Suharto and braced by the armed forces, which came to power as a result of destroying an attempted Communist coup 22 years ago—seeks to smother incipient revolutionary outbreaks with strong preemptory security actions and policies of economic redistribution.

The Philippines—where 20,000 to 22,000 New People's Army (NPA) Marxist insurgents, supported indirectly by the Soviet bloc—is waging guerrilla and political warfare against the Manila government which, under President Corazon Aquino, is responding with a controversial carrot-and-stick approach.

Indochina—where Vietnam's historic drive to dominate the Khmer and Lao people—has produced a major low-intensity conflict pitting Hanoi's Soviet-equipped occupation forces in Kampuchea (140,000) against about 55,000 Marxist-dominated Cambodian rebels.

These three LIC environments cover an interesting spectrum of challenge, response, and external involvement. In Indochina, where the problems between the Vietnamese, Khmers, and Thais go back for centuries, *the United States has joined China and ASEAN in supporting a guerrilla war* conducted by Communist and non-Communist Khmer insurgents against the Soviet-supported Vietnamese military occupation which, in turn, props up a Khmer regime in Phnom Penh. In the Philippines, a country distorted by economic stagnation and political emasculation, *the United States is supporting a reformist regime's counterinsurgency* against an indigenous Marxist LIC challenge. In Indonesia, *the United States is watching the military-backed regime of President Suharto* administer the largest and most resource-rich country in Southeast Asia as it tries to preempt revolutionary and criminal activity before they evolve into a low-intensity conflict.

Are there similarities or patterns that aid conceptualization in these three LIC environments? What are the similarities in the conditions that spawn these low-intensity conflicts? What works or does not work for the revolutionaries? For the governments? For their allies? This analysis includes these factors:

• How the social-political-economic environment may facilitate or inhibit LIC.

• Who the revolutionaries are and what they want.

132

- How the governments are responding and what may be their strengths and weaknesses.

- What kinds of external involvements are occurring.

- How the United States may best respond to each LIC.

Indonesia

The Indonesian government of President Suharto takes the threat of internal violence and low-intensity conflict, in whatever form, very seriously. Having pulled Indonesia out of the bloody abyss into which President Sukarno and the Indonesian Communist party (PKI) plunged the country in 1965, the Suharto regime's "New Order" has made its overriding goal the prevention of any return to the incendiary political-social-ideological fragmentation that nurtured the PKI "Gestapu" *putsch* of 30 September 1965. This New Order has two fundamental emphases: economic development and stabilization efforts based on exploiting Indonesia's mineral wealth, the income from which has been slowly redistributed on an uneven but growing basis—particularly in Java; and vigorous reactions to any moves by elements seeking to overturn or reverse the New Order.

As the largest and most well-endowed country in Southeast Asia, Indonesia, at 165 million people, is the region's political and demographic heavyweight. Administering this complex country has been the responsibility of President Suharto and his associates for over 20 years. It has been a difficult task, but one that has enriched Suharto, his family, and the favored elites in the Javanese power structure. And in a country experiencing the recurrent effects of fluctuating oil prices and massive overpopulation, the Suharto regime has shown little reluctance to employ coercion whenever it felt control slipping. American policy has generally viewed Indonesia from a strategic context. Accordingly, the Suharto government and its policies have received US support despite periodic discomfort with some of Jakarta's internal practices.

The Environment

Indonesia's social-political-economic environment has considerable potential for the disintegration of authority, social cohesion, and communications. As the Netherland Indies and Holland's largest colony, Indonesia was a conglomeration of societies on thousands of islands scattered 3,000 miles across the equator between Asia and Australia. Indonesia's 13,000 islands are equal in mass to three-fourths of the rest of Southeast Asia, and

133

they contain half of the entire region's people. The islands count over 350 ethnic groups, nine of which are considered major. The Javanese, about 95 million people, constitute the most important group. They dwarf the rest and are packed into 85 percent of an island about the size of North Carolina. Calculating that social and political divisions could reignite Indonesia's political tinder, the Suharto regime has consistently sought to nail *any* revolutionary activity or radical Muslim opposition that might threaten the armed forces, major economic enterprises, or the nation at large.

The heart of Indonesia is Java. Constituting less than 8 percent of the country's actual landmass, it is the political, ethnic, and economic center of the nation. Java is an island of extremes: Jakarta, with its teeming urban concentration; Surabaya, the provincial capital on the island's eastern seacoast tip; and Central-East Java, where some of the worst population cramming in the world exists. Regarding Central-East Java, Arnold Brackman wrote in 1977 that it "is Indonesia's Bengal. It shares with Bengal the problems of overpopulation, unemployment, and underemployment, land hunger, and chronic food shortages."[1] But in recent years, President Suharto's government has made major strides in easing the food problem (Java is now self-sufficient in rice). Still, Java's population increases; it may be at 95 million people today. Regarding the entire country, Douglas Paauw wrote in 1985 that "the severe inequality of Indonesia's income distribution and the presence of large unemployment and underemployment imply a massive amount of poverty—so much so that an estimated 36 percent of Indonesian households subsist below Indonesia's poverty line of a monthly income of 10,000 rupiah (about US $10)."[2] Thus, the government is in a perpetual race to keep population pressures from pushing too hard against food and jobs. Nevertheless, while there is substantial poverty and a top-heavy state-corporation-dominated economy in Indonesia, under Suharto the distribution of economic benefits seems to have been sufficient enough to preclude the kind of poverty evident, for example, in the Philippines. Moreover, under the New Order:

> Indonesia, once Asia's largest food-importer, has become self-sufficient in rice; the bulging government budget has paved the roads, built schools and hospitals, and supplied fresh water and electricity to thousands of villages. Where formerly only a handful of affluent elites existed nervously in a sea of poverty, [Suharto] has created a small middle class, estimated to number between 5 percent and 10 percent of total population.[3]

Although the Javanese dominate their modest-sized island, there are two other ethnic groups on Java's tips: the Sudanese on the west and the Madurese on the east. These three groups are culturally suspicious of each other, but violence is not a factor. Immediately across the Lombok Strait from Java are three million Hindu Balinese. In 1965, fighting between Balinese and Javanese, and between Hindu and Muslim, accounted for possibly

100,000 killings—and this was in addition to the slaughter of the Communists and their supporters, which may have added another 200,000 deaths. Then there are Sumatra, Borneo, and the Celebes group of islands, each with non-Javanese majorities. In a word, it is amazing that this country of such extraordinary ethnic and geographic diversity has not disintegrated. That the Suharto government has been able to maintain order is remarkable. The key to order has been an astute strategy of combined economic development and political authoritarianism. Civil liberties in Indonesia are not well protected; and in the mid-1980s, government-authorized "death squads" eliminated thousands of people, mostly suspected or released criminals. In 1985 and 1986, senior PKI prisoners and incarcerated Communist trade union officials, under sentence of death for many years, were executed inside Indonesian jails.

Revolutionary Activity

Indonesia's current revolutionary/criminal activity is small, scattered, and of three kinds: tiny pockets of fugitive PKI remnants, some Muslim radical elements, and scattered gangster-criminal operatives. The first two are under close government pressure or surveillance, and they constitute groups with national goals—in the first case revolutionary; in the second, religious. The criminal gangs, who sometimes blend in with the other two groups, have become more active in recent years. There is also periodic unrest among the ethnic Chinese minorities in the cities. The Muslims, whose orthodox leadership has always wanted a religious state in Indonesia, conduct a running struggle with the government over religious priorities versus state policies. In recent years, President Suharto has insisted that they endorse the "Pancasila" state philosophy; under a law passed in 1985 by the government-controlled legislature, all Indonesian social and political organizations have to accept the principles of Pancasila.

The largest and historically most dangerous revolutionary force in Indonesia, of course, has been the Communist party of Indonesia—the PKI. With roots reaching back to the 1914 when its prototype emerged as a radical labor union organizing force, the PKI has gone through three almost total transformations; and attempted to take power by force on three dramatic occasions: in 1926, in 1948, and in 1965. Staggered by its losses in 1926 and 1948, the party nevertheless reorganized and reemerged phoenix-like each time from ashes. By the 1960s, the PKI had become the largest Communist party outside the Sino-Soviet bloc. In what became one of the most frenzied bloodbaths in modern Asian history, the PKI attempted a coup d'état in September 1965 only to be ripped to shreds in the process. Still, the specter of some future Communist renewal in Indonesia, menacingly predicted by the PKI's scattered spokesmen, continues to provoke government caution.[4]

135

Always in the back of the Suharto government's plans are the memory of what happened in the mid-1960s and the experience and lessons the authorities have drawn from it. As Donald Weatherbee writes:

> [T]he possible reactivation of the PKI platform has never been dismissed in Indonesian military circles because of the difficulty in distinguishing between Communist and all other radical nationalist rhetoric. The current state and form of the PKI remains unanswered, although millions of sympathizers are thought to still exist.[5]

The failure of the Communist party's "Gestapu" *putsch* of 1965 provided the circumstances in which General Suharto and his army colleagues took power. The terrible upheaval and its legacy also illustrate why the Communists lost and have subsequently failed to gain power. It is worth revisiting the nightmare of 1964–66 to understand what brought the Suharto regime to power and how it applies the lessons learned.

In the aftermath of the PKI coup attempt of 30 September 1965, a great slaughter occurred on Java and Bali. The army, led in the breach by General Suharto, spearheaded the purge. From 200,000 to 300,000 Indonesian citizens were killed, half a million more were arrested, and 200,000 were confined to political detention camps.[6] The army sought to eliminate the PKI leadership, its affiliated organizations, and it supporters within the armed services and the police. Thousands of officers and men were arrested, suspended, or cashiered.[7] But while thousands of PKI leaders and supporters were executed by army elements in the midst of frenzied vendettas, the really wholesale carnage took place in the villages of East and Central Java and on Bali. These killings were the work of enraged Muslim civilians—often militant youths—taking revenge on Communist cadres and sympathizers who had bullied villagers, students, and the Muslim press. Communist activities had seemed directed at destroying the Islamic way of life in the midst of Sukarno's incredible mismanagement of the country at large.[8] Thus, while the army shouldered direct responsibility for eliminating the PKI leadership, the wholesale violence was carried out in village vendettas. That it got out of hand is obvious. That the army encouraged and benefited from it is also clear.

Typically for Indonesia, the patterns of the slaughters were complicated. For example, in North Sumatra the anti-Communist witch hunt was as much an ethnic clash as an ideological one. The PKI there consisted of Javanese plantation workers; they were slaughtered by anti-Javanese Sumatran Muslim youths. In Bali, indiscriminate killing erupted as nationalist elements killed PKI personnel and Muslims went after Hindus. In West Java it was a straightforward army versus Communist showdown. In Central-East Java Muslim mobs revenged themselves on PKI bullies and sympathizers. Throughout all the frenzied slaughter, the bottom line was ethnicity and religion. Realizing that the army would not, or could not, dissuade others from taking action against them, mobs of Muslim and nationalist youths unleashed a village-by-village, street-by-street terror against all suspected or real Communist cadres and sympathizers. Of that nightmare, Ulf Sundharssin wrote a detailed and scholarly review of the evidence:

> The motive for such behavior may be found in the atmosphere the PKI had itself created during 1964/5. It would be insufficient to look only at the issue of the unilateral actions in which communists attempted to seize land from others. What is more important is the fact that they eradicated the harmony in the community which existed at least on the surface and had facilitated the living-together of the *santri* (staunch Muslim adherents) and *abangan* (more traditional Javanese). They branded their antagonists as "village devils," counter-revolutionary enemies of the state, and scum. They ridiculed and slandered religion which resulted in the readiness for *jihad* (holy war) in the Muslim community. In less strongly Muslim areas, such as Central Java, or Hindu Bali, non-communists were put under the same intense pressures by the PKI/BTI which caused the desire for *jihad* in East Java and Aceh. It is this reckless breaking-up of community accord by the communists which must be primarily regarded as the cause for the indiscriminate mass slaughter in 1965/6.[9]

This is not to say that the army is completely without blame for the mass killings. Sundharssin continues:

> Without the Army's anti-PKI propaganda, the massacre might not have occurred. Moreover, there were instances in every province where army officers and soldiers participated in the slaughter. But the decision to kill indiscriminately was made by those who had been most severely harassed by the PKI in previous years, namely the villagers of the non-communist *aliran* (stream).[10]

Of the 200,000 Indonesians jailed during the height of the Gestapu violence between September 1965 and January 1966, the vast majority were gradually released and rehabilitated during the first seven to 10 years of President Suharto's New Order. By the mid-1970s, although Western sources could not agree on the remaining number, probably no more than 30,000 people remained in custody; but their living conditions and situations were often extremely bad. In the late 1970s, responding to the Carter administration, Vatican, The Hague, and Amnesty International remonstrances, the Suharto government implemented a series of staged, publicized releases of remaining PKI prisoners. All told, between 25,000 and 30,000 were released between 1977 and the early 1980s. In the early 1980s, most Western sources estimated that no more than 5,000 hard-core PKI and other radical personnel remained in custody. These remnants were evidently either on Buru Island in the Moluccas or in Java jails. Other sources, principally the US government, believe that the Buru jails are now empty. As of this writing, perhaps only several hundred hard-core PKI remain incarcerated. During 1985 and 1986, after a lapse of more than 15 years, the regime has begun executing some of them in prison. Prominent was Mohammed Munir, the former leader of Indonesia's Communist trade union movement, convicted in 1973 and executed in May 1985. Another three veteran PKI leaders were executed that June. Nine more Communist prisoners, among them Kamaruzaman, who had headed the PKI's Special Bureau, were executed in September 1986. Concurrent with these executions have been arrests and executions of extremist Muslims, particularly those involved in the Tanjung Priok riot of December 1984. The government seems to alternate its elimination of Communist and Muslim radicals, thereby demonstrating "fairhandedness" with extremists of both the left and the right.[11]

Recent Government Responses

In the early 1980s, the Indonesian "oil economy's years of sudden glory" came to an end. Prices went down, costs of offshore oil exploitation went up, and the government began reining in the economy.[12] The slump continued throughout 1986 and into 1987. In September 1986, the government devalued the rupiah 31 percent against the US dollar; in January 1987, President Suharto announced a 30-percent budget cut.[13] Also critical are the pressures to reduce the huge network of state-owned monopolies which dominate Indonesia's oil, gas, steel, cotton, plastics, and tin. While the Suharto regime—and the president's family members who have grown rich in these businesses—has resisted the dismantling,[14] the Indonesian economy's contraction may mean future political instability. Add to that the continuing population pressure on Java (with estimates that by the year 2000 the country at large could have over 220 million people, 60 percent of them trying to live on Java), and the tinder for renewed instability is there.

As early as 1983, as these trends began to create increasing urban unemployment in the midst of the general economic decline, gangster and recidivist criminal activity began to rise. Muslim street violence also flared up that year. The government, led by many of the same officers who has squashed Gestapu, reacted severely. Between March and August 1983, bodies began to appear in Central Java—particularly in the environs of Yogyakarta, which became a virtual "dumping ground for corpses of former but duly released convicts, of suspected but not convicted criminals, and not least, of scores of 'hangers-on' and presumably accomplices of the first two categories of victims."[15] The death toll that year was estimated to have reached between 3,000 and 4,000.

Nor was the problem confined to Java. In May 1983, the death squad campaign spread to Medan in Sumatra. That August, there was a score of killings in East and West Kalimantan (Borneo). As the violence mounted, two of the most powerful public men in Indonesia commented on it. On 21 July 1983, Gen Amir Mahmud—the speaker of the Indonesian parliament, a senior army officer, government party stalwart, and former interior minister—publicly declared that he "personally approved of the summary killings of hundreds of suspected criminals throughout the country in recent months." Mahmud added that the benefit the "feeling of tranquility" it gave to 150 million Indonesians.[16] A week later, on 28 July, Gen Ali Murtopo—vice chairman of Indonesia's Supreme Advisory Council, former information minister, a major power broker in and out of the army, and perhaps President Suharto's closest confidant—declared after a meeting with the president that the killings were justified and "in line with the rules governing the implementation of the duties of the armed forces." The killings would stop, Murtopo said, "when those who have the authority" decide the "mission is over."[17] In 1985 and 1986, the regime seems to have reined in the death squads and used the quieter method of executions inside the prisons, altering between convicted Communist extremists and Muslim radicals.

These, then, in the midst of a continuing economic contraction, are the techniques the Suharto regime has used and may use again to control low-intensity conflict challenges to its New Order. Acting on guidance from the president, the government deals with gangsters, criminals, and political extremists with the same determination it used against the PKI two decades ago, although it is mixing paramilitary actions with judicial and more customary security procedures. Thus, the Indonesian armed forces' "dual function"—the internal security and economic development responsibilities they have exercised since 1965—continues. The Java power elite brooked no challenges to the system's structure and advantages, which they still enjoy.

From the Indonesian experience, therefore, comes this "model" for regime response to a low-intensity conflict challenge in the Southeast Asian context: (1) decisive, repeated intelligence, police, and military actions against criminal and revolutionary threats whether secular or religious; (2) reliance on village cohesion and traditional ways of life as a bulwark against Communist appeals and tactics; and (3) as the economy permits, distribution of economic benefits evenly enough for the society's tolerances. Identifying these regime policies in one LIC environment—in this case Indonesia—is useful. Whether governments in other Southeast Asian LIC environments may adopt them, and then translate them into effective actions, is an entirely different question.

The Philippines

The Philippine government of Corazon Aquino inherited one of the most chronically stricken economies and atrophied political systems in Southeast Asia. Having capitalized on a military revolt against President Ferdinand

Marcos, which allowed the contested election outcome of February 1986 to place her in office, the popular Mrs Aquino has had to deal with problems so drastic as to seem overwhelming: a current account foreign debt ($28 billion) equal to 80 percent of the country's gross national product (GNP); a systematic hobbling for 20 years of Filipino political institutions by Marcos; Marxist and Muslim separatist guerrilla wars; a shifting security relationship with the United States; and instability within the Aquino cabinets and the armed forces. Working with Vice President Salvador Laurel's base of strength—a popular political umbrella group, United Nationalist Democratic Organization (UNIDO), based in Luzon—and still retaining her popularity, Mrs Aquino has been attempting to build support abroad (particularly in the United States and Japan) as she weathers internal pressures from left and right. Since she dismissed her first cabinet on 23 November 1986, shifting coalitions of opposition groups have pressed the Aquino-Laurel government for concessions. Thus, the guerrilla warfare and cease-fires that the Communists and the Muslims conduct against the Manila government take place within the broader context of political instability at the center and social-political-economic malaise in the country at large.

United States interests in the Philippines are critical, and they include use of military bases that we have relied on since acquiring the Philippines and Guam in December 1898 as a result of the Spanish-American War. The American-Philippine relationship conformed to no preexisting pattern of colonial administration—it was a special arrangement involving what the US Supreme Court called "unincorporated territory."[18] Almost from the start, Washington and most of the American public viewed our administration of the Philippines as transitory, to prepare the Filipinos for independence—although independence was delayed by Japan's invasion and not consummated until 4 July 1946.

American tutelage of the Philippines left a legacy that included linking the Philippine economy with the American economy, Philippine reliance on the United States for external security, use of English as the common language, acceptance of the goal of universal education, and the imposition of an American social-political overlay on the already Hispanicized and fragmented Philippine culture.[19] Other important factors included the Military Bases Agreement of March 1947 which, as amended in 1965 and 1979, has afforded the United States essentially unencumbered use of major military facilities at Clark Air Base, Subic Bay naval installation, and associated support and communications facilities. There also has been increasing Philippine sovereignty and increasing US compensation. According to the bilateral Mutual Defense Treaty of August 1951, each party considers that "an armed attack in the Pacific area on either of the Parties would be dangerous to its own peace and safety," and each "would act to meet the common dangers in accordance with their respective constitutional processes."[20] The Mutual Defense Assistance Agreement of 1953 set the terms of US-Philippine military cooperation and provided the legal basis for US security assistance to the Philippines (equipment, training, and logistics support).

In the new Aquino era, American interests in the Philippines tend to focus on the following priorities:

• Retaining the Philippines as a US friend and ally, thereby permitting continued use of the military facilities.

• Maintaining US investments and special economic privileges in the country while expanding terms of trade in mutually beneficial ways.

• Encouraging a rebuilding of the Philippines market economy.

• Backing the Aquino-Laurel-Ramos government (and, indirectly, its internal security efforts).

The Environment

Like Indonesia, the Philippines is an island-nation. But of the more than 7,000 islands, only two of them are major: Luzon in the north, almost entirely Roman Catholic; and Mindanao in the south, nearly totally Muslim. The Philippines forms the northeastern tip of the Malay archipelago chain on the outer "fringe" of Southeast Asia. At 55 million people with a GNP of about $34 billion, Philippine per capita income is about $400 per year—lowest of the ASEAN countries, but double that of Vietnam. Further, the Philippine GNP has actually been contracting for the past three years; and the past year and one-half of political instability has done nothing to arrest it.[21]

The Philippines' main exports are sugar, coconut oil, timber, and some minerals. It also exports people, especially domestic servants and low-wage laborers. Lying along the Western Pacific typhoon belt, the Philippines has a harsh tropical climate by most yardsticks; and every year it is hit by five or six typhoons which do considerable economic damage. The country has many active volcanoes, and the total Philippines coastline is longer than the US coastline. Filipinos are fishing, farming, and seafaring people; and piracy, smuggling, violence, and gunrunning are common—especially in the south.

The Philippines has one of the more unfortunate political legacies in Southeast Asia. They were exposed historically to an interaction among various ethnic groups and racial migrations. Among the earliest inhabitants were Negritos. They were followed by Malays and, later, Chinese and Arabs.

But they never experienced a central government or major cultural legacy from mainland Asia, as did so many other Southeast Asian societies. One result was that Filipinos tended to live in villages and hamlets isolated from each other. Being comparatively isolated from the rest of Southeast Asia, and given the islands' geographic fragmentation, another critical result has been an identity problem for the Philippine people.[22] Suffering from the lack of a strong precolonial identity, compared to other Southeast Asian peoples, Filipino ethnic/national consciousness is underdeveloped. As David Joel Steinberg writes:

> There is little indigenous history that predates the arrival of the foreigners. Unlike Indonesia, Thailand, or Vietnam, in which great cultures and societies flourished prior to the arrival of the Westerners, the Philippines lacked a long recorded history when Islamic influence was first felt in the fourteenth century. When Magellan sailed to Cebu in 1521, there was still only a local form of political structure and economic development; there was no central government, no sense of insular identity, and no notion of a historical past.[23]

Revolutionary Activity

The Philippines changed colonial ownership between Spain and the United States at the end of the nineteenth century in the midst of an insurrection led by a ruthless guerrilla chieftain named Emilio Aguinaldo. Aguinaldo lost his insurrection but, as the first major guerrilla leader in modern Philippine history, he set an example for future revolutionaries. It was the Japanese invasion 40 years later that produced the next serious nationalist reaction in the Philippines, a popular one:

> The guerrilla movement had the open sympathy of the whole population, and the Japanese proved incapable of stifling it despite savage repression. Filipinos battled on in large measure because they had come of age as a nation.[24]

It was during World War II in the midst of the anti-Japanese struggle that a particular group of guerrillas in central Luzon, the Hukbalahaps (Huks), became prominent. After the war, their goals were economic as well as nationalistic. They continued their activities, refused to surrender their weapons, and they focused on land reform and political activity in the 1950s. Primarily a peasant organization under Communist trappings, and led by the dynamic Luis Taruc, the Huks' agrarian uprising grew after World War II. But their appeal was arrested by President Ramón Magsaysay's popular administration and his skillful combination of land reform and security measures. The Huks' soon degenerated into a Mafia-style extortion operation.

Then, during the 1960s, guerrillas reappeared in traditional Huk areas; but this time they were ideologically intense and led by university-trained intellectuals, often from elite or upwardly mobile families. Despairing at the Philippines' growing socioeconomic paralysis, the leaders moved to organize radical political actions, the Marxists among them splitting between Moscow and Beijing.

The predecessor of the current Communist party of the Philippines began as a pro-Chinese Maoist party in the mid-1960s. While still formally independent, it began in the late 1960s to show increasing links to the Communist Party of the Soviet Union (CPSU). Then, in December 1968, its leader, José Maria Sison, broke with the urban-based traditional Partido Komunistang Pilipias (PKP), which was the CPSU's associate in the Philippines, and formed the pro-Maoist Communist party of the Philippines (CPP).

The military appendage of Sison's CPP, the New People's Army (NPA), emerged in the early 1970s around Clark Air Base in southern Luzon. It was unable to capitalize on the country's revolutionary conditions, however, and was further weakened by astute Marcos security policies. Unable to organize enough rural bases to launch a nationwide offensive, the CCP reverted to positions of caution and organization-building, Sison coming around to the Moscow view that the CPP should downplay armed struggle and concentrate on political struggle. Chinese support dropped off.

Then Moscow began to cultivate the Marcos administration with a view toward gaining diplomatic relations. The effort paid off in 1976, when ambassadors were exchanged. As the 1980s approached, the CPSU and the CPP developed an increasing common interest in promoting a united front against Marcos by exploiting the labor sector and forming various solidarity groups. Still denying their connection with each other, indeed actively criticizing each other in public disinformation campaigns, the CPSU and the CPP entered into a clandestine arms arrangement (mainly AK-47s) with PLO elements in 1981. By mid-1983, the CPP had dropped most Maoist jargon and was openly pro-Soviet. Sison, who had been jailed by Marcos and then released by Aquino, was succeeded by Rodolfo Salas, who was himself captured in September 1986. Salas has been kept under government custody on the insistence of Philippine military authorities.

With the assassination of Benigno Aquino in August 1983, both the CPP and the CPSU believed the revolutionary conditions in the country were improving. The Kremlin increased the size of the Soviet mission in Manila from about 60 to 90. Its clandestine and disinformation activities increased, and it funded "peace" conference held at the University of the Philippines. The NPA moved into heightened military action as the Marcos regime grew more unstable and Soviet financial support to the NPA increased. Throughout late 1986 and early 1987, reports grew of financial support and arms shipments to the CPP by Soviet-bloc allies—including Vietnam and the Japanese Communist party, as well as the CPSU.[25]

Ferdinand Marcos was elected in 1965 and reelected in 1969. In 1972,

143

amidst corruption, economic decline, and rising political violence, Marcos declared martial law. All constitutional vestiges of legal political activity were eventually swept away. Rule by executive decree became the norm. Government intervention in the economy and a resulting morass of mismanagement and favoritism escalated.[26] As the Marcos government grew corrupt, the Marxist challenge escalated—now in the form of the remodeled, pro-Soviet CPP and its NPA. Operating principally in northern and southeastern Luzon, the emboldened NPA opposed Marcos's rule at every turn. As Marcos came under mounting public criticism in the 1980s, especially following Benigno Aquino's August 1983 murder while he was in custody of government security men, NPA recruitments jumped—from a reported 8,000 to 10,000 armed members in 1983 to 12,000 the next year to upwards of 20,000 in 1987.[27]

Of less current danger than the NPA, but of continuing concern, is the Muslim secessionist violence in the deep south. This violence is now focused around two guerrilla factions known as the Moro National Liberation Front (MNLF) and the Moro Islamic Liberation Front (MILF).[28] Boiling over in late 1972, the Muslim rebellion had tied up nearly 100,000 government troops by the late 1970s. It may have been costing the Marcos government over $1 million a day. But Marcos made some gains against the Muslims: Their arms supplies from nearby Sabah were reduced, various socioeconomic programs were launched in Mindanao, and some rebel elements were granted amnesty or bought off. The "Tripoli Agreement," which pledged "autonomy" in selected areas of Mindanao, was signed. Cease-fires were announced and referendums on local rule in 13 southern provinces were held.

But these measures did not end the fighting. Subsequent claims by Manila that the violence was a mere "police-action" were belied by reality. In November 1979, President Marcos revealed that between 500,000 and 1,000,000 civilians had been displaced by the fighting and that between 30,000 and 50,000 of them had been killed in the last six years.[29] Despite continuing attempts by the Marcos government to buy off, amnesty, or eliminate the rebel leadership, the fighting continued in the 1980s. When Mrs Aquino inherited the government, the demoralized armed forces of the Philippines faced both a growing NPA threat and a continuing Moro secession effort. Mrs Aquino currently employs a combined talk-and-fight strategy toward the Muslim rebels.[30]

Government Response

The Aquino-Laurel government initially moved energetically to try and speed the Philippine recovery from the corruption and decay of the Marcos era. The low-intensity conflict challenges from the Marxists and the Mus-

144

lims were serious, but they were not the first priority on Mrs Aquino's agenda. That priority alternated between rekindling the country's stricken economy and stabilizing her leadership of the government. In economic affairs, Manila sought to dismantle the huge legacy of "crony capitalism" (state enterprises) fostered by Marcos, stop capital flight and inflation, and (particularly with US and Japanese help) reattract foreign investment. Mrs Aquino believes that the best way to put people to work and reduce the reasons for taking up arms is to get the economy working again, but she has had her attention constantly sidetracked by other problems. For example, when she flew to Japan in November 1986 to seek new loans, she had to extract public promises from both Defense Minister Enrile and Armed Forces Chief Ramos that they would not support any coup attempts. Finally, on 23 November 1986, in the midst of new coup rumors, Mrs Aquino dissolved her cabinet (in part to force Enrile out).[31]

In the midst of this instability, Aquino's approach toward the insurgents has involved both the carrot and the stick. The Aquino government has conducted a variety of negotiations with both Marxist and Muslim guerrillas, and she has met personally with senior representatives of both the CPP and the MNLF, offering amnesty, varieties of home rule, and jobs to those who would lay down arms. She also told CPP representatives that they could compete in the legal political process—much as the Japanese Communist Party does—if they would renounce violence.

Defense Minister Enrile and Armed Forces Chief Ramos continued operations against some NPA forces in the fall of 1986, usually as a reaction to Communist-initiated attacks. Several announced truces broke down. On 1 November, the NPA, through its front group, and perhaps to bolster Mrs Aquino's position against Enrile, offered a 100-day cease-fire.[32] A 60-day cease-fire arrangement finally took effect on 10 December 1986. But President Aquino was continually pushed by the military not to stop all action against hard-core NPA elements. By February 1987, as the cease-fire neared its conclusion, the NPA was preparing for a return to armed action should negotiations with Manila on an extension break down.[33] When they did subsequently break down, Mrs Aquino said her peace initiatives had failed and that the time had come for military victory over both Communist insurgents and right-wing terrorists.[34]

In comparison with the Suharto government's consistent security response and comparatively effective economic policies, the Aquino-Laurel administration in Manila has only begun to find its writ as an effective government. Not surprisingly, it has failed to produce a firm, consistent approach to the insurgents and their threats; nor has it nurtured an economic recovery. Challenged from both within and without her government, Mrs Aquino's response to the LIC being waged by the NPA continues to alternate between conciliation and confrontation. Moreover, the country's economic situation remains extremely serious—the oligarchical pattern of wealth distortion hardly having been altered since Mrs Aquino took over from Marcos in February 1986.

In summary, the Philippine response to low-intensity conflict has not succeeded. Government security forces, riven by factionalism, have failed to root out the revolutionary hard core; nor has the government co-opted the insurgents' support base with economic/political programs. And the government's economic policies have failed to halt the perpetuation of enormous imbalances within the society.

Indochina

The current conflict in Kampuchea (Cambodia)* is the most complex struggle in Southeast Asia, and it involves layers of violence and competition among at least eight actors. At center stage is the fratricide within Cambodia. It pits Communists against Communists and nationalists: The Vietnamese client regime in Phnom Penh, nominally led by Hanoi-affiliated Heng Samrin, against the guerrilla warfare conducted by the Prince Norodom Sihanouk-led tripartite "Democratic Coalition Government of Kampuchea," operating out of Thai-Cambodian border bases. Exacerbating the Cambodian conflict are two historic antagonists in mainland Southeast Asia, the Socialist Republic of Vietnam and the Kingdom of Thailand. Vietnamese-Thai enmity goes back for centuries, and each views Cambodia as a critical territorial buffer. Indochina and ASEAN make up the next layer in the Indochina conflict—the Indochinese governments in Vientiane and Phnom Penh being subordinate to Hanoi's foreign policy dictates while Thailand, ASEAN's "frontline" state, seeks, with partial success, diplomatic and military support from the other five ASEAN states. Finally, the Soviets, the Chinese, and the Americans factor into the Indochina equation as backers of Hanoi and the rest of Indochina (USSR) on the one side with Bangkok, Sihanouk, and ASEAN (China, USA), on the other.

No party to the Indochina conflict is an innocent victim except the quarter million refugees strung out along the Thai-Cambodian frontier. The war in Cambodia could not continue without the anarchy which has characterized Khmer politics for over two decades. Moreover, the Vietnamese and the Thais, who have long coveted (and sometimes grabbed)

---

*The name Kampuchea, or Kambuja, is traditional. It first appears in Cambodia about the tenth century in reference to the people, the "Kambu-ja," born of Kambu. In modern times, the name has passed into European languages; in English as Cambodia. The term *Khmer*, a native ethnic term, is both current and relevant. We use the name Cambodia except when emphasizing titles such as People's Republic of Kampuchea (PRK) or Democratic Kampuchea (DK).

pieces of Khmer (and Lao) territory, now have armies crammed with resources and lucrative income sources resulting from the war and the refugee black markets. The confrontation between ASEAN and Indochina has divided Southeast Asia, making it easier for external powers to exploit the area's problems. And, of course, Soviet, Chinese, and American hard-line policy interests are indirectly affected by the violence in Indochina, which fuels Sino-Soviet geopolitical rivalry.

United States interests in the Kampuchean conflict largely derive from the fact of the other contestants' involvement. ASEAN, which leads Southeast Asian economic performance, is confronting Soviet-Vietnamese power in Indochina and therefore it automatically receives US support. Sino-Soviet competition in Indochina also indirectly benefits US interests to some extent because it ties down Chinese and Russian resources in this economically backward area. But the Kampuchean conflict also extends Soviet access to Indochina and gives Moscow another reason for perpetuating its military power projection into Southeast Asia. Thus a settlement of the Kampuchean conflict, or its de-escalation, would convert much of the competition from military to economic forms of activities, and this would obviously play into ASEAN's and the United States' hands.

The Environment

Cambodia constitutes about one-fifth of Indochina's territory, but it has only about one-tenth the population, currently numbering about six million people. This small population was reduced—drastically—in the murderous years of Pol Pot's Khmer Rouge rule between April 1975 and December 1978. In the last 20 years, Cambodia has gone through pulverizing experiences—from coup to civil war to the Khmer Rouge social purification experiment to foreign occupation and a concurrent low-intensity conflict. Few nations in recent history have suffered as terribly as Cambodia. Between the Lon Nol coup of March 1970 and Vietnam's December 1978 invasion, about two million Cambodians died, 75 percent of them under the "peacetime" rule of the Khmer Rouge.[35]

It has been Cambodia's historic fate to spawn the most brilliant culture in mainland Southeast Asia, to quarrel over which Cambodians would dominate it, and to be surrounded by larger territorially and ethnically jealous countries who have, with assistance from Cambodian intriguers, sought to destroy that culture. From the Thai and Burmese invasions in the fourteenth and fifteenth centuries to the resultant fracturing of the Khmer state, to the incessant Vietnamese and Thai pressures of the eighteenth century, to French occupation and colonization in the nineteenth and twentieth centuries, to the most recent Vietnamese military occupation, the Khmer people—pacific in manners and countenance but often warlike

147

and revenge-minded when they saw the chance to extend their domain—have usually been at risk from the outside.[36] The Vietnamese and the Thais, who sought retribution, and who since the fourteenth century have a record of digesting pieces of Cambodian territory chunk by chunk, constitute the handles of the vise in which Cambodia remains caught. This pressure is something all Cambodians understand. It is no surprise that in the 1850s the Norodom emperors in Phnom Penh, attempting to preserve a Khmer identity over the Angkor monuments, solicited French colonialism as protection against the Vietnamese and Thais. In return for Cambodian supplications, the French hand rested relatively lightly on Cambodia at first: the Royal family retained its privileges, and the Khmer's great cultural relics and structures (i.e., Angkor Wat and Angkor Thom) were protected and maintained. But then came increasingly heavy French taxation in the twentieth century. With part of the funds used outside Cambodia, with forced labor commonplace, and with exorbitant Chinese lending rates becoming widespread, the effects produced anti-French tax riots and several prominent assassinations in Cambodia after World War I.

Revolutionary Activity

The Second World War collapsed French authority in Cambodia even though only about 8,000 Japanese troops actually occupied the country. In the countryside, armed groups, gangs, and other elements roamed; and the Cambodian Communists and freedom fighters (Issarak), supported by Vietnamese cadres, moved about with increasing freedom. Arbitrary justice, violent death, and acts of revenge became commonplace. Surfacing in 1950–51 under Vietnamese tutelage, Khmer revolutionaries, led by Son Ngoc Minh,[37] announced the creation of the Khmer People's Revolutionary party (KPRP).[38] Led by a few hundred members, the KPRP united against French and Prince Sihanouk's opposition. Underneath, however, the KPRP contained a contentious spectrum of socialists and nationalists, the most murderous being the Marxist-Leninists.

In July–August 1954, under provisions of the Geneva Indochina Accords, between 1,000 and 2,000 Vietnamese-trained or -oriented Cambodian Communists—referred to by many non-Communists as "Khmer Vietminh" and led by Son Ngoc Minh—left Cambodia for Ho Chi Minh's newly independent Democratic Republic of Vietnam, where they were given sanctuary and further training. They were kept in reserve while another, more Maoist, group of Cambodian Marxist-Leninists were active. Enjoying secret Chinese assistance and support, and demonstrating various intellectual and organizational links to the French Communist party, these French- and Chinese-indoctrinated Khmer Maoists were soon led by Ieng Sary and a disappointed young student turned radio repairman named

Saloth Sar (Pol Pot), a Marxist-Leninist who had demonstrated an anti-Vietnamese bent early in his student years.[39] They "took over the virtually defunct remnant of the Vietnamese-created party. That party, which they later renamed the Kampuchean Communist party, guided what [Cambodia's leader, Prince] Sihanouk called the Khmer Rouge."[40] By 1963, Pol Pot had emerged as the acting secretary-general of the Communist party. Sihanouk reacted vigorously as leftist violence increased in Cambodia, and the Khmer Rouge leadership soon fled Phnom Penh for the countryside. In 1966–67, as violence escalated across Indochina, Pol Pot's forces began, with Chinese support but Vietnamese skepticism,[41] their guerrilla war against the Sihanouk government.

Against the background of changing events in Cambodia—particularly the Lon Nol coup of March 1970, and the spillover effects of North Vietnamese preparation for the 1972 Easter offensive against Saigon—the Khmer Communists began to settle old, and new, scores. When Hanoi reinfiltrated its Khmer cadres into Cambodia, latecomers on a full-blown revolutionary scene, in preparation for the fall of Lon Nol, Pol Pot's Khmer Rouge faction hunted down the Hanoi cadres; a host of liquidations and massacres began, continuing well into the late 1970s.[42]

The catastrophic result of the Khmer Rouge-Pol Pot rule between April 1975 and December 1978 is now well documented. In Pol Pot's "Democratic Kampuchea," the only "progressive" classes were poor peasants. All others—particularly the urban workers, but also, of course, all educated people, administrators, businessmen, army officers, policemen, minorities, and previous Lon Nol or Sihanouk functionaries—became enemies of the Angkar (organization). The people of the land ruled by the Angkar were referred to as opokar (instruments).

Beginning on 17 April 1975, all urban dwellers were rapidly deported to the countryside—upwards of 3.5 million people were herded out of the cities (2.5 million in Phnom Penh alone) within 36 hours. The most pitiful scenes occurred at the overcrowded hospitals, orphanages, and convalescent homes.[43] The forced marches continued until "resettlement" (i.e., group living in the fields or sleeping tents by the sides of the roads) was accomplished and the exhausted evacuees organized into work brigades. Gradually, Cambodia transformed into a gigantic work site divided into seven zones with as near total supervision of human activity as the Angkar's toughs could effect. During the Khmer Rouge's 45 months in power, upwards of 1.5 million Cambodians either starved to death, died due to forced work and disease, or were murdered.[44] The deceased's bones came to litter the countryside. Where possible, the Angkar kept detailed photographic evidence of the tortures and executions. The most gruesome records were preserved at a Phnom Penh secondary school that had been converted to a prison that the Khmer Rouge reserved for the most important "social negatives." In the countryside, more expedient methods were used.

149

As a rule, a villager receives a paper ordering him to report to the Angkar Leu. He is taken there at night, by soldiers. From there he goes to his place of death. To save bullets, the necks of the condemned are usually broken with the handle of a pick. "One shouldn't waste cartridges on those people," they say. The young soldiers have been nicknamed *A-ksae nylon* (nylon rope) or *A-ksae teo* (telephone wire) because that is what they use to bind the condemned person before killing him. Moreover, they make no secret of the fact that they enjoy killing.[45]

In keeping with the social philosophy of the Khmer Rouge experiment, all aspects of Westernization and most traditional elements of Cambodian culture were targeted for obliteration. Religion was banned, bonzes disappeared, currency was abolished, markets were dismantled, and the entire country's economy and social life was communalized. Libraries and museums were destroyed or vandalized, and some of the great cultural edifices at Angkor were desecrated. Thousands of Buddhist drawings and sculptures were damaged. The Buddhist monk population, traditional custodians of primary education in Cambodia, shrank from 80,000 to 30,000. Ninety-five percent of the 2,400 temples in the country were damaged or destroyed, as were 70,000 volumes of the national library's 100,000-book collection. The number of doctors in the country shrank to 10 percent of its pre-1975 levels. Today, no universities function in Kampuchea; and most industry is gone. Such is the record of "Democratic Kampuchea."[46]

By the time Vietnamese forces invaded in December 1978, following two years of border clashes largely instigated by the Khmer Rouge, Hanoi's partisan Khmer elements inside Kampuchea had been so crippled that installing Heng Samrin (who had been part, briefly, of the Democratic Kampuchea regime in the eastern provinces adjacent to Vietnam before he later fled) and about 1,000 other Hanoi-trained or -affiliated Khmer cadres was like trying to graft branches onto a blistered tree with no roots. Thus, although the "party" installed in Phnom Penh by Vietnam's army claims to be the original KPRP that was created in 1951, it was in fact both the remnants of an authentic Cambodian Communist apparatus and the "enfeebled vehicle of Hanoi's long-standing desire for an Indochina federation under its control."[47]

When the Khmer Rouge were thrown out of Phnom Penh, they fled to prearranged redoubts on the Thai border amidst the confusion and pathos of thousands of refugee families. Gradually, a disparate group of anti-Vietnamese resistance elements, Pol Pot's remnants being the largest, came together under an umbrella organization led by the mercurial, but seemingly indefatigable, Prince Sihanouk. Formally structured in July 1982 as a tripartite political entity, the movement is called the Coalition Government of Democratic Kampuchea (CGDK). Recent estimates put the CGDK's force strength this way: Khmer Rouge forces number about 35,000, mainly armed with Chinese weapons; Sihanouk's Moulinaka (Movement for the National Liberation of Kampuchea) consists of about 10,000 troops using

Chinese and some ASEAN weapons; and Son Sann's Khmer People's National Liberation Front (KPNLF), also non-Communist and bitterly anti-Khmer Rouge, and armed with Chinese and ASEAN weapons, number about 13,500. There is then a total active CGDK complement of about 58,500 armed personnel.[48] Coordination and trust among these armed forces is poor.

Government Response

When the Vietnamese invaded Cambodia on 24 December 1978, 200,000 first-line troops crashed across the border in a Soviet-style blitzkrieg. Two weeks later, on 7 January 1979, Phnom Penh fell. The Vietnamese quickly installed Heng Samrin, the pro-Vietnamese Marxist and previous DK eastern-zone leader. He has remained in power ever since. With Samrin came other anti-Pol Pot Marxists, particularly Pen Sovann and Hun Sen. Once it had set up the KPRP, Hanoi found it had to build a government from scratch. The KPRP had gone the complete cycle from anti-French resistance fighters to pro-Vietnamese cadres and troops evacuated to North Vietnam, to a client regime in exile for over 20 years, to a remolded client regime installed in Phnom Penh—all under the tutelage of the Vietnamese Communists.

Like the Russians in Afghanistan, the Vietnamese have sought to stabilize Kampuchea (and Laos) first by exercising military control, then by fashioning a pliant and competent client regime to serve Vietnam's broader interests—a secure and stable rear zone in Kampuchea and Laos as Vietnam addresses the larger and more dangerous threat from the north (China). The Vietnamese Communists' perception of themselves as the successor force to the French throughout *all* of Indochina has roots back to the 1930s, but did not gain operational impetus until the early 1950s. The notion of a Marxist *mission civilatrice* for the region, a region seen as a "single strategic unit, a single battlefield," in Vo Nguyen Giap's words, became the predominant Vietnamese Communist party view. Today, despite leadership changes, this continues to be Hanoi's view.[49]

When Vietnamese officers entered Phnom Penh in January 1979, they found a shattered Khmer administrative apparatus; and the Khmer Communists who liberated the country with them had neither the numbers nor the competence to fully staff even the upper levels of their own PRK administration. Nevertheless, the vacuum left by the Khmer Rouge provided opportunities for the PRK-Vietnamese regime. They invited back with some success the small remaining groups of educated elite, technical and administrative personnel, teachers, and officials who had hidden out or fled during the nightmare years. As a result, "PRK society [now] comprises a very thin stratum of proven revolutionary socialists in most of the top

151

administrative offices and positions of authority, and below them, through-out the administration and service occupations, people from the same groups who occupied such positions before 1975."[50]

In order to preclude mass starvation, the Vietnamese quickly directed a food policy of total laissez-faire; the peasants were allowed to consume anything they could grow, no questions asked, and market prices were established by supply and demand.[51]

Class divisions have reemerged, albeit to a very limited degree; and women, who constitute 60 percent of Cambodia's population, have of necessity moved out from traditional roles. But the hereditary elite, the prewar entrepreneurial classes, the old officer corps, and of course the university faculties, are gone—no doubt permanently.

The Kampuchean operation has not been easy for Vietnam. Economically strapped by its expeditionary venture in Kampuchea and by its moribund economy at home, the Socialist Republic of Vietnam, more than a decade after Saigon's "liberation," displays one of the lowest standards of living in Southeast Asia—indeed in the entire third world. And Hanoi has drawn down its forces in Kampuchea to about 140,000, relying on a meager Phnom Penh-KPRP army of about 35,000 actives supplemented by Khmer labor battalions. But the Vietnamese, who field some of the best infantry and armour in the world, have found that about 50,000 anti-Vietnamese resistance fighters (whose core remain the Khmer Rouge) are able to keep Kampuchea's western and northern borders unstable. Thus Hanoi's attention remains distracted from the state-building tasks it would prefer to concentrate on.

The Kampuchean low-intensity conflict is relatively more costly for the Vietnamese and the PRK than for the resistance. As they prop up Phnom Penh's forces, Vietnamese battalions conduct search and destroy operations against the resistance's guerrillas and base camps. In the 1984–85 campaign, the resistance camps at Sok Sanh, Phnom Malai, Ampil, and Tatum were demolished. Vietnamese cross-border pursuit and artillery barrages into Thailand have occurred since 1980. In spite of these setbacks, Sihanouk's resistance, operating from relocated base areas in Thailand, keeps up the costs of the Vietnamese occupation with a hit-and-run strategy, staging periodic attacks close to Phnom Penh. And the resistance's bases in Thailand are more secure than were Vietnam's base camps in Cambodia during the Second Indochina War. Furthermore, Sihanouk and his lieutenants relentlessly work the diplomatic problem in capital after capital, hoping to gradually tire Hanoi of the contest.

Policy and Personnel Shifts in Hanoi

The grinding effects of the low-intensity conflict in Kampuchea and the economic poverty and mismanagement at home in Vietnam began to produce gradual changes in Hanoi's policies in the mid-1980s. With an underfed population, a nearly valueless currency, a per capita annual income that ranks among the world's lowest, openly flourishing black markets, raging inflation, and shortages in most consumer goods, the Vietnamese economy is a case study in socialist disaster. To keep up the war economy, the Soviets have been pumping in up to $2 billion in assistance each year.

Moscow's "return" on its investment in Vietnam is reflected in its tight strategic grip on Vietnamese bases, anchored in a 25-year bilateral defense treaty inked only weeks before Vietnam invaded Kampuchea in late 1978. Soviet naval and air forces operate principally out of Cam Ranh Bay and Da Nang. By late 1986, 25 to 35 Soviet naval vessels using Cam Ranh Bay included four to six submarines while eight Bear (Tu–95) long-range bombers and 16 Badger (Tu–16) medium-range bombers were flying out of Da Nang. These are "the only Russian strike aircraft deployed anywhere in the world beyond Soviet borders."[52] What Leonid Brezhnev called "this important outpost for peace and socialism in Southeast Asia" shows no signs of changing its utility to Moscow.

Important changes in the Vietnamese Communist leadership apparatus came in late 1986, following a year of self-criticism and argument among Vietnam's ruling elite. The three oldest surviving Stalinists, men who had led the party for almost half a century, were retired at the Sixth Congress of the Communist party of Vietnam in December. Truong Chinh, 79-year-old party secretary and state president; Pham Van Dong, 80-year-old premier; and 76-year-old Le Duc Tho, party strategist and Henry Kissinger's opposite at the Paris peace negotiations, were all dropped.[53] Moving to the top was the party's prominent economic reformer, 73-year-old Nguyen Van Linh. A former party administrator of Ho Chi Minh City (Saigon), Linh had spent most of his party career in the south. With Linh came more influence for like-minded reformers and economists such as Vo Van Keit and Vo Chi Cong.[54] A major cabinet reshuffle also occurred in Phnom Penh.[55]

Prince Sihanouk, sensing the opportunity to exploit the movement in Vietnam's power structure, became more active at the turn of the year; and Hanoi, again, seemed to respond favorably to the notion of a future presence for Sihanouk in a demilitarized Kampuchea. The Soviets, hoping to enlarge their diplomatic clout in Indochina, have said they would like to join any negotiation.[56]

The low-intensity conflict in Kampuchea has dragged on because neither the Vietnamese and their Phnom Penh clients nor the Sihanouk-led resistance is able to achieve a decisive victory or force a showdown which could lead to a victory. The war is a stalemate. Like the Aquino government in Manila, the Heng Samrin regime has yet to establish its writ as an effective government. It is nearly completely dependent on external protection. And unlike the Suharto government in Indonesia, Phnom Penh's authorities have neither an overarching philosophy nor (as yet) a national development plan. Without Hanoi's forces, the army of the People's Republic of Kampuchea would be defeated by the larger and more experienced CGDK forces whose core are the grim, battle-hardened Khmer Rouge.

Thus, Hanoi props up and perpetuates a client regime in Phnom Penh; but it cannot legitimate that regime or leave it unsupported. The Cambodian people, who have benefited from their release from Pol Pot's nightmare and undoubtedly would rather be occupied by a foreign army than reexperience Khmer Rouge rule, have yet to genuinely identify with the Heng Samrin regime. Thus, a brittle clientism characterizes the government while a low-cost destabilizing strategy characterizes the insurgents. Sihanouk, as the only truly authentic and neutral hope for tortured Cambodia, may yet come back to administer some kind of coalition Cambodian government as an ultimate compromise choice among all parties.

Conclusion

The low-intensity conflict environments analyzed in this study—Indonesia, the Philippines, and Kampuchea—are all unique and unrelated. Each is a special case without direct connection to the other. United States interests in these LIC environments and their outcomes are also different in each case. But that is not to say that a US response to one LIC will not be without effect on the others. Asian governments and guerrillas observe what the United States does or does not do.

Indonesia is the fifth largest country in the world, a substantial demographic factor in East Asia, and the most richly endowed country in the Southeast Asian subregion. By dint of population and location, Indonesia must figure prominently in future US policies toward Southeast Asia. A high-level American official, not known for his humility, once posed a rhetorical question to a group of Americans traveling to Southeast Asia in the late 1970s. He asked, "What has Indonesia ever done for the United States?" The answer to that question is both obvious and crucial: Under Suharto, Indonesia destroyed one of the largest and most dangerous Communist revolutionary movements in East Asia. And Suharto has stabilized and gradually modernized the country in one of the most astonishing turnarounds in any third world drama. That is what Indonesia has done for the United States; and for Southeast Asia, ASEAN, and, of course, for itself.

The Philippines figures even more prominently and directly in United States interests in Southeast Asia. The two countries have a special relationship, and US military power in the region—projected, in part, on behalf of ASEAN—depends on two critically located (and nonreplicable) Philippine military installations: the Subic Bay naval complex and Clark Air

Base. American military operations out of those Philippine bases underwrite the strategic balance in Southeast Asia—a balance which wavered dangerously following the Indochina collapse in the mid-1970s.

The war in Kampuchea, while it perhaps ought to be of less significance to the United States than events in the Philippines and Indonesia, impacts US interests because so many other countries—both friendly and adversarial—are involved. Wherever the Soviets are in East Asia, the United States automatically must be alert. And when a de facto treaty ally like Thailand has its security threatened, that too concerns the United States.

In making suggestions about US policy toward these three Southeast Asian low-intensity conflict environments, one must take care not to treat the violence separately from the broader societal and cultural environments which produce it. Recommendations to the Jakarta or Manila governments, or to the Sihanouk guerrilla forces, on how to improve their security operations or their combat efficiency would miss the point. The origins and foundations of the instability and violence in these countries are deep and long-standing; thus, program guidance and tactical suggestions on how to put out fires (or fan them) are irrelevant.

By contrast, this study concludes that the problems causing the upheavals and violence in Indonesia, the Philippines, and Kampuchea are not going to go away soon—and US influence on these problems is minimal. In each case, American influence is filtered through a host government with problems or an opposition movement under pressure; and it is those authorities and instruments that determine the effectiveness of US policies.

Toward Indonesia, American policy has consistently taken a geopolitical stance and, with the exception of some human rights pressures on Jakarta during the Carter administration, Washington has kept relations cordial with the Suharto regime despite its internal policies. And it is hard to quarrel with that approach because Indonesia's record of stability and development for the past 20 years anchors ASEAN and ASEAN's progress. One has only to recall the nightmare of Sukarno and his aggression against neighboring countries to picture what a radical, or chaotic, Indonesia would do to ASEAN; and to imagine the new opportunities it would create for Moscow and Beijing in Southeast Asia.

In applying its New Order, the Suharto regime has, in addition to its own skills and cunning, something that neither the Philippines nor Kampuchea has: oil and gas wealth. These minerals may be the single most important ingredient in the regime's ability to keep the lid on as the frightening population growth continues; Jakarta can usually anticipate the economic pie growing as it slowly redistributes pieces of the pie to the millions of new mouths that must be fed every year. So US policy toward Indonesia, and its government's preemptive policy toward internal threats, should concentrate on economics more than anything else. Indonesia simply needs to slow down, then stop, its population growth while accelerating its resettlement programs. That is the fundamental economic, political, and security requirement for this major country. American policy ought to bend every effort to help it achieve that goal.

In the Philippines, United States policy under the Reagan administration has been lucky. The transition from Marcos to Aquino was relatively quick and bloodless. A democratic system has been rekindled in the Philippines and the US-Philippine special relationship has survived the departure of an American-protected, and extremely greedy, dictator and his wife. Now a very different kind of transition and challenge is under way in the Philippines, one which the United States is supporting—the building of a democratic polity by a nonauthoritarian regime attempting to pull the country out of years of socioeconomic malaise.

The key to American policies toward the Philippines' efforts to quell its low-intensity conflicts lies in broader kinds of policy supports. We must continue backing the democratic triumvirate in Manila of Aquino-Laurel-Ramos, seek to get the Philippine debt bridged until the economy can be rekindled, support the Aquino government's new constitution, support the dismantling of oligarchical patterns in both the economy and the armed forces, and push Manila for a more effective counterinsurgency effort.

Can a democratic and reformist pro-American administration in the Philippines rebuild the institutions of government and rekindle the economy in the midst of hope, poverty, and violence? It will take years to be successful. US policy must calibrate for the long haul and must work with the Aquino government on all these fronts simultaneously. The insurgent challenges in the Philippines are symptoms, not causes. The causes are much deeper—at heart they are structural, cultural, and psychological.

Regarding Indochina and the conflict in Kampuchea, two fundamental choices lie before US policymakers, although Washington's ability to make either choice make a difference on the battlefield is very limited. In the first policy option, the United States can continue its choice of backing Chinese and Thai support to the Sihanouk-led rebels, which in turn gives Hanoi and Moscow counterincentives to push for their own military solution. The second policy option would have the United States seek a neutralization of, and power-sharing within, Kampuchea. In this option, the United States might offer economic and diplomatic inducements to Hanoi, and perhaps to Phnom Penh, and Moscow.

The first option, which is current United States policy, seeks to keep Hanoi grinding itself down in Kampuchea, the objective being to so wear down the Vietnamese that some day (1990?) they will pack up and go home. This has been the aim of Sihanouk's guerrilla commanders and of China. ASEAN, however, splits on the issue. Thailand and Singapore are the hardliners; the others are opposed or not sure. The second US policy option of negotiations could have a more complex result: While it would loosen Vietnam's grip on Kampuchea and separate Thai and Vietnamese forces, the

156

Chinese might be the major winner—if they could see installed in Phnom Penh and anti-Vietnamese Khmer clique.

But a transition in Phnom Penh involving Khmer nationalists might not necessarily favor either China or Vietnam. And a real neutralization of Kampuchea, perhaps resulting from a diplomatic conference, would have the advantage of converting a violent contest into an economic and political one—thus playing into skills that ASEAN and the United States bring to bear. Whichever policy track the United States adopts in the future, it is clear that low-intensity conflict in Kampuchea is the product of complex multilateral activities. Steering the competition toward a more preferred outcome is the central task of US and ASEAN policy.

Low-intensity conflicts in Southeast Asia are political struggles. They reflect political, social, and economic ruptures and breakdowns in these societies. They express demands for fundamental changes in the power distribution. The violence in these conflicts, a reflection of the deeper issues, is used to gain larger ends, not the other way around. To the extent that United States policymakers understand the thoroughly political nature of these conflict environments and comprehend the political implications of the kinds of programs and policies they recommend, they will help rather than harm American interest.

NOTES

1. Arnold C. Brackman, *Indonesia: Suharto's Road* (New York: American-Asian Educational Exchange, 1973), 13.

2. Douglas S. Paauw, "The Indonesian Economy in the 1980s," *Economic Bulletin for Asia and the Pacific* 31 (December 1980): 41.

3. Shim Jae Hoon, "Indonesia: Breaking Old Ground," *Far Eastern Economic Review*, 20 November 1986, 46. Also see Donald E. Weatherbee, "Indonesia in 1985: Chills and Thaws," *Asian Survey*, February 1986, 144–45.

4. Organized by the Dutch Marxist Hendricus Sneevliet in Java in 1914 under the name Indies Social Democrat Association, the Indonesian Communist organization gradually broadened its appeal while changing its name to the Communist Association of Indonesia (PKI) in 1920 and finally the Communist party of Indonesia (PKI) in 1924. Independent of Bolshevik Russia and the Comintern, the PKI moved into action against Dutch authorities in the 1920s aligning itself with radical Muslim groups and using a variety of provocative tactics against the authorities. In the fall of 1926, driven by premature enthusiasm, strong-arm tactics, and a rush for power by local branches, PKI agents tried to create a general uprising. The result was disastrous as anti-Communist villagers and then the colonial police and intelligence services extinguished the Java-based uprising. The Dutch arrested some 13,000 people, executed those found responsible for murder, and sentenced over 4,000 to long prison terms.

The revolt of 1948 was a different matter. In the two decades since 1926 a new generation of PKI leadership, prominently pro-Soviet, took charge. In the midst of Indonesia's emergence from colonial to independent status, the Japanese occupation, and the Sukarno collaborationist administration, the PKI split bitterly between Stalinists and nationalists. Hemmed in by socialist parties and preempted by the Dutch-PKI military conflict, as in 1926, the PKI again headed into disaster: premature planning, fragmented command and control, gangsterism, and lack of support. When the Dutch reinvaded in late 1948, they again went after the PKI remnants. See Leslie Palmier, *Communists in Indonesia: Power Pursued in Vain* (Garden City, N.Y.: Anchor Books, 1973), passim.

5. Donald E. Weatherbee, "Phoenix Supine: The Indonesian Communist Party and Armed Struggle," in *Armed Communist Movements in Southeast Asia*, ed. Lim Joo-Jock and Vani S. (Hampshire, England: Gower, 1983), 47.

6. Brackman, 11.

7. David Jenkins, *Suharto and His Generals: Indonesian Military Politics 1975–1983* (Ithaca, N.Y.: Cornell Modern Indonesian Project, 1984), 3–4.

8. Sukarno's legacy has been well documented. Only half-sane at the end of his rule, the Indonesian president drove Indonesia into chaos. Flamboyant and mercurial, his methods of governing used fragmentation and isolation. He deliberately set the country's parties, groups, and military forces one against another. He split the armed services and police agencies into separate fiefdoms, commands, and paramilitary units. Sukarno sowed economic chaos as well: By 1960 almost all rational economic planning, fiscal policy, and pragmatism had disintegrated. By 1965 inflation was 650 percent. To cover the problems Sukarno launched military strikes against neighboring countries, and railed against the United Nations, the United States, and Japan.

9. Ulf Sundharssin, *The Road To Power: Indonesia Military Politics, 1945–1967* (Kuala Lumpur: Oxford University Press, 1982), 218–19.

10. Ibid., 219.

11. Harold Crouch, "Postponed Executions May Have Political Messages," *Far Eastern Economic Review*, 20 November 1986, 50.

12. Donald K. Emmerson, "Indonesia in 1983: Plus Ça Change . . ." *Asian Survey*, February 1984, 140–43.

13. Barbara Crossette, "Jakarta, Citing Oil Prices, Set Austerity Budget," *New York Times*, 7 January 1987, D-2.

14. Steven Jones and Raphael Pura, "All in the Family: Indonesian Decrees Help Suharto's Friends and Relatives Prosper," *Wall Street Journal*, 24 November 1986, 1, 22.

15. Justus van Der Kroef, "'Petrus': Patterns of Prophylactic Murder in Indonesia," *Asian Survey*, July 1985, 748.

16. Ibid., 750.

17. Ibid.

18. The Philippines became an American possession on 6 February 1899.

19. Claude A. Buss, *The United States and the Philippines: Background for Policy* (Washington, D.C.: American Enterprise Institute, 1977), 1–22.

20. The United States and the Philippines are also tied together by the Southeast Asia Collective Defense Treaty, known as the Manila Pact, which was signed in 1954. The Southeast Asia Treaty Organization (SEATO) was dissolved in 1977, but the Manila Pact continues.

21. In mid-April 1987, Philippine Finance Minister Jaime Ongpin indicated the country's current account foreign debt stood at $28.2 billion.

22. See, for example, Benigno S. Aquino, "What's Wrong With the Philippines?" *Foreign Affairs*, July 1968, 770–79.

23. David Joel Steinberg, *The Philippines: A Singular and a Plural Place* (Boulder, Colo.: Westview Press, 1982), 33–34.

24. Ibid., 53.

25. The details are in Leif R. Rosenberger, "Philippine Communism and the Soviet Union," *Survey*, vol. 29, no. 1 (Spring 1985); and Rosenberger, "Philippine Communism: The Continuing Threat and the Aquino Challenge" in *East Asian Conflict Zones: Prospects for De-escalation and Stability*, ed. Lawrence E. Grinter and Young W. Kihl (New York: St. Martin's

Press, September 1987). The most recent news reports include Tom Breen's articles in the *Washington Times*, 10 October 1986, 6A; 9 March 1987, 1A; and 24 March 1987, 1A, 6A.

26. For details see Robert A. Manning, "The Philippines in Crisis," *Foreign Affairs*, Winter 1984–1985, 393–98.

27. Ibid., citing US Defense Department data, 402; and Carl H. Lande and Richard Hooley, "Aquino Takes Charge," *Foreign Affairs*, Summer 1986, 1096–97. US Assistant Secretary of Defense Richard Armitage estimated in March 1987 that NPA strength was up to 24,430. *New York Times*, 22 March 1987, 9.

28. See, for early background on the MNLF, Lela Garner Noble, "The Moro National Liberation Front," *Pacific Affairs*, Fall 1976, 405–24.

29. Lawrence E. Grinter, drawing on *Far-Eastern Economic Review* and *Washington Post* reports in his *The Philippine Bases: Continuing Utility in a Changing Strategic Context*, National Defense University Monograph no. 80–2 (Washington, D.C.: NDU Press, 1980), 42, 48.

30. *New York Times*, 10 April 1987, A5.

31. *Atlanta Constitution*, 24 November 1986, 1-A, 14-A; and *Wall Street Journal*, 24 November 1986, 37.

32. *New York Times,* 2 November 1986, 3.

33. See, for example, Clayton Jones, "Filipino Communists: guns mostly silent, but economic war blazes," *Christian Science Monitor*, 21 January 1987, 1, 32.

35. Most scholarly research on Pol Pot's rule concludes that one-fifth of the Khmer population, or 1.5 million human beings, died during the Khmer Rouge reign. All told, between 1970 and 1980, accounting for about 600,000 war dead, 850,000 refugees leaving the country, and 1.5 million deaths under the Khmer Rouge due to starvation, disease, forced labor and liquidations, Cambodia lost about 30 percent of its population. Today women comprise about 60 percent of Cambodia's population. See Ben Kiernan, *How Pol Pot Came to Power* (London: Verso, 1985); Kimmo Kiljunen, ed., *Kampuchea: Decade of Genocide*, Report of a Finnish Inquiry Commission (London: Zed Press, 1985), 30–34, 43, 47; and Francois Ponchaud, *Cambodia: Year Zero* (New York: Holt, Rinehart and Winston, 1977), 70–71.

36. In Southeast Asia the Khmers are known as valiant fighters. During the First Indochina War they were tough combatants for the French—especially against the Vietminh. Cambodians show sincerity and friendship for anyone who has done them favors, and Therevada Buddhism preaches serenity and pity for the unfortunate, but the Khmer concept of forgiveness is complicated: Forgiving someone can be a sign of weakness. Revenge and gratuitous brutality, common among the Khmer, have long historical roots. As Francois Ponchaud wrote in *Cambodia: Year Zero*, 141,

> In practice the nationalist myth that says "we can always come to an understanding among Khmers" turned out to be untrue. The lust for revenge—the timid man's form of violence—has run its course implacably, even at the risk of the country's annihilation.

Also see Michael Vickery, *Cambodia: 1975–1982* (Boston, Mass.: South End Press, 1984), 4–8.

37. Michael Vickery, *Kampuchea: Politics, Economics and Society* (London: Frances Pinter, 1986), 15.

38. Vietnamese tutelage of the Khmer and Lao Communist parties is well documented. See, for example, Dennis J. Duncanson, *Government and Revolution in Vietnam* (London: Oxford University Press, 1968), 170, 397; and Stephen J. Morris, "Vietnam's Vietnam," *The Atlantic Monthly*, January 1985, 76–77.

39. Vickery, *Kampuchea*, 12.

40. Morris, 77.

41. From that point on, Pol Pot's faction within the Khmer Communist movement evidently concluded that the Vietnamese meant to hobble or retard them in order to control the pace

of events in Kampuchea. William J. Duiker, *Vietnam: Nation in Revolution* (Boulder, Colo.: Westview Press, 1983), 142.

42. Vickery, *Kampuchea*, 21, 39.

43. An eyewitness account is Ponchaud, 6–7, 52, 87–107.

44. The Khmer Rouge extermination rate was the subject of widely variant interpretation, ranging from "tens of thousands" to three million. Taking into account war deaths, disease, starvation, forced labor, and a *minimum* of a half-million Khmer Rouge-ordered killings, a figure approaching 1.5-million deaths results. Two important sources are Vickery, *Kampuchea*, 184–88; and Craig Etcheson, *The Rise and Demise of Democratic Kampuchea* (Boulder, Colo.: Westview Press, 1984), 143–49.

45. Ponchaud, 66.

46. Kiljunen, 39–41; Vickery, *Cambodia*, 92, 115, 117, 134, 141; and Ponchaud, 126–34.

47. Morris, 77.

48. Estimates vary. These are composite figures from a variety of sources. See, for example, Kiljunen, 54–56; *Far Eastern Economic Review*, 24 October 1985, 44; and 10 July 1986, 11–12.

49. William S. Turley, "Vietnam/Indochina: Hanoi's Challenge to Southeast Asian Regional Order," in *Asian-Pacific Security: Emerging Challenges and Responses*, ed. Young W. Kihl and Lawrence E. Grinter (Boulder, Colo.: Lynne Rienner Publishers, Inc., 1986), 181–85.

50. Vickery, *Kampuchea*, 56.

51. Ibid., 44, 131.

52. Benjamin F. Schemmer, "The Pacific Naval Balance," *Armed Forces Journal*, April 1984, 38–40; and *The Military Balance 1985-1986* (London: International Institute for Strategic Studies) as cited in Bernard Gordon, "The Third Indochina Conflict," *Foreign Affairs*, Fall 1986, 80. Also see Leszek Buszynski, *Soviet Foreign Policy and Southeast Asia* (New York: St. Martin's Press, 1986), 204–5. Evident Soviet reluctance to make the facilities permanent undoubtedly reflects Vietnamese sensitivities.

53. Le Duan, the 78-year-old previous VCP leader, had died in July 1986.

54. *New York Times*, 19 December 1986, A–7.

55. Ibid., 12 December 1986, A–10.

56. Also see, for example, Vietnam Foreign Minister Nguyen Co Thach's comment to veteran Indochina reporter Robert Shaplen, in Shaplen's "The Captivity of Cambodia," *The New Yorker*, 5 May 1986, 52. Also see *Far Eastern Economic Review*, 1 January 1987, 11–12. Also relevant is Buszynski, 239–42.

US Policy and Strategic Planning
For Low-Intensity Conflict

Jerome W. Klingaman

The authors of the preceding studies have examined their areas of specialty for important policy and strategy implications that lie within the vast realm of low-intensity conflict. The results of those examinations are relevant at two levels of policy and strategy development. Individually, the narratives provide basic points of departure for developing policies and strategic guidance in specific countries and conflict situations. Collectively, they provide a larger body of evidence contributing to the development, refinement, and interpretation of general, long-term strategies for low-intensity conflict situations. This final narrative concludes the authors' works by briefly assessing this larger body of evidence for its implications at the second level of strategic planning. The assessment focuses on specific implications relevant to our understanding of low-intensity conflict, and it draws from these implications a critical perspective on the broad policy guidelines contained in present and future low-intensity conflict strategies. Low-intensity conflict has only recently entered the strategy development process at the national level, but it is likely to remain in the forefront of official concern for the remainder of this century and beyond.

Formulating Strategy for Low-Intensity Conflict

The US government is presently searching for appropriate ways and means to respond purposefully and with national unity against a variety of threats currently classified under the term *low-intensity conflict* (LIC). As stated in the current *National Security Strategy of the United States,* these threats "take place at levels below conventional war but above the routine, peaceful competition among states."[1] To ensure that national strategy properly accounts for future threats impinging on America's security, the secretary of defense's Bipartisan Commission on Integrated Long-Term Strategy is currently charting the broad guidelines for defense technology and strategy for the next 20 years.[2] Significant threats identified by the commission will provide the background for an in-depth analysis of our present national defense strategy. A Regional Conflicts Working Group

161

supporting the commission is examining "the strategic implications of future political violence in the form of sabotage, terrorism, paramilitary criminality, insurgency, and interstate wars which do not pit the armed forces of the United States against the Soviet Union."[3] Their findings and recommendations will be included in the commission's Long-Term Strategy Report, which may, in turn, support the president's Annual National Security Strategy Report to the US Congress. According to Senator John Warner, ranking Republican Armed Services Committee member, "These two reports will assist the members of Congress as we measure the value and relevance of individual programs from Pentagon spending to foreign assistance." The two documents will also provide a clear statement to the American people of the way in which we intend to turn our national and defense goals into reality. As Senator Warner states,"Informed public debate on these goals, strategies, and available options must reflect an awareness of the dangerous complexities facing the United States."[4] Beyond these two reports, the evidence presented by the Regional Conflicts Working Group may lead to the development of an updated strategy for low-intensity conflict and ultimately to specific defense capabilities for dealing with this threat.

The goal of strategy analysis, review, and development is a credible defense posture that combines various economic, political, informational, and military instruments of national power. A national security strategy provides basic licensing authority and guidance for general implementing strategies and for country-specific programs developed by the US Defense Department and by other agencies, departments, and independent establishments of the US government. It also furnishes a bridge between broad policy objectives and specific defense initiatives for developing force structures, doctrines, and training programs. Combined with the implementing strategies, a national strategy for low-intensity conflict underwrites all civilian and military defense capabilities that will ultimately be brought to bear on the LIC problem.

The Problem of Definition

At this level of defense planning, we are dealing with general strategies in which concepts, objectives, and capabilities are addressed in a very basic formulation of policy guidance. Developing a broad conceptual framework for such guidance necessarily relies on a certain amount of generalization; and generalizations can be misleading, especially in a field where it is difficult to define the scope and nature of the threat. Low-intensity conflict is just such a field. While the need for a LIC strategy is clear to most people in the government, the definitional boundaries of LIC are not as apparent. Since the term *low-intensity conflict* possesses no referential framework of

162

its own, aside from a stipulated content made up of conflict elements such as insurgency, terrorism, subversion, and so forth, there is no consensus on the upper and lower limits of the realm. As a result, the strategy development process almost invariably finds itself impaled on the thorn of semantic relativism and subject to endless debate over the number and types of conflict elements that should be included. Also, there is considerable disagreement over fundamental causes and critical centers of gravity within each of the conflict elements. Because of the term's highly relative meaning and many possible connotations, it lacks utility in precisely those instances where an unequivocal understanding is crucial to national security—in pinning down the types of low-intensity conflict that must be addressed through policy, strategy, doctrine, and force structure initiatives. Because the conflict elements are often complex in nature, and because they vary from situation to situation, generalizing on causes, centers of gravity, and appropriate response mechanisms, produce results that are forever open to interpretation.

A generalization is often seized upon as a total account of the causes underlying a particular conflict or as a complete, definitive answer to the problem. Some people will argue, for instance, that the Soviet objective of controlling global basing, critical maritime chokepoints, and strategic resources is the primary cause of third world instability and armed conflict. Such an argument has little to offer in the way of practical solutions, since going to the source is a very risky business; but it suggests that stability can be restored by simply removing Soviet influence from the affected countries. Others argue that such instability and conflict are the direct result of high population densities, poverty, or a lack of political self-determination, and that the answers are social development, economic aid, and a democratic process.

The present strategy development process has attempted to properly circumscribe the LIC realm and cut through all such simplistic notions. Still, it is impossible to account for every variant of low-intensity conflict in a way that avoids either a possible misapplication of the general guidance or a misinterpretation of the threat itself. In some cases, there may be no ready solution to the problem, or at least no solution that can be carried out through American involvement without sacrificing the highest ideals of our society. This is not to say that where there are no immediate answers we must fall back on the counsel of despair. Sometimes even the questions themselves are useful in sharpening the wisdom of a foreign policy that might otherwise lead to political embarrassment or failure. In other cases, strategic guidance derived from generalizations may have to be altered significantly when constructing strategies for specific countries and situations. In all cases, the generalizations must be carefully assessed for their application to specific threats and conflict situations.

The lack of conceptual clarity inherent in such a highly relative term as

163

low-intensity conflict continually frustrates the best attempts at definition, and it complicates the strategy development process. We might wonder, then, why we do not relieve ourselves of this semantic burden and turn to more explicit language that accurately identifies specific threats having special significance to US security interests at levels below conventional war and above the routine, peaceful competition among states. The answer itself holds significant implications for US foreign policy and strategy development. It also provides a starting point for assessing strategy implications contained in the previous chapters.

Explicit Language: The Fall from Grace

The term *low-intensity conflict* is a euphemism that arose during the early post-Vietnam era. It was used to replace the traditional terminology of revolutionary war, a terminology that symbolized to some extent America's failure to prevail during a bitter and disastrous experience in Southeast Asia. In such terms as *insurgency, counterinsurgency,* and *guerrilla warfare,* many people believed they could read the graveyard inscriptions of ill-fated adventurism in US foreign policy, and no one read those inscriptions more clearly than the US defense establishment, even though there were others who argued that insurgent warfare was alive and well and would return to threaten our security interests in other parts of the world. The military entered the war with counterinsurgency advisers to assist the Republic of South Vietnam in defeating Vietcong guerrillas. As the war progressed, however, the value of a low-order counterinsurgency strategy was lost in the face of mounting military initiatives by North Vietnam to reunify the country under Hanoi's leadership—initiatives that did not necessarily coincide with the political and revolutionary ambitions of the Vietcong.

With backing from the administration, US military planners seized upon the widening commitment of North Vietnamese regulars in the South as an opportunity to abandon the counterinsurgency effort and concentrate on what they considered to be the primary perpetrator of the war—North Vietnam. At the same time, the United States was looking for a way to shorten the war and bring about a negotiated settlement that satisfied the need for measurable, near-term results. A settlement required pressure, and pressure required a substantial increase in firepower and logistics support. With a land invasion of North Vietnam out of the question, Washington attempted to signal Hanoi that it could not win without facing the risk of substantial escalation. That signal included an intense bombing campaign in the North and a massive buildup of US troop strength in the South. Counterinsurgency thus gave way to a policy of graduated response and escalation.

Washington's signal failed to offset Hanoi, and American political resolve finally gave out in 1973. In the end, America's strategic aims in Vietnam were defeated not by military force but through a campaign of intense political and psychological warfare waged by North Vietnam and its allies. In the aftermath of the struggle, the principles of low-order counterrevolutionary warfare were swept away in a flood of criticism against indecisive military actions and self-imposed constraints that many believed had led to an excessively long engagement, the withholding of decisive combat measures, and the wearing down of our political and moral resolve.

Given North Vietnam's incredible perseverance and motivation to win at any cost—all of which were impossible to anticipate in 1960—one might argue that the initial counterinsurgency effort in South Vietnam did not fail for its own lack of merit and should not be held singularly responsible for what happened in the end. Such an argument, however, fails to alter the perception that US support of counterguerrilla operations during the early phases of the conflict was a tentative and ill-advised response that drew the United States into an ever-deepening morass of political blind alleys and fatal commitments.

The United States returned from Vietnam with an aversion to the perils of extended military intervention in foreign internal conflicts deeply imbedded in its political and moral conscience, an aversion that led to a complete reassessment of our foreign policy initiatives in the third world. Our failure to prevail in Vietnam manifested itself during the postwar years in an almost total rejection of warfighting strategies and capabilities for all revolutionary conflicts and insurgencies, including those impinging on US security interests in our own hemisphere. Insurgency, counterinsurgency, and guerrilla warfare were too closely identified with unpopular, protracted struggles of psychological attrition; and during the post-Vietnam era, even the terms themselves were eliminated from official use. Today, the terminology of revolutionary war is subsumed under the broad generic classification *low-intensity conflict,* where it presently resides with other definitional elements in a confusing array of terms, meanings, and relationships. Low-intensity conflict now denotes an ever-expanding realm of threats and response measures that fall short of engagement between conventional military forces. Because the term carries almost no semantic value of its own, the size and content of that realm vary according to the operational interests of planners and staff agencies within the US government and Defense Department.

The Significance of Low-Intensity Conflict

Low-intensity conflict is more than a euphemism, however. Despite lack of agreement over the definitional elements, the persistence of this term suggests growing recognition that US security interests are threatened, and

165

will continue to be threatened, by a distinct class of closely related unconventional conflicts lying outside the reach of conventional strategies and response mechanisms. That we are moving away from the paralyzing effects of Vietnam is suggested by recent efforts to develop strategies, doctrines, and specialized response capabilities for LIC. *National Security Strategy of the United States,* published in January 1987, contains the first substantial policy guidance on low-intensity conflict.[5] Counterterrorism, support for democratic resistance movements, and military assistance to developing nations are specific components of this document. A companion National Security Decision Directive expands the guidance and provides a licensing foundation for the development of implementing civilian and military strategies. The 1986 Goldwater-Nichols Defense Reorganization Act assigns responsibility for strategy development and implementation to the Office of the Secretary of Defense, the Joint Chiefs of Staff, and the commanders in chief of the unified and specified combatant commands.

An annual National Strategy Report, now required under the same act, reflects a shift in congressional interest from the minutiae of Defense Department acquisition programs to the level of strategy analysis and review.[6] Much of that interest is generated by concern over the relevance of our present defense strategies and programs—geared predominantly for deterrence and high-intensity, conventional warfare—to low-intensity threats that cannot be deterred in the conventional sense and that do not yield to conventional solutions. The Defense Reorganization Act also mandated a new assistant secretary of defense for low-intensity conflict and special operations, and it reorganized all active and reserve special operations forces under a newly created United States Special Operations Command located at MacDill AFB, Florida. Elsewhere within the Department of Defense, there is renewed interest in joint and service doctrines for low-intensity conflict, and specialized military capabilities are being enlarged for certain contingencies that fall within the LIC envelope.

In keeping with general agreement that LIC involves the use of force up to, but not including, sustained engagement between conventional forces, the LIC realm also includes such low-order, peacetime "crises" as attempted coups, kidnappings, civil disorders, assassinations, and armed expropriations. By drawing in civilian components of the government such as the State Department, the Central Intelligence Agency, the Drug Enforcement Administration, the US Information Agency, and the Commerce Department, the list expands even more. We now find other specific threats to national security: coercive diplomacy, disinformation, subversion, illegal drug traffic, extortion, blackmail, and the precipitous curtailment of strategic resources.

Included in the LIC realm are potential US response measures that range all the way from diplomatic and economic sanctions to the use of military force. Defense doctrine proposes a variety of military responses to deal with the threats listed above. The response to insurgency is *counterinsurgency* (the original term replaced by LIC). The response to terrorism is counterterrorism, either in the reactive, retaliatory mode or the proactive, preemptive mode. Certain crises and conflict situations may be dealt with through peacetime contingency operations such as raids, rescues, surgical attacks, and special intelligence missions. If military operations are required to restore or maintain peace between belligerent groups or states, US military units may act as a peacekeeping force. Also, it is conceivable that US forces may be called on to support an internal resistance movement against a regime hostile to US security.

Strategy Implications

Although it is possible to detect the existence or potential of all these LIC elements in the conflict situations described earlier in this book, the central theme dominating the narratives is revolutionary conflict and insurgency. It is a theme that overshadows all other aspects of the LIC realm. This observation coincides with Sam Sarkesian's statement that "the substantive dimensions of [LIC] evolve primarily from revolutionary and counterrevolutionary strategy and causes."[7] In most cases, the other definitional elements of LIC are either manifestations of revolt or responses to it. Even in Doctor Ware's study on the Middle East, where one might expect to find a lengthy treatment of terrorism, the central issues are revolution and insurgency. Terrorism surfaces as a manifestation of some form of revolution, either as a tactic of guerrilla warfare or as an extension of the revolutionary ambitions of a state or group. The question is: How much can we draw from this observation as a basis for developing general strategy?

A General Statement of the Problem

If the substantive dimensions of LIC are revolution and counterrevolution, a long-term LIC strategy should be grounded in a similar context, at least theoretically. In actual practice, however, the great differences among the conflict situations alluded to in the previous studies suggest the extreme difficulty of constructing a general LIC strategy that applies in specific instances. Even if we accept the proposition that the major conflict elements of LIC are grounded in revolution, our very notion of revolution changes considerably from one region to another. In some cases, Central America and most of Southeast Asia, for example, revolution may often be a means of seeking to eliminate economic and political disparities in social orders that have been governed for decades, even centuries, by outmoded class systems and oppressive, self-serving governments. In the process of change and modernization, old, conservative regimes are brought down and replaced by new ones that seek new forms of national identity and independence among the community of nations—forms that do not always coincide with American ideals and interests.

In the Middle East, our notion of revolution enlarges considerably. In Iran and Afghanistan, revolution may be a conservative reaction to forces of change and modernization that threaten cultural identity and traditional belief systems. In contrast to Nicaragua, where a pro-Soviet political base was established through a revolution that replaced the existing Somoza regime and brought the Sandinistas to power, the leaders of the government in Iran are, themselves, agents of revolution—insurgents, if you will, bent on purifying the world of Islam. As a policy-strategy model for the United States, the familiar principles of insurgency and counterinsurgency in Central America are almost impossible to apply in the Middle East.

In moving from the Middle East to countries on the USSR's southern borders, the history of low-intensity conflict again alters our concept of the origins and manifestations of revolution, presenting an entirely different set of problems for strategy development. During the central Asian campaigns of the 1920s, pro-Soviet political cadres were implanted through coup d'état, and coup d'état was turned into revolution for Sovietizing society. Conventional Soviet forces were then used to counter the ensuing insurgency waged by anti-Soviet counterrevolutionary forces while the cadre expanded and solidified its political base. This process is going on today in Afghanistan.

In every one of these conflict situations, one can undoubtedly identify common seeds of revolt in social, economic, and political grievances that must be addressed in long-term planning for assisting friends and allies. With respect to support of developing nations and democratic resistance movements, our current LIC strategy recognizes that "long-term political and economic development will reduce the underlying causes of instability [in] the third world, help undermine the attractiveness of totalitarian regimes, and eventually lead to conditions favorable to US and Western interests."[8] Free trade, private enterprise, economic expansion, and economic independence must be facilitated through US developmental assistance and economic aid programs. The strategy also recognizes that indirect applications of US military force, primarily through security assistance, are the most appropriate means to help foreign military institutions protect their citizens and governments.[9] This strategy reflects a hard-won sensitivity to the multidimensional characteristics of revolutionary conflict. It properly seeks internal solutions within the affected nations through a nationally coordinated effort that balances political objectives with military means. Such balance is essential in a strategy that seeks to avoid the risk of active military involvement at levels that are both politically unacceptable and tactically inappropriate. This strategy is based on the premise that lack of political and economic development in the third world is the major cause of low-intensity conflict; and it may, indeed, be a major cause—but let us be sure we understand what we mean by "cause." Perhaps the correct term is *condition*.

Complicating Factors

Poverty, class oppression, and political disenfranchisement may be necessary conditions of revolution, but they are not sufficient to generate revolutionary conflict.[10] Given the necessary conditions of economic or political grievances, another condition must be met to ignite the fires of revolution; and it is this condition that complicates the development of a general strategy for LIC. It is also the condition that establishes significant differences among revolutionary conflicts, confuses the legitimacy of the revolution, and is often the main obstacle in overcoming the conflicts. The complicating factor is the *ideological content* of the revolutionary movement. That content—itself a necessary though not sufficient condition— furnishes the catalyst to focus grievances on the perceived failure of a state to act in the best interests of the people. Together, the grievances and the catalysts function as necessary and sufficient conditions that will set a revolution in motion and sustain its momentum during the course of an entire generation or longer. What makes the conflict situations so different and so difficult to deal with is not simply the grievances themselves, but rather the way in which the expression of those grievances is inspired, organized, and focused. This is not to say that eliminating economic and political instability is simple, for it is not. But the catalysts that bind together the various elements of modern revolution are highly resistant to reform measures aimed at eliminating the political and economic tensions that "caused" the revolution in the first place. The most resistant are those found in revolutions hostile to US interests, and the most familiar are those where Marxist-Leninist programs of Soviet origin furnish the political-ideological models for revolutionary discipline, organization, and direction. Models such as these transform insurgency—armed tactical operations with possibly limited political goals—into a programmatic enterprise possessing what Bernard Fall calls "a political rationale" for overthrowing the existing government.

Doctor Weathers presents Mario Vargas Llosa's explanation of the rationale for guerrilla warfare in Central America. The "settling of accounts between privileged sectors of society" referred to by Llosa alters somewhat the common view of disaffected peasants rising in revolt against the government. At the peasant level, there are, indeed, genuine grievances—preexisting conditions of revolt, conditions that have existed for generations in

169

many countries around the world. The revolution does not start here, however. On one side of the "privileged sector" is a deeply entrenched, oppressive military bureaucracy. On the other side is a collection of intellectuals and militant middle class who have been pushed out of the power system, exploited by the government, and subjected to outside influences that create a sense of political awareness and an awakening of conscience. The genuine, well-meaning objective of the middle class and intellectuals is the leveling out of social, economic, and political disparities on behalf of the peasants—a "settling of accounts." Lacking a democratic process and a voice to effect change, and wanting action now in the face of seemingly immovable opposition, force is seen as the only viable alternative. As "Walkman" Lawson once remarked in a somewhat different context, "Most people who can communicate, communicate. Those who can't, carry guns."[11] And so, the poor, the voiceless, and the dispossessed draw themselves to the edge of insurrection.

Moving beyond that edge, an armed insurgency might be able to extract limited concessions from the government. But if the primary objective is the overthrow of the government, the insurgency must be equipped with a solid political foundation and a theory of revolution that incorporates the necessary administrative, organizational, and operational instruments; in other words, an infrastructure. A revolutionist does not at this point seek an appropriate theory or infrastructure; it was already in place during the early days when a hard-core leadership of Marxist-Leninists established the catalytic effect by focusing the people's attention on ancient grievances. It will remain firmly entrenched during the recruiting, organizing, training, and equipping of guerrillas and political cadres. During the protracted phase of the guerrilla war, it will manipulate world opinion and provide tactical direction in the conduct of military operations. In the end, it will carry the revolutionary leadership to power on the backs of those who wanted to accelerate the processes of change and modernization—but who only traded one form of totalitarianism for another.

The complication posed by this catalyst is evident in Doctor Grinter's account of Southeast Asia where US security interests are caught up in a violent expression of legitimate needs and aspirations that have been co-opted by nondemocratic programs that subordinate personal freedom to the survival of the revolutionary state. In the Philippines and Indonesia, it is difficult for the nonspecialist to determine how much of the revolutionary momentum is based on a broad, popular mandate to change the existing order and how much is based purely on the political initiatives of those who would transform a nation or the entire world into a monolithic society for the sake of a Marxist or Maoist ideology.

Ware identifies an important variant of the catalyst when he states that Khomeini used religion to mobilize a politically uninformed mass against secularism in Iran and against the forces of Western imperialism. The

170

ideological content here is not Marxist-Leninism or Maoism, but an old vision of the cosmic order reborn in a new mandate for ordering man's relationship to man and man's relationship to God and the universe. In Doctor Blank's work on Afghanistan, religion surfaces again as the catalyst that binds together, if only temporarily, the various mujahidin factions in their holy war against the Soviet invaders and the Afghan government. Another variant—tribalism—is emphasized in Doctor Ofcansky's account of ethnic rivalry in Africa.

US strategy for countering insurgent violence against friends and allies is also complicated by a conflict between legitimate revolutionary aims and Soviet initiatives in the third world. As this author has stated elsewhere, the revolutionary aspirations of many lesser developed nations will probably be carried forward and realized, with or without Soviet support, under the influence of expanding communications, education, and technology. As a social phenomenon, the process is probably inevitable.[12] One of the most difficult problems for US strategic planners is that by providing the material resources and the political-ideological rationale for revolution in the third world, the Soviets and their allies in Cuba and the Eastern bloc have already aligned themselves with forces of change that might eventually prevail. This alignment plays a crucial role in Soviet global strategy. Unable to achieve economic parity with other major industrial societies on the basis of free trade and international competition, the Soviets seek to redress the economic balance of power through indirect means that avoid a direct confrontation between themselves and the United States. Through revolutionary warfare waged by surrogates and proxies, they can exercise a relatively cheap, low-risk option for denying international markets, natural resources, and strategic positions to the United States and its allies. Specific Soviet objectives will be to force a gradual drawdown of US political leverage, prestige, and physical presence overseas, and to erode US economic viability in the world trade centers. As many other authors have noted, the Soviets can pursue their limited war objectives with little likelihood of a stiff US response due to the unacceptable risks of direct superpower confrontation.

Counterrevolution

A leading question for defense planners is: How do we promulgate national strategy to eliminate or reduce the threat that revolutionary warfare poses to US and allied security interests without denying the processes of social and political evolution in the underdeveloped nations? A convincing answer to this question begins with the recognition that the unwillingness of a nation to deal fairly with its own people is, itself, a threat to national security—theirs as well as ours. If we ever hope to separate the Soviets and their agents from the revolutionary processes, we must begin by encouraging friends and allies to initiate political-economic reform measures that offer, at a bare minimum, demonstrable evidence that the leaders are acting in the best interests of the people. This does not mean that the United States can in all cases implant democracy as an alternative political system or that US economic assistance can eliminate poverty in the third world; it cannot. It does not even suggest that eliminating poverty is a necessary condition for countering revolution; it is not. It does, however, suggest that US diplomatic initiatives must, wherever possible, be brought to bear in promoting some form of representative government that engenders among the people a sense of national identity and participation in the affairs of state. If a nation is threatened by insurgent violence, it is at least the people's own nation that is being threatened. Most certainly, the strategic initiative must be preserved through economic means, but the issues affecting regional security are primarily political, not economic.

On Reform

Some might argue that reform initiatives are sufficient to remove what is widely termed the *root causes* underlying the revolutionary movement. In eliminating social, economic, and political injustices that fuel the revolution, the catalytic agent has nothing to work on. In time, the agent simply loses strength and dissipates. This sounds correct. The object, after all, is to capture the political initiative from the revolutionary movement—a goal that requires political mobilization in favor of the defending regime. In actual practice, however, the elimination of insurgent violence against a government is not likely to occur through reform alone. In Central and South America, and in certain parts of Southeast Asia, the catalyst contains an imported element of revolutionary leadership whose ambitions extend considerably beyond the legitimate aims of the revolutionary rank and file. The point that is often missed by the advocates of diplomacy and reform is that the leaders of these revolutionary movements do not want reform—they want total control of the state. No amount of reform or political compromise will satisfy the revolutionary aspirations of a hard-core Maoist or Marxist-Leninist leadership. In fact, reform is a threat to the leadership of any revolutionary movement bent on acquiring power at any cost. In the Philippines, for instance, the continuation of repressive policies under the Marcos regime actually served the political interests of the Communist party of the Philippines (CPP). The longer the Marcos regime stayed in power, the more time the CPP had to consolidate a political-economic infrastructure throughout the island complex, particularly on Luzon.

In some cases, reforms initiated by the state are capable of actually producing conditions that lead to insurgent violence. Muhammed Reza Pah-

172

lavi's modernizing reforms in Iran, for instance, were too much, too soon. In Afghanistan, a revolution of radical social reform initiated in 1978 by pro-Soviet Afghan leaders produced a counterrevolution that has survived nine years of Soviet air attacks, ground offensives, and forced migration.

On Diplomacy and Political Compromise

There is, of course, more to revolt than ideological theories or the will to power. We must always anticipate the possibility of a revolutionary mandate at the grass-roots level of any insurgency. But there is more at foot here than a revolution of the people. Proponents of counterinsurgency strategies based purely on economic and political reform must come to terms with the fact that the objectives of the sponsoring parties are rarely negotiable. Compromise solutions play an active role in achieving revolutionary ends in the Marxist-Leninist system, but only as a tactic for implanting, legitimizing, and enlarging a political infrastructure that eventually chokes out all competing elements. A revolutionary movement aimed at establishing a totalitarian state cannot achieve its goal, or even survive, on compromise solutions that entail an actual sharing of power. As with economic reforms that take the steam out of the peasant support base, diplomacy and political compromise hold little attraction for a revolution that must arrive at power with all its political, economic, informational, and military control instruments intact. Insurgent leaders will not negotiate away what they can win militarily. Drawing hard-core revolutionaries into the electoral process is no more likely than their allowing it to continue once they have come to power. If they were to come to power through the vote alone, they would not be able to bring with them a monopoly on military force to protect and sustain their programs against hostile elements of the previous military structure if that structure were capable of wielding considerable force and was firmly entrenched as a national institution. The Sandinistas did not, of course, meet with such opposition when they took control of Nicaragua in 1979. The previous military structure had not been a broad-based national institution with an extensive fighting capability. The *Guardia Nacional* was a relatively small presidential enforcement and protection instrument that owed its allegiance to Samoza. When Samoza's power base was destroyed in the political arena, the *Guardia Nacional* found itself without a sponsor and with no political or economic viability of its own. The political and economic sectors had been almost totally under state control. The Sandinistas possess a much larger fighting force today— a force that owes its allegiance and source of power to the Sandinista leadership, not to a body of legislation that stands over and above the authority of one party or regime—an interesting point for students of contra strategy.

The Use of Force

The uncompromising nature of the revolutionary catalyst manifests itself in the insurgent's willingness and, indeed, need to use force as a substitute for denied or otherwise unobtainable political leverage against the government. The insurgent can and must be engaged politically through social, economic, and institutional government reform; but reform takes time. The host government must be protected for whatever time is required for those initiatives to take effect, and that requires counterforce. The principal targets of reform is the revolutionary support base—the people. The principal targets of counterforce should be those who espouse violence while denying the logic and meaning of reform. This requires penetrating the insurgent's infrastructure and eliminating the catalyst. The principal instruments for dealing with an infrastructure are intelligence agencies and police or paramilitary forces. Beyond the infrastructure, military forces may be required to offset the main thrust of guerrilla offensives. Force thus becomes one of several instruments that must be incorporated into the host nation's internal defense strategy. US military training and supply assistance to a third world ally will be appropriate in many instances as an adjunct to a much larger foreign assistance program, but such training and assistance will be difficult to apply efficiently if the host government is incapable of dealing with the revolutionary infrastructure. As with all other major aspects of host nation's internal defense program, dealing with a hostile infrastructure requires an internal solution. US participation and influence in this area will probably be minimal due to the necessary heavy reliance on political, judicial, informational, and law enforcement instruments.

Integration

Pulling together all the capabilities needed to implement reform, to eliminate the insurgent infrastructure, and to provide physical protection of the host government establishes an imperative for combining all instruments of national power into a single, integrated internal defense and development program made up of both civilian and military elements. The most important implication for US defense planning is that our own civilian and military instruments must be similarly integrated for supporting friends and allies. The objective of such a move is a nationally coordinated effort that addresses the multidimensional aspects of revolutionary war—but the key term here is *integration*, not merely coordination. Applying foreign assistance programs that are not mutually supporting, or that shore up a missing or deficient capability in only one area when the host nation is equally lacking in other areas, can waste valuable resources and may only contribute to the insurgents' strategy of extending the conflict.

174

Revolution

The implications that can be derived from the internal dynamics of revolutionary war suggest that we reexamine our strategy for assisting resistance movements. So far, our assistance has been directed almost exclusively to military aid for armed tactical operations for insurgency; and we have often provided that assistance without a clear indication of objectives, rationale, or correct methodology. The problems of organization, administration, direction, and legitimacy in a resistance movement hold not only for insurgency against non-Communist states but also for insurgencies (the Marxist term is *counterrevolution*) that rebound on Communist states after they have taken power. An infrastructure with political, economic, social, and informational components is no less important to an anti-Communist resistance movement than it is to a resistance of Communist origin. If the aims of the resistance are revolutionary, there must be a revolutionary vision and a means of translating that vision into a popular revolutionary mandate.

It can be argued that popular support is not a necessary condition for overthrowing a government and capturing power through guerrilla operations. The murderous assault of the Khmer Rouge against the Republic of Cambodia supports such an argument. A successful revolution, however, is one that survives after it has come to power and that requires more than a purely military solution. The insurgent may succeed in capturing power without the support of the people, but he will eventually need that support to govern the nation. Moreover, for the purpose of establishing US policy and strategy for assisting resistance movements, the *most* successful revolution should be defined as one that shows promise of surviving, without resort to the draconian methods of a totalitarian police state, over a long period of time on the basis of broad, popular support and democratic rule. Long-term survival on this basis requires a long-range strategy that reaches considerably beyond immediate military objectives. Because the struggle is primarily political, the strategy must focus on political objectives, even when the means of achieving those objectives are economic. For instance, the development of an extensive, independent, property-owning middle class is one of the most important initiatives that can be taken toward securing the survival of a democratic institution once it is in place. A broad-based middle class—with the freedom to develop an independent local economy, private enterprise, and international trade—provides a mechanism for preventing state domination of the economic scene. A middle class also provides a source of constant pressure for expanding that freedom toward greater equality in the social and political sectors. By extending economic freedom, civil and political liberties, and the rule of law to the people, the government receives the continuing support it needs to survive. Such an initiative is an ambitious undertaking that may not be possible in

175

every case. Where the initiative does show promise as part of the revolutionary vision, however, it must be planned for in advance; and it may require US assistance.

In the same fashion as successful counterinsurgency, a successful revolution involves programs in the social, economic, and political sectors. These programs should be an integral part of the revolutionary planning process from the very beginning. They should be expanded during the guerrilla conflict phase and carried over into the posthostilities era. Military actions must be carefully integrated into the nation-building and reform initiatives. The infrastructure required to administer and direct these initiatives must also provide public information devices for mobilizing political support within the nation, gaining outside support for the revolutionary movement, and reducing support of the enemy regime. The same infrastructure provides a means for dealing with such issues as human rights and social welfare, government propaganda, and the internal control of insurgent forces. All such actions must be underwritten by a political rationale and managed through an administrative apparatus that functions through a broad communications and intelligence network. Where the theoretical and practical foundations of such a coordinated enterprise are lacking, US strategic aims in supporting resistance movements will be very difficult to achieve. In Nicaragua, for example, the contras initiated tactical operations before they established an infrastructure to coordinate military means with political and social objectives. As a result, the legitimacy and future of the contra movement are still in doubt among skeptics of contra aid.

There is also considerable doubt as to the utility and moral significance of supporting resistance movements that are incapable of achieving anything more than limited tactical operations. A resistance movement that lacks the means of mobilizing and sustaining significant political support within the nation is likely to have difficulty obtaining political and materiel assistance from outside sources. In Chile, Allende's socialist program collapsed for lack of both internal and external support. Since Allende's fall, the leftist guerrilla movement has not made significant progress because it too lacks sufficient domestic and foreign backing.

Lacking the support needed to mount a sustained and serious military offensive, the revolutionary movement is in a poor position to negotiate lasting concessions from the incumbent regime. If the resistance proves incapable of carrying the insurgency across the threshold into revolutionary takeover through either political or military means, it may not even be able to negotiate its own survival when outside support comes to an end. The remaining alternatives are endless fighting with dwindling resources, escape into exile, or unconditional surrender.

There may be instances where our support of resistance movements should include developmental initiatives in the social, economic, and political sectors. To provide a means of launching and sustaining these initiatives, commensurate with US interests and where not prohibited by law, our assistance may also be required in developing a revolutionary infrastructure with all its organizational and administrative devices. Adjusting to this larger dimension of revolutionary conflict will be difficult for the United States because we lack a modern theory of revolution. Our own democracy had its origins in a revolution, but American democratic institutions and values are neither based on, nor dependent on, an ideological rationale of promoting and expanding the revolutionary process throughout the world. Unlike the Soviet model for Marxist-Leninist government, democracy is not structured for such an enterprise. Nor should it be. But the survival of our free institutions may depend on a competitive strategy for containment that includes not only military aid but also assistance in organizing, coordinating, and focusing the efforts of those who seek alternatives to totalitarian forms of government.

Counterterrorism

International terrorism originating in the Middle East is a manifestation of revolution directed both internally and externally. Where it takes place externally, the United States and other industrialized nations are often the targets of violence. Treating terrorism within the political-social context of revolution in those regions where this type of conflict originates, however, may be impossible. For we are left with the question of what strategy or strategies do these political-social factors inform? The Islamist revolutionary process assumes a form and content that differs considerably from the types of local, internal conflicts we generally associate with revolutions founded on Marxist-Leninist models. We are dealing here with a form of revolution that renders inoperative our standard counterrevolutionary strategy of military assistance combined with social, economic, and political reform. In Iran, for instance, the government has already focused attention on the failure of secular rule to satisfy social, economic, and political needs. The regime itself has taken up reform as the means of restoring "a just and perfect society," both within and without. Moreover, the clerical leaders of this regime have provided an alternative—a return to Islamism and a holy crusade against internal corruption and the forces of Western imperialism. What we are faced with is not an internal revolution directed against the state, but rather the state directing revolution against much of the Western world with reform being its principal objective. The terrorist movements that carry on this crusade, whether they are state sponsored or not, live within systems of ideological principles that are completely impervious to social, economic, and political reform from the outside.

It seems reasonable to look for solutions to terrorism by eliminating its causes; but in some cases, there may be no "causes" amenable to solution. How, for instance, do we construct a foreign policy or strategy to neutralize a terrorist movement that is opposed to and totally isolated from all rationally founded formal institutions of government and society, their own as well as ours? In time, we may discover political and economic paths that lead to accommodation and the elimination of terrorism. Given the uncompromising, radical motivations behind international terrorism, however, that path will be very difficult to find. And where we are unable to achieve diplomatic closure and penetrate the arid, philosophically closed doctrines that justify terrorist violence, there will be few options short of forceful deterrence for protecting the rights and safety of our citizens and free institutions.

NOTES

1. *National Security Strategy of the United States* (The White House, January 1987), 32.

2. Quoted in Arnold F. Klick, "Formulation of Strategy," *National Defense* LXXI, no. 428 (May–June, 1987): 74.

3. "A U.S. Strategy For Low-Intensity Conflict" (Proposal for the Commission on Integrated Long-Term Strategy by the Regional Conflicts Working Group, 15 June 1987 draft), 1.

4. Klick, 75.

5. *National Security Strategy of the United States,* 32.

6. Klick, 75.

7. Sam C. Sarkesian, "Low-Intensity Conflict: Concepts, Principles, and Policy Guidelines," *Air University Review* XXXVI, no. 2 (January–February 1985): 5.

8. *National Security Strategy of the United States,* 33.

9. Ibid., 33.

10. The argument that poverty does not "cause" revolution is advanced in Col Rod Paschall's article "Marxist Counterinsurgencies," *Parameters* XVI, no. 2 (Summer 1986): 3. The "causes" of revolt are related to necessary and sufficient conditions in the essay, "Terror and Peace: 'The Root Cause' Fallacy," *Time,* 22 September 1986, 97.

11. Quoted in Gregory Jaynes's article "This Is Against My Rights," *Time,* 6 July 1987, 42.

12. Jerome W. Klingaman, "Policy and Strategy Foundations for Low-Intensity Warfare," keynote speech to an international forum on low-intensity warfare, Paris, France. Contained in *CADRE Papers,* Report No. AU-ARI-CP-86-2, Air University Press, Maxwell AFB, Ala, September 1986, 6.